D1569454

God's Mind in That Music

God's Mind in That Music

Theological Explorations through
the Music of John Coltrane

For James Cone,
In thanks for all your great work

JAMIE HOWISON

Foreword by Don E. Saliers

![CASCADE logo] CASCADE *Books* · Eugene, Oregon

GOD'S MIND IN THAT MUSIC
Theological Explorations through the Music of John Coltrane

Copyright © 2012 Jamie Howison. All rights reserved. Except for brief quotations in critical publications or reviews, no part of this book may be reproduced in any manner without prior written permission from the publisher. Write: Permissions, Wipf and Stock Publishers, 199 W. 8th Ave., Suite 3, Eugene, OR 97401.

Cascade Books
An Imprint of Wipf and Stock Publishers
199 W. 8th Ave., Suite 3
Eugene, OR 97401

www.wipfandstock.com

ISBN 13: 978-1-62032-156-0

Scripture quotations are from the New Revised Standard Version Bible, copyright 1989, Division of Christian Education of the National Council of the Churches of Christ in the United States of America. Used by permission. All rights reserved.

Excerpted from "Sonny's Blues" © 1957 by James Baldwin. Copyright renewed. Originally published in *Partisan Review*. Collected in *Going to Meet the Man*, published by Vintage Books. Used by arrangement with the James Baldwin Estate.

An early version of chapter 9 was published as "God's Mind in the Music: How Coltrane Deepened My Theology of the Triune God" in *Didaskalia* (Fall 2009).

Cataloging-in-Publication data:

Howison, Jamie.

God's mind in that music : theological explorations through the music of John Coltrane / Jamie Howison.

xii + 232 p. ; 23 cm. — Includes bibliographical references and index(es).

ISBN 13: 978-1-62032-156-0

1. Coltrane, John, 1926–1967—Criticism and interpretation. 2. Jazz musicians—United States—Biography. 3. Jazz—Religious Aspects. I. Title.

ML419 C645 H48 2012

Manufactured in the U.S.A.

For Catherine, who not only made it possible for me to head off on the study leave that eventually led to this book, but who has always told me that I needed to keep writing.

I haven't heard anything higher than "The Father and the Son and the Holy Ghost" from the *Meditations* album. I would often play it at four in the morning, the traditional time for meditation. I could hear God's mind in that music, influencing John Coltrane. I heard the Supreme One playing music through John Coltrane's mind.

—**Carlos Santana**

Contents

Foreword

This book asks the question, "What does jazz have to do with theology?" Most of us do not put jazz and theology together, yet when it comes to the music of John Coltrane, we have to. Jamie Howison's love of jazz and honest theology enters John Coltrane's music and his soul, his anguish and his ecstasy, in these pages. Coltrane is for him a "theological musician." So there is something here for "church types" and the spiritually searching reader, but also for the fan, the critic, and the curious about Coltrane.

Anyone who knows the least bit about jazz has heard of John Coltrane. Yet for most of us, his life and his music remain enigmatic, and more than a bit challenging. His music, like his life, was intense, complex, and full of tension and contradiction, yet capable of enormous love and spiritual desire. All of these will be found in the chapters that follow—an account that takes us into Coltrane's turmoil without sentimentality. Unafraid of the religious and spiritual dimensions, Howison knows how to listen well, and thus how to encourage any reader to listen with new ears for that "love supreme" which Coltrane sought to sound and reveal in his playing. Be prepared for an honest portrait from a theologically trained lover of jazz who has done his homework. Howison brings, without apology, his own religious and theological convictions to the task, bringing voices as diverse as St. Augustine, William James, and Dorothee Soelle into conversation with Coltrane.

It is perhaps a cliché to observe that John Coltrane desired to play all the notes available in the universe. Yet in so doing he conjoins lyricism and severe distortion of tone and the ability to "swing." The music he heard within himself is mind and sensibility shattering, thus John Coltrane is adored and vilified by critics and fans alike. He was not beyond criticism, as some devotees may have claimed. Yet in reading his life the way this author does we come to understand that Coltrane is an Archimedean point, giving us a "place to stand" to survey the history and the future of jazz. For the readers of this book, that place was profoundly religious as well—owing so much to the black church tradition and to Coltrane's childhood formation in the African Methodist Episcopal Zion Church. His was both a prophetic visionary and, I would argue, a kind of priestly witness in the sacrament of sound.

I am impressed with the many detailed interpretations of Coltrane's most important recordings: most especially the album *A Love Supreme,* detailed in chapter 7. Citing Cornel West, who called that 1964 record a "masterpiece of the greatest musical artist of our time and the grand exemplar of twentieth-century black spirituality," Howison claims, as does West, this music to be a form of prayer. But individual tracks such as "Naima" (his first wife's name) and "Alabama" also can be heard this way. There is a profound range of pain (societal, racial, and personal) in Coltrane. His music during the 1960s evokes the struggles of the civil rights movement. The bombing of the Sixteenth Street Baptist Church in Birmingham is a back-story in his composition and performance. There we hear the "stubborn resilience of the blues" and the psalmic and God-haunted lament. "Alabama" bears a powerful relationship to the trauma and to the subsequent search for justice. One can hear in his music the anguish of that longer history of slavery and its devastating aftermath. At the same time we become aware in Howison's account of the ambiguities of Coltrane's personal life and loves. His own movement between self-deception and truthfulness is sounded both in the music and in his written self-expression. All of this is why it seems appropriate to observe that "conversion" is central to hearing *A Love Supreme.*

The later move in Coltrane toward free jazz develops a difficult musical vocabulary that taxes the player, the range of the instrument itself, and certainly the listener's hearing. Coltrane pushes sound and tactility that simply defies standard ordering and expectations. He breaks so many assumptions and expectations within the inherited jazz traditions coming through the 40s, 50s, and early 60s. Howison lets us in on many of the stories behind the recordings, stories that describe the environment in which the jazz of Coltrane's groups were living. Group improvisation is clearly for Howison, as it was for McCoy Tyner, Coltrane, and other collaborators, a spiritual experience. Jazz collaboration, deeply embedded in a history of playing together, is understood as sounding of the spiritual and religious roots of a people.

Of the forty-minute long recording of *Ascension*, in his review for *Down Beat* Bill Mathieu said, "this is possibly the most powerful human sound ever recorded." Howison's deeply empathetic exploration of *Ascension*—with its biblical overtones of the ascension of Christ—is written with a deep humility before the subject. Even if you, the reader, have no concern for theology, you will find yourself, as I have, wondering about Coltrane's encounter and wrestling with God—"His OMNIPOTENCE" as he writes in the notes to *A Love Supreme*. He was and remains, for each new generation's hearing, a child of American black church and its music and spiritual cultures. There spiritual lament and doxology, the cry of suffering and the shout of redemption, are always waiting to be rediscovered.

I find myself reading these pages on multiple levels, just as we must listen to Coltrane's music on multiple levels. The book is not a piece of music criticism, though it offers detailed critical insights into a whole range of the recordings. This is not a standard biography, though it is dense with biographical details. It is not about church theology, but it takes us into the mystery of why the Trinitarian God is an improviser—via the work of the Holy Spirit. It is not an essay in religious spirituality, though it will provoke real questions about God and acoustic imagination, especially about what it means to live *coram deo* (before the presence of God). All four of these concerns are interwoven. I think of them as "sounded," and as giving a telling counterpoint. This mirrors the life and music of John Coltrane.

There is really only one appropriate response to this book: to take up listening again to the range of Coltrane's recordings, perhaps especially to *A Love Supreme*. This is, of course, a demanding task. His music can assault, explode, scream, sound chaotic, and take us into somatic and emotional realms we may not understand—at least not at first. Just like author Howison, we will have to give ourselves time with Coltrane. I think I can begin to say that I can now hear Coltrane "praying" through his horn. The closest analogy here, it seems to me, is the wild range we find in the biblical psalms: lament, complaint, anguish, even paranoia, but right alongside utter thanksgiving and ecstatic praise. "Let everything that breathes praise the Lord" (Ps 150). John Coltrane lived and breathed and still can set us on edge, listening for the grandeur and misery of being human in the presence of God.

Don E. Saliers
Atlanta
May 2012

Introduction

A visiting friend and I were listening to a jazz trio one Sunday morning in an Anglican church. The trio led off with a prelude by John Coltrane, and then accompanied the singing of hymns and responses. For the offering they played a piece by Thelonious Monk. While the ushers passed the plates between the rows the bass tromped out the vintage, the piano danced on the head of a pin and the saxophone reached deep into the invisible joinery of mortise and tenon in the high-raftered interior of the building. As the notes slowly resolved again into three musicians stationed below the altar with their instruments, my friend leaned over and said, *Today I believe in God.*

—John Terpstra, *Skin Boat*

You have to be careful back here . . . this music will make you weep.

—Unnamed customer, Melody Record Shop, Washington D.C.

A steamy hot day in Washington, D.C., and we were done for the day with museums and monuments. I'd taken refuge from the heat and congestion at the Melody Record Shop on Connecticut Avenue, giving myself a blissful hour to see if I couldn't find some hidden gem tucked away in the midst of the store's considerable stock. As is often the case in CD and record stores, the jazz section was located off near the back, far from the racks that were attracting most of the traffic. Making my way through the John Coltrane discs, I hadn't noticed the arrival of another jazz

1

fan. His warning—"You have to be careful back here . . . this music will make you weep"—was like a little shot to the ribs, and I looked up to meet the eyes of a thin, graying African-American man. "It will," he said, slowly shaking his head from side to side. I nodded and smiled, and we returned to our respective searches, though our conversation continued in little bits and pieces. "You know this one?" he asked, holding up a copy of *The Complete Village Vanguard Recordings, 1961* by Bill Evans. "This man can play."

"Oh yeah, I love Bill Evans," I responded, "particularly from that era. I don't have the complete sessions, but I've got the single disc edition, which I've listened to a lot." And as we continued flipping through the discs, we chatted about the music we each owned, and which old and worn vinyl records we had begun to replace with CDs. He seemed to like the fact that my tastes were rooted mostly in the 1950s and 60s. And then the conversation shifted.

"I have a nine year old granddaughter, and she's a dancer. You should see her dance when I have Bill Evans on the stereo. Once she started to dance as we were walking across this bridge . . . she was just humming one of his tunes, and dancing . . . made me cry. I'll start now, if I think about it too much."

Our silence resumed, punctuated by the slightly muffled click-click-click sound made as each of us flipped our way through row after row of plastic CD jewel cases. Then out of nowhere he said, "And you knew that Evans was a heroin addict?" His eyes were locked firmly on the disc in his hand. "He played with such beauty and such sadness, through all of that pain."

"Heroin took a lot of them," I said, and now it was my turn to hold the long pause. I suppose I was giving him space to back away from what seemed to be an almost painfully personal moment, and then when I did speak I said, "But for all that the scene was tangled up in drugs and addiction, I love the music of that time." Another pause—shorter this time. "I got to see Sonny Rollins a couple of months ago, at our jazz festival back home in Winnipeg. He was astonishing."

"Oh Sonny, he plays with such power, and at his age too." Again he was slowly shaking his head from side to side, this time looking as if he was receding into some deep aural memory. "Son," he said, "I'm going to have to leave you here on your own, before I really do start to cry." And with that, he turned and made his way down the narrow aisle, out the door and into the heat of the August afternoon.

That sort of thing just happens with people who love jazz music. Sometimes it is in a music store, but most often it is at a live venue. Even in a concert hall it isn't unusual to find yourself talking with someone you've never met before, though it is in the smaller clubs that it is really common. Sitting up at the bar or at one of the often tightly packed tables, conversations just seem to begin, and before you know it you're sharing the story of a great show you saw last week or last year—with older fans it might be a great show from decades back—or recommending a great new recording from some as yet largely unknown player. Occasionally there is a competitive edge to these exchanges, with a touch of bragging about who you have seen live, as each tries to establish just how much the other actually knows or loves this music, but even that is all part of the culture. After all, part of the legacy of jazz music is the famous "cutting sessions" and head-to-head battles of musicians looking to demonstrate their worth, but more on that later.

It is striking, too, the degree to which emotionally charged words are used to describe experiences connected to the music. My acquaintance at the D.C. record store was quite willing to talk not only of the beauty, but also of the deep sadness of the music he loved, and to confess to a complete stranger how close he was to weeping. Other times I've had people tell me how a particular show moved them, "blew them away," or left them emotionally drained. When jazz fans get into these kinds of conversations, it isn't so much a case of boasting as it is an expression of the desire to share something of a peak experience; an experience that embodied something particularly powerful and occasionally even transcendent.

In a 2007 videotaped interview given for the archives of the National Jazz Museum in Harlem, bass player Reggie Workman recounts a story from his mid-sixties stint with Art Blakey's Jazz Messengers. As was typical for Blakey, in that incarnation of the Messengers he had gathered a group of young and promising musicians, and was forming, pushing, and disciplining them into shape as a mature performing unit. The band was on tour in California, and one night when they took the stage Blakey discovered that Dizzy Gillespie and Billy Eckstine were sitting at the front table. As Workman tells the story, the confident and demanding bandleader "became like a little child in the presence of Billy and Dizzy," who numbered amongst his own mentors and heroes. Workman recalls how Blakey pushed himself to play even harder than usual, wanting so much to earn the respect of these two musicians whom he held in such high esteem. His young band took up the challenge, and as Workman tells it, the audience experienced something rare and precious. "The music went so high," he says, his voice trailing off to the point where he is rendered, quite literally, speechless. "No words," he barely manages to say as he fights off the tears. "No words."

It is an astonishing thing to watch this veteran musician fall into silence, head bowed and hand held to his teary eyes, overwhelmed and humbled in his memory of having been a part of something that transcended musical prowess and technique. It is particularly astonishing that his response was so powerful some forty years after the event. In the interview, Workman is also clear that the audience was not incidental to the whole. Gillespie and Eckstine, of course, were a part of that audience, but of the others Workman says, "Anybody who was in the club that night experienced something that they will never—and had never—experienced before."

It isn't only live performances that do it, either. A few years back I presided at the funeral of a man from our church, who in a state of deep depression and despair had taken his own life. More than just a church member, Terry was also someone I counted as a friend, which made the funeral all the more painful. Why hadn't I known about his depression? Why didn't I see this coming? Why hadn't he reached out to me? All the questions people ask when someone they know commits suicide. The funeral service took place in the city, but the burial was in a small town church yard about an hour's drive away, and as I got into my car I slipped Terence Blanchard's *A Tale of God's Will* into the stereo, thinking it a good opportunity to give the album my first close listening. Subtitled *Requiem for Katrina*, Blanchard's album is a sustained, sorrowful, and extraordinarily dignified meditation on the devastation of New Orleans under the force of Hurricane Katrina. It was a remarkably apt soundtrack for my drive, and as I turned off the main highway onto the road that would take me into that little town the disc reached "Funeral Dirge," a song that voices both deep lament and powerful resilience. By the time the song ended, tears were streaming down my face, and I had to drive around the town for another five minutes just to get my bearings.

Yet, even as I drove that loop, I found I had to give "Funeral Dirge" a second listening. The resilience—I needed the resilience as much as I needed the visceral release that had come with the tears.

I had occasion to speak with Blanchard about this prior to a set at New York's Jazz Standard night club, and after thanking him for what I described as a "devastatingly beautiful" work, he told me that others had shared similar experiences around the way in which the album had been both cathartic and healing. Blanchard then added that it was "one of those records I don't even feel that I made," and that it "just came to us, like a gift."

Needless to say, it is not only jazz music that can work to touch emotions, unlock grief, express joy, or bring about peak experiences. Yet there may be something very particular about a music that is so defined by improvisational freedom, collectivity, and live performance that makes jazz particularly suited to this kind of work.

And while I am interested in making the claim that jazz can be a theologically and spiritually expressive and insightful form, for years it was routinely dismissed as being at best lowbrow. In James Baldwin's classic short story "Sonny's Blues," when the title character tells his older brother that he wants to be a jazz musician, the concerned brother muses to himself that, "It seemed—beneath him, somehow. I had never thought about it before, had never been forced to, but I suppose I had always put jazz musicians in a class with what Daddy called 'good-time people.'"[1]

Even worse, jazz was often written off as brothel music, "jungle music," or even the devil's music. This sort of view was held not only by those in the church, but as Neil Leonard points out also by those committed to what he calls "classical music orthodoxy." "[T]he church-like music orthodoxy found that contagious jazz, springing in wild luxuriance from the black subsoil, was blatantly irrational, full of raw sensuality that defied common decency and the sober purposefulness of the received ethic."[2] This stuff was dangerous.

1. Baldwin, "Sonny's Blues," 31.
2. Leonard, *Jazz: Myth and Religion*, 15–16.

Yet the evangelical theologian, William Edgar—himself a jazz musician—can write that, "In studying the emergence of jazz, it is impossible to extricate the religious element without completely altering the history of its formation."[3] Even more to the point, jazz giant Dizzy Gillespie once commented that, "Like most black musicians, most of my inspiration, especially with rhythms and harmonies, came from the church. I first learned about rhythms there and all about how music could transport people spiritually."[4] To this, the liturgical theologian Don Saliers—also a musician with a taste for jazz—adds another layer of insight, when he writes, "So it is that in the twentieth century, gospel music and jazz emerged as the peculiar fusion of African and European musical traditions in the Americas, and has made its way into liturgical and theological domains. As Alice Coltrane, creative musician and wife of saxophonist John Coltrane is reported to have said, 'to play jazz *is* to worship—to be in church.'"[5]

The so-called devil's music seems to have made some serious inroads into the world of the church. Or better, the time came when people began to recognize that jazz has some pretty deep roots in the church, and that to find ways to honor that connection might be a good thing for both the church and for jazz.

The honoring of this connection is hardly new. Over the years, influential jazz musicians such as Art Tatum and Louis Armstrong were unafraid to draw on hymnody as part of their repertoire, while the 1960s witnessed the production of jazz mass settings by Paul Horn (*Jazz Suite on the Mass Texts*, 1965) and Mary Lou Williams (*Music for Peace*, revised as *Mary Lou's Mass*, 1964), as well as the first two of Duke Ellington's three "Sacred Concerts." This is the same period in which the Reverend John Garcia Gensel began his pioneering jazz ministry in New York City. Initiated in 1960, and originally based out of Advent Lutheran Church in the Upper West Side, in 1965 the jazz ministry followed Gensel to St Peter's Lutheran Church on Lexington Avenue, and it was in that context that a weekly Sunday afternoon jazz vespers liturgy was introduced. As described by Gensel's friend and former ministry colleague Dale Lind, "It started as a request from the musicians themselves,

3. Edgar, "The Deep Joy of Jazz," para. 4.

4. Leonard, *Jazz: Myth and Religion*, 47.

5. Saliers, *Music and Theology*, 18.

who desired to participate in a worship service where they could play their own music as an offering of praise for the glory of God at a time which would accommodate their late night lifestyle in which they usually performed in jazz clubs until four o'clock in the morning."[6] It was, in short, a liturgical ministry connected to the needs, gifts, and spiritual yearnings of the community that Gensel sought to serve as pastor.

During this same period, many jazz musicians were actively exploring theological and spiritual truths through their music. Often as not, however, these explorations reflected the move many African-American musicians were making to embrace Islam, the Nation of Islam, various forms of Eastern religious spirituality, or some other more esoteric spiritual system. In part, this movement was precipitated by the often critical and condemning position held by the church in its attitude toward jazz, though as we shall see other factors also played a role.

And of course, these were also the years in which John Coltrane was pursuing his most spiritual music, notably *A Love Supreme* (1965), described in the album liner notes as "a humble offering to Him," and "An attempt to say 'THANK YOU GOD' through our work, even as we do in our hearts and with our tongues." Though certainly Coltrane's best known and best-selling record, *A Love Supreme* marks something of a beginning point in his musical search, as opposed to an ending or culmination. While describing the album as "the consummate product of an assimilation process in which Coltrane sums up five years of musical experiences and perceptions," the German jazz writer and musician Ekkehard Jost claims that, "The step from *A Love Supreme* . . . to *Ascension* which Coltrane recorded a half-year later meant more for his musical growth that any step before."[7] Or as John Coltrane remarked to Nat Hentoff in an interview for the liner notes to the 1966 *Meditations* album, "Once you become aware of this force for unity in life, you can't ever forget it. It becomes part of everything you do. In that respect, this is an extension of *A Love Supreme*."

It is precisely this searching spiritual quality in Coltrane's musical and personal vision that seems to draw people. Coltrane's grip on so many, many listeners (even to the point of some fans

6. Lind, "John Garcia Gensel," 222.
7. Jost, *Free Jazz*, 32.

becoming quite literally disciples) is not simply a matter of his musical and technical excellence. Rather it is his stature as a quintessential *seeker*—a seeker with a horn, but also with a heart, a mind, and a tireless passion—that has made him such an iconic figure. In a 1987 article in *The Atlantic Monthly*, Edward Strickland wrote of "Coltrane's journey from hard-bop saxist to daring harmonic and modal improviser to dying prophet speaking in tongues," ending the piece with the following: "The whole spectrum of Coltrane's music—the world-weary melancholy and transcendental yearning that ultimately recall Bach more than [Charlie] Parker, the jungle calls and glossolalic shrieks, the whirlwind runs and spare elegies for murdered children and a murderous plant—is at root merely a suffering man's breath. The quality of that music reminds us that the root of the word inspiration is 'breathing upon.' This country has not produced a greater musician."[8]

Coltrane seems to *draw* people to his music, to his story, and to the oftentimes enigmatic quality of his personality. Less than a decade after his untimely death in 1967, a Coltrane publishing industry emerged, with two biographies arriving in 1975 and a third in 1976. Rather than slowing down, the past two decades have actually witnessed an acceleration in the production of Coltrane books, including very carefully researched and quite scholarly works—Lewis Porter's *John Coltrane: His Life and Music* and the exhaustive *John Coltrane Reference*—along with more popular, less technical book such as Ben Ratliff's *Coltrane: The Story of a Sound*. In writing my book I am adding one more title to the ever-expanding catalogue, though the approach that I am taking is as much an exploration of the convergence of music and theology as it is a study of this particular musician.

And clearly *this* particular musician *has* drawn me, both with his music and through his story. Working with the interviews, reviews, liner notes, and articles published during his life and with the abundance of material published since his death, I have taken a long view of things. In this I particularly appreciate Herman Gray's observation that at some point the person of John Coltrane was turned into "the mythical and iconic figure" of Trane, a "symbolic

---

8. Strickland, "What Coltrane Wanted," 102.

act" which "ultimately comes at a price."[9] I trust that in writing this book I have managed to avoid mistaking a myth for the man.

In terms of the general shape and perspective of this book, it will be important to begin by offering something of an overview of the way in which theology has tended to understand music. Certainly not meant to be an exhaustive treatment, I will offer a rather personal picture of how my own theological engagement with this music has unfolded. This section will also include a review of some of the theological work that has been done on jazz, blues, and the spirituals. This latter area is not uncontested, and to presume to do anything like an exhaustive study would be foolish. Yet to *not* look at these issues would be to render this study shallow and ultimately rootless, which is a deep problem for both theology and jazz.

It will be necessary to then consider a set of questions around the origins of jazz music and specifically its roots in the black church tradition. As will become quite apparent, questions related to the origins of jazz music are also not undisputed or uncontroversial. This is a matter of some importance to my reading of John Coltrane, as I understand at least part of his theological significance as being tied to his deep roots in the black church tradition.

This will then lead to a chapter dealing with the outlines of Coltrane's life, which to my mind is indispensable in understanding his creative work and vision. This assumption does cut directly against the grain of a text-based post-structuralist approach to reading cultural texts, but in this case I would argue that it is frankly impossible to fully appreciate the musical statement without knowing the background narrative. I will not, however, try to presume too much in terms of the specifics of Coltrane's beliefs and theology. Many have succumbed to the temptation to try to claim Coltrane as their own and to presume to have him represent positions that he himself never clearly articulated. I take very seriously the observation offered me by the musician and Coltrane scholar Dr. Lewis Porter, who suggested it is highly problematic to try "guessing what someone thought after they have passed away." As Porter observed, "Virtually everything Coltrane ever said on the topic [of religion and spirituality] is included in my book, and as I'm sure you've noticed, it's not much."[10] I will attempt to walk a

9. Gray, "Coltrane and the Practice of Freedom," 35.
10. Porter, e-mail correspondence.

fine line between recognizing the way in which Coltrane's music is anchored in his personal story, without presuming to actually know his mind and heart.

This will mark the transition toward the second section of the book, which is a series of seven theological reflections offered through a hearing of specific pieces of Coltrane's music. I have subtitled this book *Theological Explorations through the Music of John Coltrane*, but to be honest I am only going to be able to do justice to just a few pieces and/or works. Even then, to say that I am going to "do justice" to them is probably a stretch, given all that I *don't* know about music, about theology, and about my subject's inner life.

It is important to offer a confessional word or two about what I don't know when it comes to writing a book dealing with the convergence of jazz and theology; about my own limitations as a researcher and writer. To frame things more positively, I need to be clear as to the particular place from which I am offering this work.

First off, I am not a musician and I bring to this project only a very rudimentary understanding of music theory. Although I struggled through several years of music lessons as a child and adolescent, all that remains from those days is a basic ability to read music and a willingness to sing as part of a church congregation. I'm sure that for some readers, this will immediately compromise the value of anything I might have to say about music. I want to suggest, however, that what it does is position me differently; I am a listener, and what I hear might well be different from what a trained musician hears. John Coltrane himself voiced some real hesitation about the idea that listeners necessarily needed to come with a theoretical framework in order to be able to hear and appreciate his music. In the liner notes to the *Transition* album, the jazz writer Nat Hentoff recounts the following: "'The music has to speak for itself,' John Coltrane said once when I asked him for a structural exegesis of one of his composition-performances. 'I'd much rather,' he continued, 'you didn't put anything technical in the notes. It might get in the way of people finding out what there is in the music for them.'" As I've already suggested in my retelling of the story of Reggie Workman and Art Blakey, every time any of us goes to hear live music, we are at least potentially a part of its creation. In a consideration of musical improvisation, Jeremy Begbie refers to what he calls "occasional constraints" (as opposed to the "musical constraints," which in jazz are things such as meter and harmonic sequence), listing firstly, "the physical space in which the improvisation occurs and its attendant sounds"; secondly, "the other improvising participants . . . the music they produce, *and the audience*"; and finally, "the disposition of the improviser him/herself."[11] The audience is a part of what shapes the music. In reflecting on his work with the Wayne Shorter quartet, bass player John Patitucci spoke of how an improvisational piece begins to build through risk-taking and a shared willingness to trust the other members of the band. At some point, he commented, it "spills right into the audience," and the way in which the members of that audience engage this challenge to be open and to risk and trust impacts what the musicians then create.[12] Put more simply, Duke Ellington once remarked, "If I hear a sigh of pleasure from the dance floor, it becomes part of our music."[13]

Second, while I have been immersed in the world of theology for most of my adult life, aside from three years as a theological student at Trinity College in Toronto this immersion has largely taken place outside of the world of the academy. I have not ignored or been in any way dismissive of the theological work done in the academic world, and in fact in various contexts I have worked collaboratively with scholars—including a seven-year tenure on the Primate's Theological Commission of the Anglican Church of Canada—but I am first and foremost a preacher. My theological wrestlings and whatever insights they might produce really begin and end in that context, as week after week I am challenged to speak something truthful into the life of a gathered community. This is by no means a bad starting point, but it is a very particular one, quite different from the starting point of the academic theologian.

I have to admit to experiencing some real delight when in reading Tommy Lott's essay, "When Bar Walkers Preach: John Coltrane and the Crisis of the Black Intellectual," I first encountered Cornel West's idea of the "organic intellectual." For West, the academic world produces and nurtures a particular kind of intellectual, which he identifies as the "literate intellectual," but he also

11. Begbie, *Theology, Music and Time*, 205. Italics added.
12. Patitucci, personal interview.
13. Gracyk, "Jazz," 184.

11

recognizes and celebrates the presence of this other stream in the black intellectual tradition, exemplified by musicians and preachers. As Lott observes, some of how West works with his distinction can be problematic, yet the very idea that the preacher (and the musician) have a significant role in the shaping of a shared intellectual life is important. And while West evidently characterizes the organic intellectual as "being less alienated for having found support from strong traditions grounded within black communities,"[14] I am not at all interested in dismissing the academic theologian as functioning only within the proverbial ivory tower, "alienated" from the organic life of the Christian community. To be fair, given West's profile as a very public intellectual, I suspect he himself is quite disinterested in being confined to that ivory tower. The significant point here is to acknowledge the need for theology to be done in the church and community as well as in the university and seminary. In this book, I write as an organic, parish-based intellectual attempting to offer a sustained reflection on the work of another, albeit very different, organic intellectual. Underlying this project is a powerful assumption that not only do the church and academy need each other, but also that both need to engage music—and in fact the arts in general—as a potent source of theological insight and wisdom. I will return to Lott's essay at a later point in this book, but for now I simply need to acknowledge the encouragement that it gave me as I set out on my research for this project.

In embracing that designation, I had to wrestle with one of the other realities that I bring to this work. Both Lott and West are dealing specifically with the black church and the black intellectual tradition, and both might be inclined to say that things are very different in my Euro-Canadian cultural and racial context. Clearly the place and prominence of a preacher coming from a highly pluralistic, twenty-first-century Canadian urban setting is utterly different from that which both of John Coltrane's preacher grandfathers would have known in their respective home communities in North Carolina. In fact, my context is utterly different from that of a preacher in a black congregation in current day Harlem. This was brought home to me in a very vivid way when I attended the funeral of the musician and educator Dr. Billy Taylor, held at Manhattan's Riverside Church on January 10, 2011. Though Riverside's

14. Lott, "Bar Walkers," 103.

own minister offered a formal invocation and words of welcome, there was little question that the person who had the real authority on the platform was Dr. Calvin O. Butts, III, the senior pastor of Harlem's Abyssinian Baptist Church. By his very presence at the front of the church, Butts clearly commanded the attention of the predominantly black congregation. More, as the memorial drew to a close and without any warning, he called the noted jazz pianist Ramsey Lewis to come out from his place in the pew to play an impromptu version of the old hymn, "Precious Lord." As he did this, Butts came across as having an entirely unselfconscious sense of authority, such that no one—least of all Lewis himself—would have questioned the wisdom or prudence of his making such an impromptu request. Frankly, in my cultural and ecclesial context, I have no experience of anything even close to that kind of authority.

At a fairly early stage of my research for this book I read James Cone's important work, *The Spirituals and the Blues*. I had made arrangements to spend a research month in New York City, and had been appointed as a scholar-in-residence at the Burke Library at Union Theological Seminary (which more or less proves my point about not wanting to be dismissive of the academy . . .). Given the importance of his book, and being that Dr. Cone is based at Union, I settled in to give *The Spirituals and the Blues* a close reading. All of three pages in, I discovered that Cone is, "convinced that it is not possible to render an authentic interpretation of black music without having shared and participated in the experience that created it. Black music must be *lived* before it can be understood."[15] As Cone's introductory chapter progressed, this passionate conviction was even more clearly articulated. "I contend that there is a deeper level of experience which transcends the tools of 'objective' historical research. And that experience is available only to those who share the *spirit* and participate in the *faith* of the people who created these songs. I am referring to the power and energy released in black devotion to the God of emotion."[16] "I, therefore, write about the spirituals and the blues, because *I am the blues* and my *life is a spiritual*," writes Cone in his closing statement to his introduction. "Without them, I cannot be."[17]

15. Cone, *Spirituals and Blues*, 3.
16. Ibid., 4.
17. Ibid., 7.

If one of the great theological interpreters of the blues can make such an impassioned statement about this music, what of jazz, which is very much rooted in the blues? Could a white Canadian possibly have anything significant to offer by way of an engagement with the work of a black American jazz musician, whose formative years were deeply shaped by the black church tradition?

With some trepidation, I arranged a telephone interview with Dr. Cone, who as it happened would not actually be in New York during my month at Union.[18] Given what I had read in his book, I was more than a bit nervous that he might tell me that I would never really be able to cross the cultural and contextual barriers, and that I might as well pack in my project. As it turned out, James Cone is far too nuanced a thinker—and far too gracious a man—to have taken such a hard line. What he did do was to offer some very good advice. In response to my question of what it might mean for a white Canadian man to be working on this sort of project, he told me, "I think you have to go to where the music has been created, and get to know the people who created it." And then referring to Adam Gussow's book *Seems Like Murder Here*, he added, "He's a white guy who paid the price, and I'll tell you he understands the blues. So when you pay the price, you can do it. But you have to pay the price."

I wondered, though, how I could possibly pay any kind of real price over the course of just four weeks in New York City. And thanks to my research grant, I'd hardly be living on the edge of suffering or poverty, and I said as much to Dr. Cone. He again suggested that I would need to "go to where the music has been created," and spend some real time in Harlem, joining local congregations for worship and listening to music in some of the neighborhood clubs. And instead of going as an observer, I'd need to actually talk with people. And so I did.

Over the course of my month in New York, I had the opportunity to join in worship with black congregations on four occasions. Cone had advised me that I'd be best to avoid the larger and more visible churches, as they tend to be harder to penetrate for a visitor, so I found my way into small and medium sized congregations where I was able to meet some people and unite my voice with theirs in worship. The congregation of Greater Hood Memorial

18. Cone, telephone interview.

African Methodist Episcopal Zion Church was particularly welcoming to this outsider (and I was the one person amongst the eighty or so people in attendance who was *clearly* the outsider), with any number of people introducing themselves to me, and Pastor Kenneth VanLew actually asking if I might be seeking a new church home. VanLew delivered an artful and impassioned sermon on Proverbs 3:1–10, giving me a real experience of what Cone meant when he told me that both black music and black preaching are, "defined more by the spirit that is generated through the sounds than through the conceptual content of what is being said." It also helped to deepen my understanding of what Wynton Marsalis meant when he compared John Coltrane's musical performance to the delivery of a sermon in the black church tradition. "The thing that is always in John Coltrane is the lyrical shout of the preacher in the heat and the full fury of attempting to transform the congregation. And that is the source of John Coltrane's power . . . when you hear it, it changes the way you perceive the world."[19]

While I certainly spent plenty of time in some of the more established clubs—Smoke, the Village Vanguard, The Jazz Standard—as well as in several of the smaller and often more experimental Greenwich Village rooms—Smalls, Bar 55, the Cornelia Street Café—I did make sure to settle in to a couple of the historic Harlem rooms as well. In both the Lenox Lounge and St. Nick's Pub I not only heard wonderful music, but also managed to share some great and rambling conversations with several of the regulars. It didn't much matter whether we were talking about the neighborhood (some thinking it wasn't what it used to be, and others very much enamored by it), professional football and the approaching Super Bowl (about which I could contribute nothing at all), the price of drinks (we could all agree that $7 for a bottled beer was too much), or the evening's music; the conversations just seemed to happen.

Anchoring my time in the neighborhood was my involvement with the National Jazz Museum in Harlem. Over the course of the month I attended eight different museum events and spent an additional couple of days working in their library and video archives. Although there are very ambitious plans in the works to build a major exhibit and performance space, at this point in its existence

19. Marsalis interview, Ken Burns' *Jazz*, episode 9.

the National Jazz Museum is more a center for educational and musical events. I have to acknowledge how much I appreciated the support of the museum's executive director, Loren Schoenberg, as well as the great jazz insights I received from the museum's co-director, Christian McBride.

Many of the people attending events at the Jazz Museum have deep roots in Harlem, and the informal conversations tended to flow easily. I was particularly delighted to have the opportunity to speak several times with Tajah Murdock, a very dignified woman of 80, who had lived much of her life in the neighborhood. As a young woman she had been a dancer at the Apollo Theater and with Count Basie's Big Band, and while she confessed to me that she had really never known what to make of the music of people like John Coltrane and Thelonious Monk, she certainly had known them. "I knew all of those people," she said, "because we all used to go to Minton's Playhouse late at night after we'd finished our show." But Tajah's heart was really for the Harlem of the 1930s and 1940s: "Harlem in those days was wonderful," she said, adding that she thought it was a real loss that so few of this current generation's musicians has any real sense of where their music originated.

All told, I probably spent as much time in Harlem as I did in any other location in the city, with the possible exception of the Burke Library at Union Theological Seminary. Based in that wonderfully rich library during many of my days, I had access to almost every theological book or journal that I needed. And because Union is connected to the Columbia University library system, I could also access the main university library as well as its fairly comprehensive music library. What wasn't available there I found quite easily during my day at the Institute for Jazz Studies at Rutgers University, in New Jersey.

Along with the library work, my time in Harlem, and many evenings spent listening to live music, the final piece of research was the series of interviews I conducted with musicians, writers, and theologians. Many of these were done in person, others over the phone or through e-mail. Many took place during my time in New York, though a number did take place both before and after my designated study leave. The willingness of so many to set aside other commitments to share a conversation, exchange correspondence, or read draft chapters was a real gift. In this regard, I need to acknowledge a whole list of people. Many are musicians, several are writers and scholars, and many of the writers are also musicians. In no particular order, thanks to John Patitucci, Jimmy Greene, Lewis Porter, David Wild, Earl MacDonald, Bill Crow, Ike Sturm, Dale Lind, Christian McBride, Loren Schoenberg, Mc-Coy Tyner, Charlie Peacock, Steve Bell, Gregory Thomas, Calvin Seerveld, William Edgar, Don Saliers, Donald Ottenhoff, Michael Boyce, Michael Gilmour, Cameron McKenzie, Alana Levandoski, Christopher Holmes, and James Cone. Also a word of thanks to Palle Pallesen Kongsgaard, for making the connection between *A Love Supreme* and the writings of Dorothee Soelle.

I also wish to thank the Louisville Institute for its financial support; John Weaver and his staff at the Burke Library of Union Theological Seminary; the staff, volunteers and regulars at the National Jazz Museum in Harlem; the staff and resident scholars at the Collegeville Institute, as well as the Benedictine community of St John's Abbey, for giving me such a rooted place to write, think, and pray; Fr. Kilian McDonnell OSB, for his encouragement; Rodney Clapp and all at Cascade; the community of my home church of saint benedict's table; my wife Catherine Pate for supporting me in taking a two-month study leave, and proceeding to renovate half of our house while I was gone. Catherine spent long hours proofing and editing my draft chapters, making it all a far more presentable project than would have otherwise been the case.

It will already be clear that I have chosen to write in a highly personal way. While it may be right and good that much theological work is done less personally and more dispassionately, in a work such as this one it is important that a sense of the author as conversation partner—and listening partner—comes through. On this count, I need to acknowledge the influence of one person in particular, for his voice greatly helped me to find my own. Both through reading his books and in sharing with him in conversation, the Christian philosopher of art and aesthetics Calvin Seerveld has been for me both a guiding light and a challenging voice. Well over a year before I wrote the first word of this book, we sat in his living room in Toronto and talked about how I was hoping to engage Coltrane's music as a source for theological reflection. Topmost in my mind were questions of authorial intent, and as our conversation progressed, it was to this question that we returned again and again. "I would not trust the art-maker as giving the final or correct answer," Cal commented. "I would like a Christian interpretive community, which is why you maybe can proceed in this music in a manner that the secular critics can't. They just think that this music is spiritual, whatever that is. I would trust your kind of insight."[20] That alone was a most reassuring message to hear, though there was another wonderful moment in which I found myself just a little humbled. "What artists think they put into it may not be what they did. Like pastors, preaching." Hmmm. But that, too, was a moment of insight, for it told this preacher that just as I am often unaware of what my sermon was communicating, so too John Coltrane would have been quite oblivious to what people—including me—might glean from one of his pieces.

And then Cal offered yet another great angle on my work: "You could think about his music as *glossalalia*, and you are the interpreter now, struggling to see what the tongues are saying . . . The key thing is in what spirit is it done? To detect the spirit in the music is very important."[21] And maybe that is at the heart of my task in this book; to attempt to discern and interpret what John Coltrane has spoken through his music. While clearly attentive to how his music unfolded in the context of his own life narrative, and sensitive to what he seems to have understood himself to be doing in the creation of his art, there is also a need—and a freedom—to engage this music from within the context of the church community. As Cal said at the very end of our conversation that day, "I think one always has to listen to the author, but not give them veto power." This approach is in keeping with Bruce Ellis Benson's assertion that what he calls "un-interpreted texts" do require interpreters and, "interpreters or readers are necessary not only for a text to have meaning but also for it simply to *be* in its fullest sense."[22] Neither the un-interpreted text nor the work of the interpreter—neither the composer nor the listener—have the final say about the meaning of the work, but rather they work together to give voice to what the text might actually have to say. In this very real sense, my work as a discerning and interpreting listener becomes a part of the improvisational freedom that characterizes the art of John Coltrane.

20. Seerveld, personal interview.
21. Ibid.
22. Benson, "Improvising Texts," 297.

Listening Guide

The only way to really engage the reflections in this book is to listen to the music, and *not* as some sort of background soundtrack to your reading. It is actually pretty tough to have Coltrane on in the background, because his music will either grab your attention and distract you from your reading, or, as in the case of a recording like "Ascension," it will just become downright irritating. Don't even try.

Even if you are familiar with these pieces, I still recommend giving each one a focused listening prior to reading the corresponding theological reflection. If this music is new to you, all the more reason to approach things in this way. Fortunately, all of my selections are quite easily available, and generally on quite affordable editions of the various albums. Almost everything here is also available for purchase as a download, though that does mean you miss out on the often very useful liner notes. If you don't want to buy before you even know if this is music that you're likely to want in your collection, your public library probably owns a decent cross-section of what you'll need. If you have a friend who is a jazz fan, she or he is guaranteed to own at least a couple of these albums that you could ask to borrow. Though be warned: your friend will inevitably offer strong opinions about the relative merits of the albums you are asking to borrow, suggest to you that my choices are somehow not quite right, and send you on your way with a small armful of other discs you really *must* listen to. It is just the way we do things.

Many of these pieces appear on various compilation albums, but purist that I am, I have chosen to go with the albums on which they were originally released. So, here goes . . .

Chapter 4—"My Favorite Things"

My Favorite Things, Atlantic 1961
Live at the Village Vanguard Again! Impulse, 1966

If you can, you should also try to lay your hands on a copy of the "Jazz Icons" DVD *John Coltrane Live in '60, '61 & '65.* I do deal with the version of "My Favorite Things" from the 1965 Belgium concert, but as bonus you also get a version from a 1961 German television program.

Chapter 5—"Naima" and "Wise One"

Giant Steps, Atlantic 1960 (for "Naima")
Crescent, Impulse 1964 (for "Wise One")

There are alternate versions of "Naima" on *Live at the Village Vanguard Again!* and on the "Jazz Icons" DVD, though for this chapter, you really do need the original.

Chapter 6—"Alabama"

Live at Birdland, Impulse 1964

"Alabama" is one of two studio tracks included on this "live" album.

Chapter 7—A Love Supreme

A Love Supreme, Impulse 1964

There is a deluxe edition of *A Love Supreme* available, which includes the only known recorded live version of the entire suite, along with some alternate studio takes of both "Acknowledgment" and "Resolution." Normally I'd say that such an extravagance isn't really necessary, but you might seriously consider purchasing this one. The alternate studio takes are interesting, but the version recorded live at the Festival Mondial du Jazz Antibes in France is what really counts here. It is fascinating to hear the very mixed reaction of the audience, which really conveys a sense that many had attended the concert expecting to hear something a little more mainstream.

Chapter 8—Ascension

Ascension, Impulse 1966

Standard CD versions of *Ascension* now come with two versions of this extended piece. You want to listen to Edition II, which somewhat confusingly will be track one on the disc. I'll explain all of this in the context of the chapter itself.

Chapter 9—"The Father and the Son and the Holy Ghost"

Meditations, Impulse 1966

A different version of the "Meditations" suite was released in 1977 as *First Meditations*. As the album title suggests, it was actually recorded prior to *Meditations*. I do offer some reflections on the differences between the two versions, though because it doesn't even include "The Father and the Son and the Holy Ghost" it is not necessary to chase down this alternate version.

Chapter 10—"Attaining"

Sun Ship, Impulse 1971

Though these recordings sessions actually predate those for *Meditations* by several months, the album itself was not released until four years after Coltrane's death. There have been a number of posthumous releases over the years, drawn both from studio sessions and from live performances. As I discuss in chapter 7, both *Sun Ship* and *Interstellar Space* (Impulse 1974) stand out as being thematically and musically coherent albums, which isn't always the case with the posthumous releases.

Of the many live albums, I'd highlight *One Down, One Up: Coltrane Live at the Half Note* (Impulse, 2005) as being a particularly good example of the work of his classic quartet at the height of its power. Rather sadly, a recording of Coltrane's final concert released on Impulse in 2001 as *The Olatunji Concert: The Last Live Recording* suffers from very poor sound, and is of little more than archival interest.

If you're really new to this, and not sure that you want to start spending a bunch of money on music you've never even heard, you could start with either *Ken Burn's Jazz: The Definitive John Coltrane* (Universal 2000) or *The Very Best of John Coltrane* (Universal 2001). Both include "My Favorite Things," "Naima," and "Alabama," along with the "Acknowledgment" section of *A Love Supreme*. However, even if you're looking to be really frugal, a copy of *A Love Supreme* complete with liner notes is pretty much an essential.

Theology's Engagement with Music

An Overview

The fact that theology has generated such an enormous range of music is impressive. But much more than this historical fact, I think, is the claim that theology worth its salt is implicitly musical. When the great Passions of Bach, or the creation by Haydn, or the mysteries of the Trinity set by Olivier Messiaen compel us to enter a deeper knowing of the theological truths, we witness this inevitable drive toward music. But not only in the 'high art' traditions of classical music; there is something also of the cosmic energy in John Coltrane's sax, or Art Tatum's prodigious harmonic re-hearing of melodies, or in the singing of Spirituals like 'Nobody Knows the Trouble I've Seen' or 'Go Tell It on the Mountain'; that gives us access to what theology tries to say.

—Don Saliers, *Music and Theology*

In the Western (European-North American) theological heritage, there are only occasional reflections on music, and most of those are negative—music as a theologically subversive activity.
—Clyde J. Steckel, "How Can Music Have Theological Significance?"

A t a glance, it would seem that the quotations with which I open this chapter are at odds with one another. There is first Saliers' statement that "theology has generated such an enormous range of music," followed by Steckel's suggestion that in the Western tradition theological reflections on music have been only occasional, and for the most part negative. The truth is that for as long as there has been a Christian religious tradition, musicians of faith have found themselves compelled to create music that expresses their engagement in that tradition . . . and theologians have wondered just what to do with it.

And the wondering of the theologians is surprising, really, when one considers that the Bible is hardly silent when it comes to music, and that for the most part the biblical assumption is that music is a part of life, and a good thing. The earliest reference to music comes in Genesis 4:21, where we read that one of the descendants of Cain was named Jubal, and "he was the ancestor of all those who play the lyre and the pipe." Jubal is listed as the brother of Jabal, "the ancestor of those who live in tents and have livestock," and as the half-brother of Tubal-cain, "who made all kinds of bronze and iron tools" (Gen 4:21–22). This seems to give to the musician a status equal to that of the herder and the smith, both of which offered essential services in that social context. It would appear that music was regarded as being equally essential to life in the everyday world.

After the Hebrew slaves made their escape through the Red Sea, praise was offered up in music; first by "Moses and the Israelites" (Exod 15:1–18), and then by Miriam "and all the women," whose considerably shorter, single verse song was accompanied "with tambourines and with dancing" (Exod 15:20–21). It is tempting to see the music and dance of the women as something of a response to the more didactic wordiness of the song offered by the men.

The great King David was said to have been a musician, and the music he offered on his lyre was the only thing that could calm Saul when he was besieged by the madness of an evil spirit (1 Sam 16:1). David apparently had music not only in his hands, but in the whole of his body as well, for on the day when the Israelites finally brought the ark of the covenant in to Jerusalem "David danced before the Lord with all his might," clad only in "a linen ephod" (2 Sam 6:14).

All you have to do is to page through the Hebrew scriptures, and you'll find example after example of how music was embedded in the passages, rituals, and markings of the community's life. And then of course there are the Psalms. The Book of Psalms as we know it is generally recognized as having been the hymnbook of what is known as "Second Temple Judaism." Back at home after the Babylonian Exile, with the long, slow process of rebuilding in view, this collection was solidified. Material referring back to the glory days of David was combined with the more recent exilic and post-exilic writings to create a collection that could speak to every season and experience of individual and communal life. What's more, it was brought together without being overly tidied, meaning that as a collection it can speak into any number of individual and community contexts. There is praise, lament, anger, celebration, and consolation. There are royal hymns right alongside of expressions of protest by those who have lost everything. Great hymns of creation roll into detailed rehearsals of the shared history as Israelites under God, yet these are followed by confessions of utter despair. There are personal and communal psalms relating to just about any experience imaginable. It is an extraordinarily courageous approach to prayer, and it is all to be sung.

The Psalms don't simply contain material about music, but in a sense embody it. Not literally of course—though there are those little bits of instruction "to the leader"—yet they do give to the reader a sense of what is worth singing about. And apparently just about everything is worth singing about.

When we come to the New Testament, there are rather fewer references to the singing of songs, and when they do occur it is not unlikely that the Psalms are in view. In fact, they are quite clearly in view in Ephesians 5:19 and Colossians 4:16, both of which refer to singing "psalms and hymns and spiritual songs." The Gospel according to Luke offers the great songs of proclamation of Zechariah, Mary, and Simeon, which the church continues to sing in our own day. And then there is the Revelation to John, in which songs of praise are sung by the "four living creatures" and "the twenty-four elders," the angels, and ultimately by every creature "in heaven and on earth and under the earth and in the sea" (Rev 4 and 5). It is almost as if in John's strange vision the new creation will be sung into being.

It is odd, then, to notice how seldom the writers of the ancient church dealt with music. Although others before him did offer occasional reflections on music—all with caution and many quite negatively—Augustine's appreciative yet ambivalent view merits a bit of extra attention. In his wonderings about the place of music in the life of the church, Augustine wrestles in the tension between his own love of music and his fear that its emotional grip will steer believers into dangerous spiritual waters. For our purposes here, the place to focus is his highly personal reflections in *The Confessions*. Although he is writing in the late fourth century, these words might just as easily have been written by someone just coming from an eighteenth-century field meeting led by John Wesley, or in fact from a twenty-first-century praise and worship service led by one of the more gifted practitioners of that genre. "How I wept during your hymns and songs! I was deeply moved by the music of the sweet chants of your Church. The sounds flowed into my ears and the truth was distilled into my heart. This caused the feelings of devotion to overflow. Tears ran, and it was good for me to have that experience."[1] Yet Augustine finds that as he more deeply engages the substance of his maturing faith it is "the words being sung" that move him, and that "when they are sung with a clear voice and entirely appropriate in modulation" he is able to "recognize the great utility of music in worship."[2] Here the music seems a kind of an aid or even a tool, which is useful in bringing emphasis to the word, but only when done properly. There is embedded in this a suspicion of music's potentially deceptive sensuality; of its ability to touch the sensate and emotional person all the while bypassing the intellect. Here Augustine's primary concern is how the created thing—in this case music—can be mistaken as an end and as a good in and of itself, rather than as something flowing from, and pointing back to, the Creator. For Augustine, this is the threat that always hovers close by for a fallen humanity.

Still, unlike many others in the ancient church, Augustine will make room for music in worship, albeit very carefully. "Thus I fluctuate between the danger of pleasure and the experience of the beneficent effect, and I am more led to put forward the opinion (not as an irrevocable view) that the custom of singing in Church is to be approved, so that through the delights of the ear the weaker mind may rise up towards the devotion of worship. Yet when it happens to me that the music moves me more than the subject of the song, I confess to commit a sin deserving punishment, and

---

1. Augustine, *Confessions*, 164.
2. Ibid., 208.

then I would prefer not to have heard the singer."[3] I do need to be careful in focusing too narrowly on the idea of the utility of music, as it might create an impression that Augustine saw music as merely an emotionally and sensually laden means by which the word could be communicated. He does stand in the long tradition winding back to Pythagoras in the sixth century BCE, who not only recognized that music was related to numbers and mathematics, but also believed that the whole of the cosmos was engaged in "the music of the spheres"; "the belief that planets and stars of different sizes emit different pitches, generating a huge, but inaudible, cosmic music."[4] This sort of an understanding was carried forward by Plato and then by Plotinus, to be fully adapted into a Christian context by Augustine. Part of the caution Augustine raises around the potential dangers of music is his sense—inherited from Plato— that what might be most important about music is to be found not in the actual playing of it, or even listening to it, but in its study. To study harmony in an almost purely mathematical sense, for instance, might give us insight into the triune God who *is* harmony. As summarized by Carol Harrison, for Augustine, "The basic, but revolutionary, insight is that God *is* music: he *is* supreme measure, number, relation, harmony, unity, and equality. When he created matter from nothing he simultaneously gave it existence by giving it music, or form—in other words measure, number, relation, harmony, unity, equality . . ."[5]

Yet as Catherine Pickstock shows in her reading of *De Musica*, Augustine is not interested in music as mere theory. The theological insights he derives are also related to the *fact* of human artistic creativity; in the recognition "that human art can truly create something new," and that this is connected to the theological truth that "human beings are situated within a universe which springs from nothing."[6]

Such a way of engaging and understanding music seems worlds away from how it is currently viewed in Western popular culture, including Christian popular culture. We did not move worlds away overnight, and the church and its theological traditions are

3. Ibid.

4. Begbie, *Resounding Truth*, 79.

5. Harrison, "Augustine and the Art of Music," 31.

6. Pickstock, "Music: Soul, City and Cosmos," 248.

very much a part of that gradually unfolding story. I am not even going to pretend to summarize the contours of the fifteen hundred years of theological thought since Augustine. However, following the work of Jeremy Begbie, I do think it important to note the differing views of three key sixteenth-century Reformers, each of whom helped shape the beginnings of modernity. And in part this is important because it will allow me to illustrate just how different is the European Protestant tradition from that which eventually surfaced in the twentieth-century African-American church.

Where Martin Luther embraces music as a good and wondrous gift from God, John Calvin is considerably more reserved. Where Luther sees the emotional impact of music as being part of its goodness—part of what enables music to enliven the words in fresh ways—Calvin is deeply suspicious of the potential sensuality of music. According to Luther, "Reason sees the world as extremely ungodly, and therefore it murmurs. The spirit sees nothing but God's benefits in the world and therefore begins to sing."[7] Calvin, on the other hand, writes, "It is true that every bad word (as St. Paul said) perverts good character, but when melody is added, that word pierces the heart much more strongly and enters within."[8]

Both Calvin and Luther, however, are quite committed to the importance of music in the life of worship. For Calvin, this takes the form of rather reserved sung settings for hymn texts based on the Psalms and other biblical texts, while Luther embraces a wide range of music, from the highly sophisticated to simple folk melodies. And Luther has no qualms about drawing on extra-biblical material as sources for sung texts.

A third major Reformation figure is Huldrych Zwingli, who moved to omit music from worship altogether. "The heart of his argument," observes Begbie, "is simply that God has not authorized music in worship, and Christ's command is that worship is to be an essentially inward, individual, and private matter."[9] Yet Zwingli was not opposed to music as such. A trained musician, to the end of his life he enjoyed music as a form of recreation, even after he had seen to it that the church organs of Zurich were destroyed. Music is to be appreciated as an art, and even recognized

7. Begbie, *Resounding Truth*, 100.
8. Ibid., 109.
9. Ibid., 115.

as being a part of the very order of things—"For no men are so stupid that they are not captivated by it, even though they are entirely ignorant of its technique."[10] For Zwingli, the issue is simply that he finds no biblical warrant for the inclusion of music in Christian worship, where the focus should be on a convicting and potentially transforming engagement with the scriptures.

For those shaped by the traditions of the African-American church, Luther probably comes closest to offering something familiar, while the thought of Calvin and Zwingli are quite utterly foreign. As the black church tradition unfolded, not only was music permissible, its absence would have been quite unfathomable. And if Jon Michael Spencer is correct in suggesting that this was a "people who drew no distinction between the sacred and the secular or the spiritual and the sexual,"[11] is it any wonder that Calvin's reservations about music's sensuality would make little sense? And even Luther would not have known what to make of Zora Neale Hurston's characterization of the spirituals as being marked by jagged harmony, intentional dissonances, and shifting keys, and all by design.[12] For Luther, this could hardly be counted as a music that is God's gift. Here Begbie's summary of Luther's sense of the role of order and of proper constraints in music is instructive: "In this view, music, the most intensely formal of the arts, the most removed from self-expression, and thus the most dissociated from the untidiness and messiness of life, has, by its grounding in cosmic order, a peculiar power to hold the forces of sin and chaos at bay, to remind us of the fundamental stability God has conferred on the world."[13] Imagine, then, what Luther might have made of jazz, particularly from the rise of bebop onwards toward the development of free jazz. And as you do that bit of imagining, it is worth noting that in some sense Luther anticipates the very concerns of the twentieth-century Calvinist thinker Hans Rookmaaker. But more on that a little later in this chapter.

It is quite important to note that within the African-American church tradition there are actually a number of quite different *traditions*, some of which were and are far more attuned to European

10. Ibid., 117.
11. Spencer, "Overview of American Popular Music," 205.
12. Lott, "Bar Walkers Preach," 107.
13. Begbie, *Resounding Truth*, 99.

musical influences. It is not particularly accurate to offer a summary that suggests that during the formative years of the African-American church there was a monolithic and definitive style of music; namely the spirituals, which over time, gave rise to black gospel music. The spirituals do play a very key role in the birth and development of the black church tradition, yet the story unfolds from that starting point in varied ways. The African Methodist Episcopal Zion churches in which John Coltrane was formed, though certainly not closed to the influence of the spirituals, would have been places in which a more conventionally European style of hymnody was normative. "The church in which Coltrane grew up was of a more staid, mainstream denomination," Salim Washington notes, and part of what was at play in the development of the various denominations and traditions were "distinct class and cultural differences," for instance between churches of the AME-Zion denomination and those of Pentecostal and holiness traditions.[14] Washington does add, however, that "his mature playing is very reminiscent of the charismata of the Holiness worship styles,"[15] which points to the way in which explorations in the jazz tradition allowed for and encouraged wider explorations; both musical and, in the case of John Coltrane, spiritual and religious.

And now, quite aware that I am skipping all too quickly across the centuries and traditions, I do need to shift into a consideration of the ways in which theology has engaged music during the twentieth century. In his 1994 essay, "How Can Music Have Theological Significance?" Clyde Steckel identifies William Edgar and Jon Michael Spencer as the two twentieth-century theologians who have offered the most substantial and serious engagement of music with theology, both during the closing decades of the century. While I would agree that these two have made significant contributions, I'm afraid Steckel's list is rather too thin.

I want to suggest that Paul Tillich's writings on culture must be taken into account here, and that when it comes to jazz the work of Hans Rookmaaker simply must be included. Similarly, for his work on the spirituals and the blues, James Cone cannot be ignored. More recently, I would point to Jeremy Begbie and Don Saliers as being particularly important voices. In fact, the first decade

14. Washington, "'Don't Let the Devil," 128–29.
15. Ibid., 129.

of the twenty-first century seems to have brought a new interest in questions of music and theology, with significant contributions in the area of classical and concert music from Catherine Pickstock, Daniel Chua, John Paul Ito, and Calvin Stapert, among many others. When it comes to rock and pop music, I would mention Tom Beaudoin and the *rockandtheology.com* project, and note that there is any number of popular, pastoral, and academic books in print on specific artists or sub-genres. I would also want to add that one of the real pioneers in this area is Steve Turner, a writer still very much at work as a music journalist and reflective Christian writer.

Theologically or even spiritually oriented writings on jazz, however, appear to be another matter. Several of the writers I have named do attend to jazz, though not usually as a primary area of interest. In the past decade or so, a few books which seek to make the connection between theology and jazz have been published, including Ann Pederson's *God, Creation and All that Jazz*, and Robert Gelinas' *Finding the Groove: Composing a Jazz-Shaped Faith*. Pederson, though, doesn't so much engage jazz as a theological source as use the music as a tool for illustrating specific theological points (of which she does an admirable job), while Gelinas does much the same thing at a more pastoral and popular level. Gelinas is actually most interested in mounting in a kind of Christian apologetic for listening to jazz, much in the same way David Nantais does for rock music in his recent *Rock-a My Soul: An Invitation to Rock Your Religion*. I actually think this is the great Achilles' heel in much of the faith-based writing about popular music; it is so often written by a fan, simply aching to have others see why it is a good thing to care about this music. While it is a far more sophisticated work at many levels, in some respects this even holds true for Karl Barth's little book on Mozart.

Not that a theological writer shouldn't be passionate about his or her subject, and I am clearly quite passionate about the music of John Coltrane. The writer, though, really needs to step back and examine the question of why the church or the theological academy should bother with music or the arts in the first place. Here I've found Paul Tillich's work on the theology of culture to be a useful starting point. While Tillich's thought develops and evolves from the time of the publication of his 1919 lecture "On the Idea of a Theology of Culture" through to his 1959 book

Theology of Culture, several ideas do remain relatively constant. As summarized in that later work, in Tillich's view "religion is being ultimately concerned about that which is and should be our ultimate concern," and in turn, "faith is the state of being grasped by an ultimate concern, and God is the name for the content of the concern."[16] His use of the terms "ultimate concern" and "ultimate reality" in his theological reflections on God, faith, and religion have very real implications for his understanding of human culture and of the artistic and poetic expressions of any given culture. In an address entitled "Art and Ultimate Reality," Tillich states, "If the idea of God includes ultimate reality, everything that expresses ultimate reality expresses God whether it intends to do so or not."[17] There is no longer a "gap between the sacred and secular realm," and there can be "no cultural creation without an ultimate concern expressed in it."[18] Visual art, music, literature, architecture, and drama all come under theological consideration, because in some manner they all speak of ultimate concern. Further, Tillich is quite explicit in his conviction that "the manifestation of the ultimate in the visual arts is not dependent on the use of works which traditionally are called religious art."[19]

In his work Tillich manages to open the door for a new theological engagement with a cultural expression such as music. In his earlier writings, he is rather optimistically certain that "the unconditioned"—or "God as the name for the content of ultimate concern"—was making itself known within the secular culture. However, largely due to the rise of Nazism and all that it represented, his thinking shifts. Tillich comes to believe that by attending to its cultural context the church could come to know the questions and ideas that demand engagement. "[It was Tillich's] conviction that what was to be found through theology of culture was primarily the ringing questions of the day, a kind of nagging activity of divine revelation alerting us to our fallenness, to our estrangement from our divine ground, to which symbols from the treasury of Christian theology could be retrieved as answers."[20] Not

16. Tillich, *Theology of Culture*, 40.
17. Tillich, "Art and Ultimate Reality," 210.
18. Tillich, *Theology of Culture*, 41–42.
19. Tillich, "Art and Ultimate Reality," 216.
20. Cobb, *Theology and Popular Culture*, 95.

that Tillich is interested in giving smug answers, or that he denies what are important and truthful voices at work outside of the walls of the church. What he really envisions is a critical and self-critical engagement of church and culture. Tillich also believes that generally the prophetic voices the church most needs to hear actually originate from outside of its own walls. "But perhaps," he writes, "one could call them participants of a 'latent Church,' a Church in which the ultimate concern which drives the manifest Church is hidden under cultural forms and deformations."[21] And the church, in hearing such voices, must be prepared to make judgments as to what is a "cultural form" and what is in fact a "deformation."

The impact of Tillich's forty years of writing and reflecting on theology and culture was to effectively establish that a cultural expression such as music is not something to be fretted over—for instance for its sensual emotionalism or its "jungle beat," as was often said about both jazz and early rock and roll. Nor is it to be uncritically absorbed by the church, as has often happened with contemporary Christian worship music. A true engagement involves both critical judgments and an openness to hearing music as a potential source for theological engagement. This is all but assumed by many of the theological writers who have gone to work in the area of music over the past fifty years.

Though he differs from Tillich in almost every way, Hans Rookmaaker's writings do provide a vivid example of a theological engagement with music. Unlike Tillich, Rookmaaker is very much interested in jazz. Writing first of the shallowness of the popular music of the early twentieth century, with palpable delight Rookmaaker declares, "Into this world burst jazz and blues. They came from quite a different background and from an unpredictable quarter, from the Negro section in the USA, from the free slaves."[22] Part of what so draws him to this music is its insistence on real substance, which he sees as being ultimately rooted in the church. "I am convinced that the realism in African-American music can be partly attributed to biblical preaching. Its influence is evident, even when the church has been abandoned by the songwriter . . . The Scriptures teach us to break with superficial escapism, pretending there is nothing wrong. In the light of this we can understand

21. Tillich, *Theology of Culture*, 51.
22. Rookmaaker, *Modern Art*, 186.

the true-to-life realism of the songs, including the secular ones, of the blacks."[23] However, much to his dismay what he identifies as "traditional jazz" (and by this he really means the jazz music of New Orleans) gives way to modern jazz. For Rookmaaker, while swing music had already marked the beginning of the slide away from the tradition, bebop is the real culprit. And in his view, bebop has far more in common with existentialist thought, beat poetry, and expressionist art than it does with jazz. "Modern jazz, if at least it is really modern, emanates from inner tension, or rather; from acute inner tension. Some artists experience this to such an extent that they are in danger of falling apart and therefore may yield to the use of narcotics. In fact, this demonstrates the very existential, very heart-rending reality of this music; it is anything but superficial entertainment. It is deeply rooted in a view of life and the world."[24]

In Rookmaaker's view, modern jazz is woefully individualistic and dangerous, both emotionally and spiritually. For all the warmth and enthusiasm with which he embraces New Orleans jazz—and he is even more enthusiastic about black gospel music, which for him is all but personified by Mahalia Jackson—Rookmaaker basically rejects all of the work of musicians such as John Coltrane. In Rookmaaker's view, from Coltrane's earliest professional days playing bebop with the likes of Dizzy Gillespie, through his tenure with both Miles Davis and Thelonious Monk, and on into the solo career which ultimately placed him on the vanguard of avant-garde and free jazz, he is simply not playing the real thing. In fact for Rookmaaker, the kind of experimental path on which Coltrane and others like him were moving is itself illustrative of the deeper problem.

> The postwar mood of despair provided fertile ground for the music. It was fashionable in a way to listen to this music in that mood of despair. This jazz that was breaching musical norms had its parallel in the beat generation, who were setting the tone in literature at that time. In the music a sort of snowball effect took place. Once the listeners had grown accustomed to the fierce sounds, it left them with a desire for more fierce stimuli. The outcome of this development was free jazz, which was bereft of any prescript. Of course

23. Ibid., 188–89.
24. Rookmaaker, *New Orleans Jazz*, 297.

you can say in retrospect that there were rules and that they were adhered to, but each time those rules were stretched so that it became more and more anarchistic.[25]

While I am in profound disagreement with Rookmaaker's conclusions, I do think that he reaches his position by way of a variation on Tillich's model of cultural engagement. Rookmaaker embraces New Orleans jazz as a vibrant cultural expression, and one coming from the margins of the dominant society no less. He has good theological warrant for this embrace, even in cases "when the church has been abandoned by the songwriter." Further, when he does come to the place of drawing his firm line between traditional and modern jazz—a line which judges even as it is drawn—this judgment is born of his critical and theological engagement with the music and with the wider culture.

In this light, it is fascinating to turn to Jeremy Begbie's reflections on jazz. Begbie is quite prepared to engage bebop, both as a musical form and as a source for his theological investigations. However, he does draw a line at the avant-garde and free jazz movements, and for reasons not entirely different from those of Rookmaaker. To be fair, Begbie does not voice anything resembling Rookmaaker's belief that the "anarchistic" character of free jazz stands as a demonstration of "the death of culture," but he does share with him a belief that it is a blind alley for jazz. In Begbie's view, in the name of freeing music from the limits of the tradition, free jazz really just represents a break from the tradition, and one that brings very little by way of true freedom. It is worth noting that built on what amounts to a "Tillichian" cultural theology of the jazz tradition, both the jazz critic Stanley Crouch and the blues and jazz scholar Albert Murray draw similarly firm lines excluding free jazz.

Begbie's theological engagement with jazz largely has to do with themes of improvisation, freedom, and constraint. Stating that in contrast to what is sometimes assumed by the casual listener, in an improvisational music such as jazz, "The improviser is *multiply* constrained."[26] For Begbie, this opens up a set of extremely important theological considerations and insights. "The freedom realised in the best improvisation is not an amorphous

25. Ibid., 378.
26. Begbie, *Theology, Music and Time*, 200.

'openness' struggling to conquer (or ignore) constraints, but a fruitful interaction between contingency and constraint. This is improvisation's distinctive contribution to learning to 'live peaceably with time,' and thus to a theology of human freedom."[27] It is in the interaction between the contingent—by which he means the things that "do not have to be" and the events that "do not have to happen"—and the constraints—both musical and "occasional," by which he mean the setting and circumstances in which the improvisation occurs—that something analogous to Christian freedom is unveiled. And it has nothing to do with being unfettered or somehow unencumbered by the tradition. "For the Christian, to be free is not fundamentally to enjoy some supposedly blank space before us, or to increase options, but to be at peace with God and one another and thus at home in a God-given world."[28] In Begbie's view, being "at peace" and "at home" is enacted in the improviser's inhabiting of the space in which the constraints interact with the contingent. Using John Coltrane along with Cecil Taylor and Ornette Coleman as prime examples, Begbie essentially suggests that in the "upheaval of jazz in the 1960s" this interaction was unbalanced. "These developments," he writes, "were marked by less dependence on pre-established formulaic elements and more on the circumstances of the occasion."[29]

It should be noted, however, that while Begbie is highly critical of Coltrane's later and increasingly free works, this does not extend to *A Love Supreme*, which he identifies as being a good example of yet another time-related theological issue: "We can look at one further form of musical tension with strong gospel overtones: delay—when an unexpected or desired fulfillment is held up, either in whole or in part. The handling of delay is a crucial musical skill."[30] And evidently, the handling of delay is a crucial theological skill as well, perhaps best cultivated in the company of the musician.

Begbie's work has had a great influence on my own understanding of the dynamic relationship between music and theology, and over the course of this book his name will come up again and

27. Ibid., 203.
28. Begbie, *Resounding Truth*, 249.
29. Begbie, *Theology, Music and Time*, 200f.
30. Begbie, *Resounding Truth*, 283.

again. Most important for my own work perhaps is his distinction between what he calls "theology for the arts" and "theology through the arts." The distinction is set out with great clarity and simplicity in a video lecture given for *Faith and Leadership*, an online resource produced by Duke University.[31] In "theology for the arts," Begbie says, the goal is to "try to understand music in the light of a theological world-view," perhaps after the manner in which Rookmaaker attempts to understand bebop jazz and expressionist art. In "theology through the arts" the questions are, "what can music or the arts bring to theology?" and "how can the particular powers of music help us unlock the great truths of the Gospel?" This is actually quite close to what Rookmaaker does in his writings on New Orleans jazz and on the music of Mahalia Jackson, for through this music his own theological vision and commitments are clearly deepened.

After making this distinction, Begbie comments that "The most wonderful things can come out of the most unpromising material." It is critical, he says, to be prepared, "always to see the possibilities, even in the most unlikely material. And sometimes I think especially in the most unlikely material."[32] This has some resonance with Tillich's insistence that the voices to which the church most needs to attend often come from outside of its own walls, though to be fair I'd have to say that Tillich's understanding of what it might mean to "unlock the great truths of the Gospel" would differ quite markedly from Begbie's. Still, both do insist that attending to "unlikely material" is extremely important; and so it should be, given how often Jesus attended to the "unlikely" in his day.

Several other writers have made significant contributions in the area of jazz and theology, and in different ways have shaped my own thought. I have already mentioned Ann Pederson's *God, Creation and All that Jazz*, but it is important to add that in her chapter on the blues she does in fact move well into Begbie's territory of theology *through* the arts. Specifically her attention to James Baldwin's short story "Sonny's Blues" confirmed my own sense of the significance of Baldwin's writing for my own work. I think Baldwin can be fairly counted as one of the "latent theologians" at work in my thought.

31. Begbie, "Theology through the Arts."
32. Ibid.

I have sought to take into account Don Saliers' sense that music can often speak what words alone cannot; that, "it is not inappropriate to speak of the 'mystery' of what is hidden in music," and that to attend carefully to music "is not a matter of more 'information' but a matter of hearing and seeing in depth what is already before us in the music."[33] A musician himself (and one who has been known to play jazz on more than just the odd occasion), Saliers' tastes run more toward Art Tatum and Oscar Peterson than to the 1960s avant-garde, yet he will not draw any simple and exclusionary lines. In response to a question regarding the challenge that comes with trying to engage Coltrane's *Ascension*, Saliers commented, "You are really talking about scales of musical value now, because music has such a wide range of possible exploration. And there are different kinds of explorations here in Coltrane's later work. I love the suggestion that he's looking to elevate [these younger musicians], who haven't thought of themselves as being front line, prodigious players. There's the other side of that, too; he is really building a new kind of communal sense. On *Ascension* that's an objective, structural feature. No denying it."[34] Still, in the manner suggested by Tillich, Saliers is not afraid to make critical and discerning judgments. In his view, this requires a "training of the ear for hearing," which is "both the discipline of 'paying attention' and the discipline of recognizing what one hears."[35]

As with Don Saliers, William Edgar is very open to a robust engagement with jazz, including the full range of Coltrane's music. And like Saliers, Edgar is both a theological scholar and a seasoned jazz musician. Aside from his 1986 book, *Taking Note of Music*—which he characterized to me as being "under-developed and in serious need of re-visiting"—most of Edgar's work on jazz has taken the form of journal and magazine articles. In 2008, he released the double CD, *Heaven in a Nightclub*, in which the music of his quartet is interspersed with brief teachings on the history of the jazz tradition. In all of these works, Edgar displays an almost boundless enthusiasm for jazz, and for how it might speak to us of the God about whom he is even more passionately enthused.

33. Saliers, *Music and Theology*, 64.
34. Saliers, telephone interview.
35. Saliers, *Music and Theology*, 67.

Edgar understands music to be first and foremost one of God's greatest gifts to humanity, and not simply on account of the joy it might bring. It is a gift of the God who has established covenant relationship with humanity, and as such it is a gift that provides a means or a language by which, and through which, the human partners in the covenant might be drawn closer to God. "All music articulates a two-way relation to spirituality," Edgar writes. "On the one hand, the spiritual and theological background gives music its special shape . . . But it works the other way around as well. Music can be the cause, the conduit that shapes the soul."[36] Not that Edgar would see this soul-shaping as being a case of music *directly* embodying God. Rather, our souls can be shaped in our being *accompanied* by music.

> Beginning at the creation, God created through music. The angels sang. I further think that every part of human activity is meant to be accompanied by—and translated with—musical realities. For me music is part of the reality of the creation, and of who we are and what we are meant to be doing, just as much as speech. Music has a special role in redemption; we're called to sing the new song once we've been transformed. There is a way in which song says as much—or even more than anything else—about who we are in our souls.[37]

And these discoveries of "who we are in our souls" are not necessarily without real challenge. For instance, Edgar writes of the music journalist Ashley Kahn, and of how after researching and writing his book on the making of *A Love Supreme,* Kahn admitted, "And, as one who was a little less assured in his agnostic or rationalist beliefs, I thought of the phrase 'opening doors.'" To this Edgar responds, "Exactly! John Coltrane's music shakes-up our agnosticism and rationalism."[38]

For Edgar's soul, "jazz says it more articulately than most," whether in praise of the glory of God, in lament over "the excruciating pain and loneliness of the fall," or in celebration of redemption. And though jazz comes out of the African-American experience, "it has also become a universal expression of creation/

36. Edgar, "Heaven in a Nightclub," 49.

37. Edgar, personal interview.

38. Edgar, "A Love Supreme," 27.

fall/redemption. It is peculiarly modern; it is my language."[39] At the heart of that language is room for improvisation, which he describes as, "musical problem solving." He finds here a favorite analogy for how God has *innovated* a new covenant with humanity. "In one way the incarnation and the atonement were God's greatest improvisatory moves. I mean, He had a problem. Here is a holy God, and here are sinful human beings, but he has love. How on earth can he, without lowering his standards, save the people he loves? And he devises this extraordinary plan, the incarnation and the atonement, whereby he can remain just and yet be the justifier of the ungodly. I take that as improvisation at the highest level."[40] For Edgar, hearing or performing improvisation in jazz provides a way of framing his theology of what God has so creatively done for humanity. More than anything, what I take from William Edgar is that sense of passion; both for jazz as a style of music, and for the creative theological potential that it holds.

I also have to acknowledge the debt I owe to James Cone, yet another passionate theologian for whom music is life and faith-defining. In his great book, *The Spirituals and the Blues,* Cone makes that powerful statement already cited in the introduction to this book: "I, therefore, write about the spirituals and the blues, because *I am the blues* and my *life is a spiritual*. Without them, I cannot be."[41] Everything that Cone writes in his book really unfolds from that statement, and so as I read about two of the styles of music which stand very much at the roots of jazz, I was actually reading about the formation of identity—both personal and communal—and about a very particular way of engaging faith and doubt. Cone challenged me to get behind the jazz music that I love, and to wrestle deeply with all that shaped and formed black America. Every time I was about to write a sweeping statement even vaguely connected to the black church or what gave rise to the blues or the role of racial politics in the development of jazz, I could feel James Cone peering over my shoulder.

Another theologian who has spent serious time working with the blues is Jon Michael Spencer. His book *Blues and Evil* both builds on and extends *The Spirituals and the Blues*, probably in ways with

39. Edgar, personal interview.
40. Ibid.
41. Cone, *Spirituals and the Blues*, 7.

which Cone himself would not necessarily agree. For me, though, Spencer's book did provide a very important second voice, which offered some quite remarkable insights regarding the theology that is embedded in the blues, as well as the social context in which the blues men and women practiced their craft. For Spencer, the blues players were very much the "latent theologians" of the black church.

For many years Spencer laboured to establish a discipline he called "theomusiology," which was intended to draw together the methods of musicology and ethnomusicology, and to fold them into the work of a theological interpretation of culture. I do have to confess to being a bit mystified by some of what he published in the name of this proposed discipline. It would seem that his labors came to a rather abrupt halt in the late 1990s, when *Black Sacred Music: A Journal of Theomusicology* ceased publication, and Spencer's own steady flow of books came to an end. Yet Spencer's insistence that music cannot be understood aside from its cultural and social context is critical to my work here. More specifically, Spencer pressed me to see that through his music John Coltrane was effectively pushing against the assumptions of the dominant culture. This is demonstrated both in his apparent abandonment of European conventions of musical beauty (though of course we should note that by almost any standards, there was great beauty in selections from even his latest recordings), and in his insistent drive to find knowledge not only through reading books (a very Western and European way of knowledge), but also through what he was exploring on his saxophone. One of the questions that Spencer would have us ask is, "so what are you going to do about it?" Or put in a different way, is John Coltrane managing to say some things in his musical search that the church and theological fraternity would do well to hear?

There are any number of theological threads that I'm picking up on here; Cornel West's perceptive and faith-full engagement with music and culture, to say nothing of his audacious turns of phrase; Tom Beaudoin's insightful insistence in *Virtual Faith* that theology attend to the *sensus infidelium*, or the wisdom of the those, "who profess to know little or nothing about the religious," yet who "may form, inform, or transform religious meaning for people of faith"[42]; Amos Niven Wilder's notion of "theopoetic," and all that

42. Beaudoin, *Virtual Faith*, 34.

he has to say about imagination; Daniel A. Siedell's theological work on modern art, which opened for me ways of thinking about music; Walter Brueggemann's work on the Psalms, which taught me new ways of not only hearing the cries of lament, but also of understanding the desire for vengeance. There are many more besides, as a glance through my bibliography will show.

Now, having traced something of an overview of the ways in which theology has engaged music, and having tugged on the various theological threads that have influenced my particular project, it is time to offer a similar overview of the origins and story of this music called jazz.

2

The Contested Story of Jazz

Competing Narratives, and Why They Matter

The music of Negro religion is that plaintive rhythmic melody, with its touching minor cadences, which, despite caricature and defilement, still remains the most original and beautiful expression of human life and longing yet born on American soil. Sprung from the African forests, where its counterpart can still be heard, it was adapted, changed, and intensified by the tragic soul-life of the slave, until, under the stress of law and whip, it became the one true expression of a people's sorrow, despair, and hope.

—W. E. B. Du Bois, *The Souls of Black Folk*

Jazz was born in the praise house. That is, the most significant antecedent of jazz, the Negro Spiritual, was generated in an atmosphere of newfound faith, lived out under duress . . . Spirituals were deeply comforting—but they also were about survival.

—William Edgar, "Heaven in a Nightclub"

One might think it a relatively straightforward matter to trace the history of jazz music, from its origins in the early 1900s up through to the end of John Coltrane's life in 1967. After all, that is a period of less than seven decades; surely a decently accurate chronological sketch drawn with a broad brush would do the trick? Unfortunately, that is simply not the case. In part, that has to do with the fact that the major taproot of this music is found in the blues, which is itself related to the spirituals and to the musical sensibilities brought from West Africa on the slave ships, so the story is considerably longer than just seven decades. And the very suggestion that there are strong ties connecting jazz back to the musical traditions of West Africa is not entirely uncontested.

There is general agreement that jazz originated in New Orleans shortly after the turn of the nineteenth century, and that its development was shaped primarily—though not exclusively—by African-American musicians. Identified by the jazz critic Stanley Crouch as "a hybrid" music from its beginnings—"A mix of African, European, Caribbean, and Afro-Hispanic elements"[1]— jazz drew on the spirituals and work songs of the plantations, along with the blues, ragtime, the music of the famous New Orleans brass bands, along with just about anything else that was in the musical air at the time. And while the city of New Orleans might have served as something of a melting pot for these musical influences, it was anything but integrated when it came to racial identity. The brass bands were segregated by race, with the black bands generally considered as being less schooled and sophisticated than the white ones.

Yet even that simple distinction between black and white is not entirely accurate, as there was a third racial identity very much at work in those early days. As Bruce Ellis Benson observes, "It is this third category—Creoles of color or *gens du couleur*—that undermines the binary of racial opposition." "As Creoles and Blacks were allowed to integrate (in the 1890s), they began to influence one another musically; the result was a musical 'Creolization.' Creole culture serves as a metaphor for understanding the development of jazz. *Musically,* Creoles occupied a space somewhere between white European and African American music—and that 'between-ness' helped open up a space for white musicians."[2] That Benson writes of the Creoles and blacks as being *allowed* to integrate is actually quite fascinating, in that an alternate way of reading this history understands the New Orleans Legislative Code no. 111 of 1894 as forcing Creoles of color out of the white districts and white bands and into African-American neighborhoods.[3] Though a kind of romanticism can often characterize the retelling of the origins

1. Crouch, "Negro Aesthetic of Jazz," 211.
2. Benson, "Improvising Texts," 307–8.
3. Shipton, *New History of Jazz*, 58.

of jazz, painting an almost idealized picture of racial collaboration and cultural cross-fertilization, the truth is that politics of race in post-Reconstruction Louisiana were not particularly amenable to real or sustained collaboration. In this sense, the sharing of musical styles and influences took place as much in a pressure-cooker as in a melting pot.

Another part of the story of these New Orleans roots—a story which is at least as much myth as it is history—is that if jazz music was not birthed in the brothels it certainly spent its formative years there. It is true that musicians did find work in the brothels of Storyville during its years as the city's designated red-light district (1897–1917), yet it was not only there that this new music was taking shape. It should be noted that the earliest application of the word "jazz" to music appears in 1915, just two years before Storyville was permanently closed down.[4] Put simply, the role of Storyville in the development of jazz is not nearly as important as has often been suggested. Reflecting on his years teaching a "Jazz in American Society" course at the University of Toledo, the musician and educator Joe Hendricks offers an impassioned alternate reading of things: "Remember, this is me talking to freshman kids: And what do they have for American culture? Dark cellars, mostly funky bars where women and drugs are for sale. And then on top of that, with their lying selves, they tell you and anyone else within earshot, that that nigger music was born in the whorehouses of New Orleans. The truth is that jazz is the secular music of our Christian church."[5] While Hendricks is indeed pushing us toward a very important piece of the story, in the formative years of the jazz tradition many church people would have wondered at his sanity. "Throughout the 1920s," observes Jon Michael Spencer, "debate raged regarding whether jazz could have degenerative effects on the human psyche,"[6] with concern arising as much in black church circles and amongst the black middle class as in the wider, predominantly white society. According to LeRoi Jones (later known as Amiri Baraka), through most of the first half of

4. Although there is no clear consensus as to the etymology of the word "jazz," it is often said to come from the slang for semen, "jass." In fact it is rather more likely that both "jazz" and "jass" are related to an older slang word, "jasm," meaning spirit, energy, and vigor.

5. Thomas, "Jon Hendricks," para. 6.

6. Spencer, "American Popular Music," 208.

the twentieth century, "Jazz was collected among the numerous skeletons the middle-class black man kept locked in the closet of his psyche, along with watermelons and gin, and whose rattling caused him no end of misery and self hatred."[7] It is this "self hatred" that Hendricks is driving at when he speaks so passionately of the *lie* that jazz was born in the brothel.

Yet in calling jazz "the secular music of our Christian church," Hendricks is also oversimplifying things. In the view of James Cone, it is really blues music—what he calls the "secular spirituals"—that historically filled that role. For Cone, the story of jazz is connected to the deeper story of African-American music, and in order to tell that story you have to begin with the spirituals. And in his view, even then you have to acknowledge that the spirituals themselves arose in a religious context that had "combined the memory of their [African] fathers with the Christian gospel."[8] "The spirituals," writes Cone, "are songs about black souls, 'stretching out into the outskirts of God's eternity' and affirming that divine reality which lets you know that you are a human being—no matter what white people say. Through the song, black people were able to affirm that Spirit who was continuous with their existence as free beings; and they created a new style of religious worship. They shouted and they prayed; they preached and they sang, because *they had found something.*"[9] In calling the blues "secular spirituals," part of what Cone is pressing for is an acknowledgment that those who sang and heard the blues had also "found something." They "flow from the same bedrock," he writes, "and neither is an adequate interpretation of black life without the commentary of the other."[10] Along with the spirituals, the blues are resolute in their refusal to accept the dominant culture's assertion that even after the abolition of slavery, to be black was to be less than fully human. In a sense, the central claim of both the spirituals and the blues is one that says, "I *am* a human." To the declaration "I am human," the spirituals add, "because God told me so." The blues, on the other hand, might be more inclined to add something like, "because the

7. Jones, "Jazz and the White Critic," *Black Music*, 15.
8. Cone, *Spirituals and the Blues*, 30.
9. Ibid., 29.
10. Ibid., 100.

sorrows and pleasures of this life, this body, and these passions and appetites tell me so."

Like Cone, Spencer recognizes a connection between the spirituals and the blues, and suggests that in at least some respects the blues are as theologically freighted as the spirituals of the church. "Owing much of its cosmology to the Judeo-Christian narratives and doctrines," writes Spencer, "early blues were in effect the spirituals of an 'invisible' postbellum black religion that demystified Christianity and called into question some of its doctrinal tenants."[11] Spencer identifies a series of themes that the blues engage in this way, including sin, justification, theodicy, and "the disdain of church hypocrisy, pietism, and political quietism."[12] Regarding this disdain, Spencer is particularly interested in the theme of the blues singer as the returning prodigal son, and cites the case of a Rev. Lacy who told his congregation, "I used to be a famous blues singer . . . and I told more truth in my blues than the average person tells in his church songs."[13]

Both Cone and Spencer recognize the impact of distinctly African sensibilities here, and not merely in the vocal styling or rhythmic character of the music. Both note the way in which the spirituals and the blues have resisted a typically Western dualism of body and spirit—and of sexuality and salvation—and so embrace embodiedness and emotional expression along with matters of the intellect in their expressions of what it means to be human.

Identifying the spirituals as "The first artistic gift of Afro-Americans to the world," and as an exemplification of "existential freedom in action," the theologian and culture critic Cornel West has little doubt that jazz is linked back to the resilient and even subversive music of the slave church. "At the level of form, these 'sorrow songs' contain subtle rhythmic elements alongside brooding melodies. They invoke deep passions not of self-pity or self-hatred but of lament and hope. The spirituals give artistic form to the frustrations and aspirations of a battered people constantly under siege with few human allies . . . Subsequent developments, such as the blues, jazz, and gospel music may reject or revise the Christian commitment, vocalize instruments, and add more complex

11. Spencer, *Blues and Evil*, 35–36.
12. Ibid., 53.
13. Ibid., 67.

rhythms, but the cultural crucible of such developments rests in the distinct musical articulation of Afro-American Christianity."[14] What's more, for West it is clear that this "existential freedom" has a deeply African rooting, that it "flows from the kinetic orality and affective physicality inherited from West African cultures and religions."[15] It should be emphasized that both West and Cone see the black church as having played a crucial role in shaping jazz, including the experimental and avant-garde expressions that emerged in the 1960s through the influence of people such as John Coltrane. According to West, "most black folk in the fifties listened weekly to spiritual and gospel music in black churches,"[16] a perspective echoed by James Cone: "Most of the jazz musician's early life was in the African-American community, and if you were in the community at that time you were in the church. The church was the most dominant reality in the community. I think it would be impossible to grow up black in the south, and not be a product of the church in some way . . . whether you were a member of it or not."[17] The church was simply in the air breathed by African-Americans, and this was true even as other religious and philosophical movements began to make inroads into urban black America. Even Jones/Baraka, who in 1966 could write that "the world had opened up, and the church had not"—thereby accounting for what he saw as the increased secularity of black America—also writes of how the emotionalism and spirit of the church was carried forward into jazz and into the emerging form of rhythm and blues.[18] Here it might be worth adding a more recent observation made by jazz saxophonist Steve Wilson. Asked in a *Down Beat* magazine interview about the way in which gospel music continues to influence both jazz and contemporary rhythm and blues, Wilson responded by voicing some concern over the current state of things. "A lot of contemporary r&b is style over substance, and that comes from a lot of things not coming out of the church. Everyone's trying to use all the inflections without trying to understand how the inflections

14. West, "Subversive Joy and Revolutionary Patience," 162–63.
15. Ibid., 162.
16. Ibid., 178.
17. Cone, telephone interview.
18. Jones, "The Changing Same," *Black Music*, 218f.

function, how the voice works and how a melody works so those kinds of sensibilities matter."[19]

Still, as I've already observed, from the very beginning it was not only African-Americans who were playing and shaping jazz, and so there were clearly other influences at work along with the blues and the music of the black church. Whatever the race politics, that original New Orleans hybrid of African-American, Creole, and European forms and sensibilities created something not only new, but also dynamically open to further innovation. From very early on, it was not only black and Creole musicians playing this music, but white ones as well, and its development was hardly confined to New Orleans. Bix Beiderbecke, the white trumpet player from Iowa, is often recognized as being second only to Louis Armstrong in his influence as a jazz soloist during the 1920s, a time when soloing became a defining feature of jazz. Further, very early in its development, jazz music began to spread into Europe. Even prior to the First World War, the African-American singer Charles Baker was a popular entertainer in Paris. With his three-piece band playing a mixture of ragtime and early jazz-related music, Baker claimed for himself the honor of being the man who introduced France to jazz. Through the twenties, African-American touring bands were enthusiastically received across much of Western Europe, with Paris serving as something of a hub for a growing jazz culture. Sometime around 1930, and inspired by Louis Armstrong's musical explorations, the guitarist Django Reinhardt and violinist Stéphane Grappelli began to shape their own distinctly European form of jazz. In 1932, the jazz critic Hugues Panassié established the famous Hot Club de France in Paris, which served as the base for his influential writings about what constituted "real jazz." In Panassié's view, white jazz musicians were always suspect, as were any black musicians who departed too far from what he considered to be the authentic New Orleans roots of the music.

As will become abundantly clear as this chapter progresses, debates over what is or isn't *real* jazz are almost as much a part of jazz history as the music itself. And in one way or another, these debates often get tangled into questions of race. Randall Sandke's 2010 book, *Where the Dark and the Light Folks Meet: Race and the Mythology, Politics, and Business of Jazz*, is something of a case in

19. Odell, "Backstage with Steve Wilson," 15.

point. In Sandke's view, while jazz was birthed in the melting pot that was New Orleans, during the opening three or four decades of the music's history jazz bands were by and large segregated by race. Though quite clear in his statement that "the overwhelming majority of its greatest exponents have been African-American," Sandke is also determined to demonstrate that jazz created by white musicians is also a significant part of the music's heritage. Further, he wants to illustrate that as musicians began to cross the color barrier and form integrated bands, they were effectively pioneers of a new way of understanding race. Here Sandke cites the black bassist, Milt Hinton: "We were miles ahead of everybody else. Musicians have been integrating way before society decided to do it."[20]

Sandke's book is not uncontroversial, and following its publication it sparked an enormous amount of debate both in print and online. Much of this debate has to do with his claim that while the decade of the 1960s brought about the civil rights movement, it also introduced a new kind of race politics to the music; one which continues to be felt right up to our current day, albeit in a different form. "Even today," he writes, "forward-looking African-American musicians can be criticized for deviating from norms advocated by certain black jazz authorities who feel that jazz should not stray too far from its 'tradition' of incorporating blues and swing." Meanwhile, "White musicians . . . have been accused of 'appropriating' a black style and at the same time criticized for not being able to master it."[21]

One of the critics to whom Sandke points is Stanley Crouch, a writer, novelist, and jazz critic known both for his strong views and for his fiery temperament. Since 1987, Crouch has served as artistic consultant for jazz programming at New York's Lincoln Center, a position that gives him a not inconsiderable level of influence in the North American jazz scene. While Crouch begins his important *Jazz Times* article on "The Negro Aesthetic of Jazz" by referring to its hybrid roots, he very quickly moves to warn of those who "would like to remove those elements that are essential to jazz and that came from the Negro," namely the blues and swing.[22] In his view, not only are these indispensable elements of jazz, they are also what

20. Sandke, *Dark and the Light Folks Meet*, 7.
21. Ibid., 3
22. Crouch, "Negro Aesthetic of Jazz," 211.

gives it its "Negro-American" character. Notice how intentional Crouch is about *not* using the term "African-American." "Through the creation of blues and swing, the Negro discovered two invaluable things. With the blues, a fresh melodic could be framed within a short form of three chords that added a new feeling to Western music and inspired endless variations. In swing it was a unique way of phrasing that provided an equally singular pulsation. These two innovations were neither African nor European nor Australian nor Latin nor South American; they were Negro-American."[23] In an article published the following year entitled "Putting the White Man In Charge"—an article which actually led to the termination of his relationship with *Jazz Times*—Crouch seems to have adopted a somewhat different view of the origins of this music. "Because Negroes invented jazz," he writes, "and because the very best players have so often been Negroes, the art has always been a junction for color trouble in the world of evaluation and promotion." Writing of the black avant-garde movement of the 1960s, Crouch simply dismisses "certain Negroes who cannot play [yet who] will claim to be of aesthetic significance on the basis of sociology and some irrelevant ancestral connection to Africa." He has at least as much disdain, though, for white jazz critics, who he says have tended to elevate respectably good white jazz players "far beyond their abilities in order to allow white writers to make themselves feel more comfortable about being in the role of evaluating an art from which they feel substantially alienated."[24]

Over the years, one of Crouch's regular sparring partners has been Amiri Baraka. In the early 1960s, and still writing under the name LeRoi Jones, he sketched a version of jazz history that contends that an essentially black music had been more or less domesticated by the white swing big bands of the 1930s and 1940s, only to be "restored" to its rightful place by the beboppers of the 1940s. Jones/Baraka writes of how the role of the boppers was "to drag it outside the mainstream of American culture again,"[25] though this too was short-lived. The white-dominated "cool jazz" movement of the 1950s was another instance of domestication, though for Jones/Baraka the late 1950s and 1960s would bring a new and

23. Ibid.
24. Crouch, "Putting the White Man In Charge," 232–35.
25. Jones, *Blues People*, 181.

much welcomed subversion of things. Writing that "Negro music is always radical in the context of formal American culture,"[26] he embraces the sonic explorations of musicians such as John Coltrane, Ornette Coleman, and Cecil Taylor as a right and good rebellion against the safe music—and racist attitudes—of white America.

Cornel West shares with Jones/Baraka a positive reading of the role of the bebop movement, calling it a "grand break with American mainstream music." Crediting the boppers of the 1940s with "Africanizing Afro-American jazz—with the accent on contrasting polyrhythms, the deemphasis of melody, and the increased vocalization of the saxophone,"[27] West clearly understands the African connection as being more than what Crouch so disdainfully calls an "irrelevant ancestral connection."

I had the opportunity to speak with the veteran bassist Bill Crow about these issues of race and jazz. Crow began playing professionally in the late 1940s, and over his long career worked and recorded with an astonishing array of jazz luminaries, including Stan Getz, Gerry Mulligan, Clark Terry, Zoot Simms, and Mary Lou Williams. Commenting that "the older generation was very generous," Crow spoke pointedly of the resentment and even anger that characterized many members of the new generation of black jazz musicians emerging in the early 1960s. "There was this young generation saying, 'what are you doing playing our music?' Dizzy [Gillespie] said it best; he said, 'you can't steal a gift. If you can hear it, you can have it.'" After noting that at an earlier stage the more important issue had been that of one's drug of choice—"In those days, if someone found out that you smoked pot instead of drank whiskey, it was like 'oh, you're in this club'"—Crow commented, "The same way with the music. If you exhibited an interest in jazz, you couldn't do wrong in a black neighborhood." However, in Crow's view as the radicalism of the 1960s began to unfold, "Any sense of having your jazz protecting you in the ghetto evaporated pretty quickly."[28]

It is important to state very clearly that there was no sense in which Bill Crow was expressing a longing for the America of the pre-civil rights era. Rather he was giving voice to his own

26. Ibid., 235.
27. West, "On Afro-American Popular Music," 178–79.
28. Crow, personal interview.

experience of having worked and lived in a jazz culture which pre-dated the civil rights movement, and in which the politics of race were—at least to his mind—more or less irrelevant. In this respect, Crow's experience actually lines up with some observations made by James Cone. "Jazz is more democratic than most music, and it speaks to American democracy as it should have been. That's the first time that the racial barriers really, truly broke down, among the jazz musicians. And also it broke down where they played. That's why it has been connected with democracy so much."[29]

Yet there did have to come a time when the radicalism of Jones/Baraka and of musicians such as Archie Shepp, Max Roach, and Albert Ayler was an all but necessary part of the struggle for civil rights. Metaphorically speaking, the tap had been off for so long that once the water began to flow through the pipes there was inevitably going to be a fair bit of rust in the mix. And to be very clear, I am not suggesting that it is the likes of Roach or Jones/Baraka who are the unwanted and rusty impurities. Rather the rust had formed in and through the society as a whole. This is a society that had engineered and legalized an oppressive system of segrega-tion in the American south, and tolerated the practice of lynching for well over half a century. Contrary to what many now assume, lynchings were not limited to occasional acts of violence carried out by small groups of whiskey-fueled vigilantes. Many were in fact rather well orchestrated and well attended "spectacle lynchings," in which an accused person was slowly and systemically tortured to death. In some cases, the victim was accused of a crime, but others were executed for a social violation, often having to do with the suggestion that a black man had acted in an unacceptable way toward a white woman. Crowds in the thousands gathered to watch as the accused was mutilated, burned, hanged, and often incinerated. A trade in souvenirs—pieces of bone, burned remains, fingers and toes—and in commemorative postcards flourished. This is a nation that even in the postwar 1940s found President Harry Truman's proposal for a federal anti-lynching law to be too controversial for serious consideration by Congress. It is also the society that in the urban north produced the ghettos and tolerated the sort of systemic racism and violence of which James Baldwin writes so passionately in *The Fire Next Time*. This is the world not

29. Cone, telephone interview.

only of the Gandhi-inspired vision of Martin Luther King, Jr., but also of the radicalism of Malcolm X and of his spiritual mentor Elijah Muhammad. It is the world that witnessed a resurgence of the Ku Klux Klan, bombings of churches and of the homes of pastors and other leaders of the civil rights movement, as well as the rise of the Black Panther Party, which at least at its more extreme edges was unafraid to use violence as a means to its political ends. The 1963 March on Washington has been impressed on American consciousness as one of the defining events in its modern history, yet it predates the riots in Watts by a mere two years. Between 1964 and 1968, major riots erupted in cities across the nation, including Harlem, Toledo, Newark, Minneapolis, Detroit, Chicago, and Washington. Not only were entire neighborhoods left literally in ruins, but the hope for real change—and specifically non-violent change—was all but obscured.

It is within this social context that what Jones/Baraka calls the "new black music" took shape. Pioneered by young avant-garde innovators such as Archie Shepp and Cecil Taylor, and carried forward by collectives including the Association for the Advancement of Creative Musicians (AACM)—which itself gave rise to the innovative jazz collective, the Art Ensemble of Chicago—this was a proudly and even defiantly Afro-centric movement. At its more extreme edges, it was also a movement that claimed that white musicians had no business playing jazz; arguing that it was through the writings of white critics and the business dealings of white record executives that this quintessentially black music had been co-opted and even stolen from the hands of its creators.[30] Put more positively, according to James C. Hall the tumultuous 1960s witnessed a sort of social and cultural rebellion on the part of the "African-American creative intellectuals," which was given voice through expressions such as the rise of this "new black music." "Experimentation, nationalistic and avant-garde, resulted in many African-American artists radically challenging the accepted boundaries of their art form. Most significantly, African-American artists of the 1960s attempted to assert cultural identity itself as necessary resistance to despair."[31]

30. Jones, *Black Music.* See particularly the essays, "Jazz and the White Critic," "The Jazz Avant-Garde," "New Tenor Archie Shepp Talking," and "The Changing Same (R&B and New Black Music)."

31. Hall, *Mercy, Mercy Me,* 5–6.

Yet to come into our current times and bring things full circle, in the words of the jazz writer Gregory Thomas, "I had my love of the playing of people like Phil Woods and Zoot Sims to save me from becoming a racist." "When I went to college and really learned about the trans-Atlantic slave trade and about Black Nationalism and started being railed and rolled around by that, I got angry. I could never tip over into becoming a racist—into saying 'I hate white people' or looking at all white people as white people—because of my love of Phil Woods and Zoot Sims and Paul Desmond. I couldn't go there, because they were part of me."[32]

So, other than demonstrating that the history of jazz is a contested one, where has this brought us? Acknowledging that the more extreme voices in this ongoing debate would be anything but satisfied—and that even the more moderate and nuanced ones would find points on which to differ with my reading of things—it brings me to the point of needing to take a stab at a brief overview of how jazz music has unfolded in the North American context.

Though birthed in a kind of melting pot in New Orleans in the opening decades of the twentieth century, the realities of racism and segregation meant that jazz music developed along trajectories defined by race. The music's development in its African-American context was profoundly shaped by the blues and the spirituals, as well as by the church context from which those musical forms emerged. "The black church, black-owned and black-run Christian congregations, is the fountainhead of the Afro-American spiritual-blues impulse," writes Cornel West. "Without the black church, with its African roots and Christian context, Afro-American culture—in fact, Afro-America itself—is unimaginable."[33]

Meanwhile, though certainly paying attention to what was happening in the black scene, white musicians were moving jazz along a trajectory that would produce the swing and dance bands that flourished under the leadership of people such as Benny Goodman and Tommy Dorsey. This trajectory also wound its way toward the development of the considerably less "jazzy" dance bands of leaders such as Guy Lombardo, and to the self-consciously revivalist Dixieland movement of the 1950s.

32. G. Thomas, personal interview.
33. West, "On Afro-American Popular Music," 184–85.

As the 1930s progressed, some of the bands did begin to integrate, a notable example being both the big band and smaller ensembles of Benny Goodman. In 1929, Goodman purchased a set of band arrangements from the black bandleader Fletcher Henderson, even hiring Henderson's band members to teach his own band how to play them. Within two years Goodman was hiring black musicians for recording dates, and in fact Billie Holiday's earliest recordings were done with Goodman. By the mid 1930s he had begun to include black musicians in his working band, though this did mean that he had to omit the Jim Crow south from the band's touring schedule. Notable, too, are the bands of Duke Ellington, which already in the early 1920s had found wide acceptance with both white and black audiences. In 1933 Ellington recorded "Cotton Club Medley," marking one of the earliest instances of a record made using a racially mixed band.

The advent of bebop in the mid 1940s marks a significant point in the music's history. Nurtured in the small late-night clubs of Harlem, and driven by black musicians, bebop was built on technical virtuosity, rhythmic and harmonic complexity, and a willingness to push against the norms and boundaries that had previously defined jazz. Rejected by many of the jazz critics of the day as doing violence to "traditional jazz," bebop was nonetheless embraced by an avid following that heard in it something more gripping—more challenging and even unsettling—than what was heard in the music's earlier forms. Writing of the "open, positive attitude to others" embodied by New Orleans jazz, the Reformed theologian and culture critic Hans Rookmaaker expressed a deep concern that, "a lot of modern jazz emanates from individualism, a negative attitude to society that is the result of a sense of inner discontent."[34] To this, many of the people gathered in those Harlem clubs in the post-war 1940s would have said simply, "yes, you're right." For all that the Second World War marked the defeat of the Axis of Evil, back at home racism still held sway; of course people were deeply discontent.

In time, bebop itself gave way to several new developments and experiments, including both hard bop—best thought of as a kind of carrying forward of the bop banner with an even stronger sense of the blues, gospel, and rhythm and blues—and cool jazz.

34. Rookmaaker, "Listening to Jazz," *New Orleans Jazz*, 361.

Though certainly the sessions Miles Davis recorded with a racially mixed nine-piece band and released as *Birth of the Cool* marked an extremely important step in its development, it was white musicians who drove the cool or "West Coast" movement. Cool jazz was almost entirely detached from anything to do with the blues, and even more so from the church. It was also very popular, producing major stars including Chet Baker, Stan Getz, and Dave Brubeck; all very white and very marketable to white audiences.

The year 1959 stands as something of a crucible in this story. Between June and August of that year, Dave Brubeck and his band recorded *Time Out*, the album that landed him on the cover of *Time* magazine and secured his status as a jazz superstar. Meanwhile, in New York City between March and May of that same year, four extraordinarily important jazz albums were recorded, each of which was a part of the development of a new chapter in jazz.

Mingus Ah Um by Charles Mingus looked forward by way of looking back; by paying homage to his own roots and influences in songs such as "Better Git It In Your Soul"— inspired by the preaching and singing of the black church—"Goodbye Pork Pie Hat"—a lovely and evocative farewell to the legendary Lester Young—and "Open Letter to Duke" and "Jelly Roll"—tributes to Duke Ellington and Jelly Roll Morton respectively. The album also includes the politically charged piece, "Fables of Faubus," titled for Orval Faubus, the Governor of Arkansas notorious for his 1957 stand against the integration schools in Little Rock, Arkansas.[35]

Giant Steps by John Coltrane was really his first fully realized album as a composer, and includes two songs that have gone on to become standards in the jazz repertoire; the title track "Giant Steps" and "Naima," a song composed for his first wife. While many of the tracks are characterized by the rapid-fire succession of notes which the critic Ira Gitler famously called "sheets of sound," *Giant Steps* is really Coltrane's final album in the hard bop genre. Over the next few years his explorations tended to be in the same modal vein which characterized his playing on the landmark Miles Davis album *Kind of Blue*, the best-selling jazz album of all

35. There is some debate as to whether or not Columbia Records refused to allow the lyrics to "Fables of Faubus" to be included on this version. By some accounts, the lyrics were only added in time for the 1960 Candid Records release, *Presents Charles Mingus*, though the current consensus is that Columbia did prevent Mingus from recording a version with lyrics.

time. To state things far too simply, whereas bebop and hard bop were built around chord changes—with the bass player "walking" the chord changes and the soloists building their improvisations in and around the repeated chord progressions—modal jazz is built around modal scales. While the bass player creates bass lines within a specified scale, the soloists are freed to really explore the scale on which the piece is written.

That *Giant Steps* and *Kind of Blue* were recorded within weeks of one another speaks both to Coltrane's versatility and to the rapid pace of his ongoing musical transformation. On *Kind of Blue*, Coltrane is at times almost as elegantly understated as Davis himself, only occasionally giving a taste of his sound from *Giant Steps*. This album is extremely important, and not simply because it has been something of a gateway to jazz for countless new listeners. Part of its role was to send out a signal that something new was afoot, and that jazz was nowhere near reaching either a dead end or a high point. Part of the unfolding future of jazz would be found in the modal work of John Coltrane himself, notably in his revolutionary treatment of the show tune "My Favorite Things" and in his first and greatest extended suite, *A Love Supreme*.

While *Kind of Blue* sent word out of lovely and evocative new possibilities, Ornette Coleman's *The Shape of Jazz to Come* was more like the word being uttered in a whole new language. Considered one of the first avant-garde jazz albums, the music on this record is performed by a pianoless quartet of bass, drums, cornet, and alto saxophone. Each song begins and ends with a "head" or melody, and in between the four players improvise with great freedom and without any chord structure. It is not a particularly easy listen, and in easing open the door to the avant-garde it really foreshadows the even more challenging albums that would be released by a wide range of innovators during the 1960s. Beyond a doubt, that door was now open.

This is all part of what gave shape—and inspiration—to the "new black music." Coleman and Coltrane in particular must be seen as heralds of this new movement of avant-garde and free jazz, a movement that in Cornel West's view "symbolized both grand achievements and dead ends."[36] Rejected by many of the critics, musicians, and fans, questions of the merit of this boundary-breaking

---

36. West, "On Afro-American Popular Music," 183.

and sensibility-shattering genre can still evoke passionate debate fifty years after its emergence, as is evident in the wildly dismissive writings of Stanley Crouch and the equally wildly laudatory ones of Jones/Baraka. And, whether or not Crouch likes it, it is the music in which John Coltrane was engaged during the closing years of his life. In fact, Coltrane not only participated in this music, but also helped to pioneer and promote it both by including several of the more experimental young musicians on his later recordings and by encouraging his record label, Impulse, to sign innovators such as Archie Shepp and Albert Ayler.

With all of that said, it is to the story of John Coltrane that we now turn.

3

John William Coltrane

A Life in Outline

He was like a monk. He just had so much coming through him, so many ideas, that he'd practice all the time; all the time. And hey, you can hear the results of it.

—Reggie Workman, "Harlem Speaks"

And he wasn't into women like me and Philly [Joe Jones]. He was just into playing, was all the way into music, and if a woman was standing right in front of him naked, he wouldn't have even seen her. That's how much concentration he had when he played.

—Miles Davis

Trane was no saint; he was just a man. Some people might call him a saint, but to me he's still a man—the best, most beautiful man I ever worked with.

—Rashied Ali

I believe that he was an angel.

—Elvin Jones

Settling in to begin to write this chapter, I have beside me a stack of five Coltrane biographies, a second stack of six Coltrane-related reference books, and a little pile of CD liner notes removed from the dozen or so albums that will feature most prominently in the second section of this book. Add to that the additional three biographical studies that I referenced in the libraries of Columbia

University and the Institute of Jazz Studies at Rutgers University, along with the rather extraordinary array of magazine and journal articles, interviews, and documentary work that I have chipped my way through, and I am left needing to make two very plain observations.

Firstly, no one—least of all me—should imagine that this chapter could get anywhere close to providing a full picture of the life of John Coltrane. I had to remind myself of that fact several times as I began tapping at the computer keyboard, only to delete entire paragraphs that were beginning to read like the opening section of yet another full-scale biography. I don't need to do that sort of work, partly because it has already been done by Lewis Porter—a scholar much better equipped for the task than I'll ever be—but mostly because that isn't the book I set out to write. And each time I set myself back on track, I needed to remind myself that at its heart this book is a series of theological explorations done with and through the music of John Coltrane. This biographical sketch is intended to provide only the background and context for those explorations, and so need not be comprehensive. In fact, because all but one of the pieces that I'm working with was recorded after 1960, much of my attention will be on the final decade of Coltrane's life.

Secondly, I think it is important to comment on just how much material has been produced about Coltrane's life and music. As I noted in my introduction, the first two biographies were published in 1975, just eight years after John Coltrane's death. Subsequent studies have appeared in 1976, 1987, 1993, 1996, 1998, 2001, and 2007. Some of these are on very small presses or even self-published, though the most recent is by the *New York Times* jazz critic Ben Ratliff, and is published in a very attractive edition by Farrar, Straus and Giroux. In 2008, *The John Coltrane Reference* was added to the growing list of published resources. This 821-page volume offers a painstakingly detailed chronology and discography of Coltrane's performances and recordings. Even then, in his preface the book's editor Lewis Porter notes, "We're not done. There is no end to our passion for Coltrane."[1] In 2010 two notable books were added to the growing catalogue: *Coltrane on Coltrane*—a collection of all of the known interviews he gave during his life, along with other related materials including some of his own personal

1. DeVito et al., *The John Coltrane Reference*, x.

writings—and *John Coltrane and Black America's Quest for Freedom*—described on the back cover as "A wide-ranging collection of essays and interviews featuring many of the most eminent figures in Black American music and jazz studies and performance." In 2013, *Equinox: The Music of John Coltrane*, by Todd Jenkins, is to be added to the list, offering what the publisher describes as "the first comprehensive guide to all of his recordings written with the non-musician in mind." It is quite a list of publications, and one that could easily double were you to add the books published in languages other than English.

Then there is the phenomenon of the Coltrane poem, increasingly recognized as a genre in black poetry.[2] Amiri Baraka's "AM/TRAK," A.B. Spellman's "did john's music kill him?," Jayne Cortez's "How Long Has Trane Been Gone?," and Michael Harper's "Dear John, Dear Coltrane" are notable examples from the 1960s and early 70s. Ironically, many of the early poems give voice to a fairly ideological Black Nationalism, the sort of which Coltrane didn't share. Many of these poets tended to hear anger in Coltrane's intense and searching playing, though he regularly expressed surprise when people characterized his music as sounding angry.

Just what is going on here, that this one jazz musician has attracted such attention and inspired such devotion? Part of the answer lies in the extraordinary power of his music, and part in the nature of his story itself. But there is often something else at work as well, having to do with the creation of a musical and cultural icon. Here I think it is extremely helpful to take a look at Herman Gray's essay, "John Coltrane and the Practice of Freedom." Making a significant distinction between the man and musician John Coltrane on the one hand, and "Trane the mythical and iconic figure" on the other, Gray explores the ways "we produce and reproduce Trane, continually nominating him as representative of black freedom."[3] This is clearly visible in the manner in which he is invoked by many of the writers of the Coltrane poem, but also in the way that both the black avant-garde and the black cultural and nationalist movements took hold of the iconic Trane. Of these two movements, Gray observes that, "Not surprisingly, both stories depended on an authenticating logic organized by an explicit

2. Feinstein, "From 'Alabama' to 'A Love Supreme,'" 315–27.
3. Gray, "Coltrane and the Practice of Freedom," 33.

need for a representation of who and what constituted the subject of their discourse—for both the nationalists and the avant-garde, Trane fulfilled this need. But the point is simply that this construction proceeded without Coltrane's complicity."[4]

John Coltrane took a deep interest in African music, but he was similarly interested in the music of India. He supported the work of the Olatunji Center of African Culture, playing a benefit concert there in 1967 that turned out to be the last performance of his life. However, his most public and powerful statement on matters of race and the African-American reality was the instrumental lament "Alabama," written in response to the 1963 fire-bombing of a Birmingham church that resulted in the death of four children. And while over the final five years of his life he certainly played avant-garde music, it had nothing to do with an ideological rejection of the schools of jazz in which he had been formed. "I don't want to take anything away from music; I want to add to it," he told an interviewer for *Esquire*. "I'll continue to look for truth in music as I see it, and I'll draw on all the sources I can, all the areas of music, all the things there are in the world around us to inspire me. It takes many people to effect a complete change in any system."[5]

Following his death, the tendency to reconstruct John Coltrane as "Trane" only intensified, and as Gray suggests, what we might stand to learn from the man becomes obscured behind the myth. It is to the man John Coltrane that I will seek to introduce you, and not to some mythic construction or plaster saint.

John William Coltrane was born in Hamlet, North Carolina on September 23, 1926 to J. R. and Alice Coltrane (nee Blair). Shortly after the birth, the Coltranes moved to High Point, North Carolina, to live with John's maternal grandparents. Both of his grandfathers were pastors in the African Methodist Episcopal Zion Church, though by all accounts it was the Reverend William Blair who was the patriarch of the family.[6] Although he traveled a great deal as a presiding elder of the AME Zion Church, William Blair remained a very real presence in young John's life. "[I]n my early years," he told August Blume in a 1958 interview, "I was going to

4. Ibid., 47.

5. DeVito, *Coltrane on Coltrane*, 336.

6. According to Lewis Porter, the move to High Point may have been precipitated by the Reverend Coltrane's death. Whatever the case, he had little direct influence on the life of young John. Porter, *John Coltrane*, 11.

church every Sunday and stuff like that, being under the influence of my grandfather—he was the dominating cat in the family. He was most well-versed, active politically." Speaking of his father, he added, "he never seemed to say too much."[7] Clearly a quiet and even retiring man, J.R. Coltrane worked as a tailor, though by all accounts was also a decently accomplished amateur musician.

The years 1938 and 1939 brought three deaths that would greatly change the shape of young John Coltrane's life. First, on December 11, 1938, the Reverend William Blair died at the age of seventy-nine. Less than a month later, on January 2, 1939, John's father J.W. Coltrane died of stomach cancer. Finally on April 26, 1939, John's grandmother Alice Blair died of breast cancer, meaning that in just over four months the thirteen-year old John Coltrane lost three of the most important figures in his life, most notably, of course, his father. It was precisely at this point in his life that he began to learn music, and Porter speculates, "Perhaps, in a sense, music became his father substitute. And through music, he could both express and relieve the pain he felt about his father's death, a pain he never seems to have allowed himself fully to explore."[8]

In 1942 or 1943, Coltrane's mother moved to Philadelphia to find work, leaving her son in High Point to finish high school before moving to join her. After relocating to Philadelphia, he held a number of jobs and began his musical studies in earnest. Following a brief stint in the navy—during which he played alto saxophone with the military band, and also recorded an impromptu session with a circle of friends—Coltrane returned to Philadelphia and began to pursue music as his full-time profession. It is interesting to note here that his recorded work with his navy friends is fairly mediocre in quality, giving no hint of the prodigious genius to come.

Back in Philadelphia, Coltrane found work in both jazz and rhythm-and-blues—with the bands of Joe Webb and Big Maybelle, King Kolax, Eddie "Cleanhead" Vinson, and Jimmy Heath—all the while studying music under Dennis Sandole at the Granoff Studios, supported by his veterans' benefits. In 1949 he joined the big band of Dizzy Gillespie, and in 1950 was invited to stay on with Gillespie's smaller ensemble when the big band had ceased to be

7. Blume, "Interview with John Coltrane," 12.
8. Porter, *John Coltrane*, 17.

financially viable. It was at this point that Coltrane's use of both heroin and alcohol began to cause serious problems.

In the story of jazz, substance abuse plays no small role. Life on the road always brings certain risks, but these were magnified by a romanticism surrounding the great alto sax innovator Charlie Parker. Parker was both a brilliant musician and a notorious heroin addict, and many younger players convinced themselves that there was a direct link between the two. Jimmy Heath even suggests that heroin assisted Coltrane in keeping an almost inhuman level of focus and concentration during his long, long practice sessions,[9] though in time the addictions would all but destroy his career. Over these years he would apparently use alcohol to try to break his reliance on heroin and then switch to using heroin to try to break his alcohol addiction, all the while constantly feeding a sugar craving by eating endless amounts of candy, resulting in serious problems with his teeth.

After his stint with Gillespie, in 1951 Coltrane returned to Philadelphia and remained there for the next few years, working in relative obscurity with various jazz and rhythm-and-blues bands and finishing up his studies at Granoff. For a time in 1954 he worked with the band of one of his original saxophone heroes, Johnny Hodges, and in 1955 spent a number of weeks with the organist Jimmy Smith. While both of these were significant experiences in their own right, they also indicate that at this point Coltrane was keeping his addictions sufficiently in check such that he was able to play at a demanding level.

It is the fall of 1955, however, that finds Coltrane facing two of the greatest opportunities—and challenges—of his life. On October 3, 1955 he married Juanita "Naima" Austin, the woman who would be a crucial support in helping him to face down his self-destructive addictions. A single parent with a six-year-old daughter named Saeeda, Naima was a convert to Islam, and while Coltrane did not share her religious beliefs he respected her faith and devotion.

Conversion to Islam, both in its conventional Middle Eastern form and to a lesser extent in the Black Nationalist offshoot of Elijah Muhammad's Nation of Islam, was not uncommon at this time, particularly amongst jazz musicians. Perceived by many as being a step away from the Eurocentric church tradition, the very

9. Ibid., 62.

existence of Islam caused something of a faith crisis for John Coltrane. In his 1958 interview with August Blume, after reflecting on his religious upbringing under the watchful eye of his grandfather, Coltrane offered the following:

> And after I'd say my late teens, I just started breakin' away, you know, among certain things. I was growin' up, so I questioned a lot of what I find in religion. I began to wonder about it. About two or three years later, maybe twenty-two, twenty-three, this Muslim thing came up. I got introduced to that. And that kinda shook me. A lot of my friends, you know, they went Muslim, you see. So I thought about that, anyway, it took me to something I had never thought about—you know, another religion? . . . I was like, religion man, I was always—I was disappointed when I found out how *many* religions there were . . . When I saw there were so many religions and kind of opposed somewhere to the next and so forth, you know, it screwed up my head. And, I don't know. I was kinda confused, you know. And I just couldn't believe that, uh, that every—that *one* guy could be right. Because if he's right somebody else got to be wrong, you know?[10]

Referring to a book entitled *Philosophy Made Simple*, Coltrane—who developed a reputation as a voracious reader—makes the rather startling admission that it is "the only thing I've actually read all the way through." He then adds that he had purchased a few other books, including *Language, Truth, and Logic*, by A. J. Ayer, but admits that he often doesn't "get any further than the first few pages."[11]

It is actually quite important to note that this interview takes place the year *after* Coltrane has kicked his addictions to both alcohol and heroin; something which he later describes as having been very much a spiritual awakening and a matter of grace. It is almost as if at this point Coltrane is still searching for a language with which to make sense of his own life and spiritual search. But more on this later.

John and Naima were married on October 3, 1955 in Baltimore at the end of his first week in the Miles Davis band. Though only a few months older than Coltrane, Miles Davis had been recording since 1945, and his tenure with the legendary Charlie Parker had

10. Blume, "Interview with John Coltrane," 12–13.
11. Ibid., 10.

basically assured him of star status. An invitation to join the Davis band meant a musician's profile would instantly be raised, but it also meant that fans and jazz writers alike would be highly critical in their appraisal of a new member's abilities. Coltrane was no exception in this respect, and in spite of his track record with the likes of Dizzy Gillespie and Johnny Hodges, he was treated as a young and unproven upstart. Davis himself, on the other hand, was clear: "[A]fter we started playing together for a while, I knew that this guy was a bad motherfucker who was just the voice I needed on tenor to set off my voice."[12] By the end of that first month, the band was in the studio recording the tracks for *Round about Midnight*, Davis' first album in what would become his thirty-year tenure with Columbia Records. Less than a month later the group was back in the studio, this time laying down tracks for Prestige Records, with which Davis was still under contractual obligation. The band toured steadily through the remainder of 1955, meaning that with the exception of the very rare weeks off when Coltrane could go home to Philadelphia, he was seldom able to spend time with his new wife. Naima and her daughter Saeeda moved to Manhattan in June 1956, where she could spend at least some time with her husband during the band's frequent New York engagements.

Trying to balance the demands of his music with the realities of domestic life, Coltrane was increasingly losing himself to his addictions. In November 1956, after being warned by Davis to straighten out, John moved his family back to Philadelphia to live with his mother. However, Coltrane's addictions were anything but in check, so in April 1957 Davis finally fired him.

This is where the *telling* of the story becomes interesting, and where one gets a real sense of Gray's distinction between the man John Coltrane and the mythic figure of Trane. The story of the iconic Trane defeating his addictions is a highly dramatic one, which would work beautifully as a personal testimony in the church tradition in which John Coltrane was actually formed. In this version, a friend issues a wake-up call—and in different variations it is Reggie Workman, Sun Ra, or Miles Davis—and so he moves back to Philadelphia where he has his wife and mother lock him into his bedroom, instructing them to bring him nothing other than water for sustenance. After a period of time—in one variation it is four

12. Porter, *John Coltrane*, 98.

days, in others as long as two weeks—he emerges straight, sober, and spiritually transformed, ready to live the rest of his life in a whole new light. It is actually worth taking a moment to examine three different accounts of this story. First from J. C. Thomas's 1975 biography, *Chasin' the Trane*:

> With God's grace, he believed, and his own determination, all things were possible. His readings in religion and philosophy had convinced him that he should now cleanse himself of physical and psychological impurities and dedicate his music to God, in whom he believed with increasing involvement each passing day.
>
> Then he excused himself, first to the bathroom to clean up, and next to retire to his room. Like a prisoner, but a self-sentenced one, he would subsist on water alone. He would fast, not sweat, it out; and he would not walk again among his family until he was clean. From time to time Naima or John's mother would knock on his door, asking him if he was all right. He would either say "Yes" or "May I have some more water?" He only left his bedroom for the bathroom; he went nowhere else in the apartment while he was going through his ordeal. The two women in his life prayed for him.

Thomas concludes by remarking, "And when it was over, that was it; no more poison in Coltrane's system."[13]

The version in John Fraim's 1996 book *Spirit Catcher* has a similar tone, though this time it culminates with Coltrane setting out on his life-long search for what Fraim calls "the mysterious sound":

> He then retreated into his room, where he would battle the terrible pains of withdrawal for the next few days. He would live solely on water and leave the room only to go to the bathroom. During the days he spent most of his time praying and asking for God's help to see him through this ordeal. When he spoke with Naima his thoughts were jumbled. Clearly, some incredible event was taking place in that room.
>
> One morning, about four days later, he walked out of his room and announced to the family that he was no longer addicted to heroin or alcohol. There was a certain look of tranquility on his face, a certain awestruck expression. He was extremely quiet.

13. J.C. Thomas, *Chasin' the Trane*, 83.

Naima, concerned about his silence, asked him if something was wrong. He looked at her and told her that he had a dream in which he heard this droning sound. "It was so beautiful," he told her. She asked him to describe it and he tried but found it impossible. He then went over to the piano and attempted to play. But after a few minutes he gave up.

With this event, the search for the mysterious sound began.[14]

And finally, an excerpt from Eric Nisenson's 1993 biography, *Ascension:*

> It happened when he finally decided to free himself from the addictions. He lay down in a room in his mother's house and instructed his wife to bring him only water. By this time, alcohol was more of a problem than heroin, and his withdrawal was at first painful and dark. His wife and mother didn't think he would make it; he became sick and agitated, both physically and psychologically. Early on during this period, he said, he was somehow touched by God, with whom he made a deal of sorts: get him through this torment and he would devote his talent to God, he would make music that would bring people to experience the same kind of revelations he was witnessing. Believe or doubt him, but after this experience he was able to calm down and wait out his cure. He lay quietly in bed, eating nothing, drinking only water, exorcising the demons that had plagued him for years.[15]

It is notable that Nisenson goes on to comment that, "As with any legend—and Coltrane became a genuine jazz legend—the truth was more complicated than the myth."[16] At first glance it seems as if Nisenson is suggesting that he might be telling a story that is a little bigger and richer than the one that was actually lived out that week in the house in Philadelphia. However, he then goes on to write about how, "us 'sophisticates' who make up the bulk of the jazz audience tend to blanche these days upon reading of somebody's religious experience."[17] It would seem that his reference to "legend" is really a sort of apologetic on behalf of the gifted and

14 Fraim, *Spirit Catcher,* 34–35.

15. Nisenson, *Ascension,* 40.

16. Ibid., 41.

17. Ibid.

artistic John Coltrane, that we not lump his religiosity in with that of "Jimmy Swaggart, Jim Jones, Jerry Falwell, Jim and Tammy Faye Bakker, and assorted gurus and cults."[18] Whatever Nisenson understands himself to be doing, he is only too happy to offer a version of the drug withdrawal story that belongs with the narrative of Trane. It just might not have much to do with John Coltrane.

Now, compare these accounts with what Lewis Porter writes in *John Coltrane: His Life and Music*. During these weeks in Philadelphia, Porter suggests, "Coltrane was not sulking at having lost the engagement with Davis. On the contrary, he took this opportunity to get his career and his personal life together. He had begun rehearsing informally with Thelonious Monk. And he played as a leader in Philadelphia."[19] While acknowledging that, "Coltrane's friends and family helped him to quit cold turkey,"[20] Porter rather simply states "Coltrane won the battle against heroin during that period of between one and two weeks—he may have had a few more bouts with alcohol before beating it for good—and, rejuvenated, he began to work harder than ever on his music."[21] Noting just how understated his version of the events is compared to the others, I asked Porter what had informed this, and he replied simply, "I talked to people no one else had talked to; Philadelphia people." He then continued,

> So often what you read is a part of the truth, and you're just not getting the whole story. Did he lock himself in a room? Yes, in the daytime before he went out to the gig. He was gigging that week as far as I can tell. According to at least one person I interviewed that was when he was actually quitting. Then he would go back home and kind of shut the door and say to Naima, if anyone comes by—especially you-know-who or those kind of people—don't let them in. So it wasn't that he literally didn't move from his room for a week, but he tried to isolate himself when he wasn't performing I guess would be a better way of putting it.[22]

The record shows that from the date that he was fired by Miles Davis—probably April 14, 1957—Coltrane worked fairly steadily,

18. Ibid.
19. Porter, *John Coltrane*, 105.
20. Ibid., 106.
21. Ibid.
22. Porter, personal interview.

even recording with Thelonious Monk on April 16. He was also involved in recordings on April 18, 19, and 20, and again on May 17, and by July was playing regularly in New York as a member of the Thelonious Monk Quartet. As Porter suggests, it also appears that he was leading a Philadelphia-based band during that spring, and gigging regularly. This does not downplay the significance or authenticity of his triumph over his addictions, nor does it make it any less a spiritual and grace-filled experience. What it does is suggest that Coltrane's struggle with his addictions was lived out in a more work-a-day world, and one in which he needed to keep putting one foot in front of the other as he learned to cope with his own cravings. Further, the fact that he may have had "a few more bouts with alcohol" serves to frame this experience as something closer to that of any one of us who struggles with addiction, and to keep us at least a step away from the mythic Trane.

In interviews from the late 1950s and very early 1960s, Coltrane offers only veiled references to his experiences with addiction and recovery. In a 1958 *Down Beat* interview with Ira Gitler, he comments that he learned how important it is to "Live cleanly . . . Do right . . . ," adding that, "You can improve as a player by improving as a person. It's a duty we owe ourselves."[23] In another interview from 1958—this one with Bob Snead for the *Cleveland Call and Post*—Coltrane admits that, "Some years ago I went into a period of depression and almost gave up. I thank God for enabling me to pull out of it. My wife Nita was a great help to me, also."[24] And while he did evidently speak very openly about his addictions in a 1960 interview with the Swedish jazz writer Bjorn Fremer, he requested that the information be omitted from the published article.[25]

This reticence to speak openly about his addictions might have come from a simple desire to sidestep the stigma of addictions, and to keep his private life and struggles out of public view. However, it might also be fairly suggested that at this stage John Coltrane did not yet have the language—musical or otherwise—to say what he most needed to say about these experiences. And perhaps, too, he was aware that at this point his life was anything

23. Gitler, "Trane on Track," 43.
24. Snead, "Jazz Profile," 46.
25. Fremer, "The John Coltrane Story," 61.

but free of complexities and struggles, and so was hesitant to say anything that might be misconstrued as a sort of testimonial to his own personal righteousness. In short, Coltrane may have been aware that there was still work to be done.

In August 1957 the family moved back to New York, where Coltrane continued to work with the Thelonious Monk Quartet through the fall. Of this experience, he would later recall, "Working with Monk brought me close to a musical architect of the highest order. I felt I learned from him in every way—through the senses, theoretically, technically."[26] When in January 1958 he was invited to return to play with the band of Miles Davis, Coltrane carried those lessons with him, playing the long rapid-fire lines that Ira Gitler famously labeled "sheets of sound." And while he'd always been known for his dedicated practicing, he was now becoming the monk-like figure to whom Reggie Workman refers in one of the quotes with which this chapter opens. It is easy to speculate that at least in part this was an addiction substitute, or maybe even an addiction in its own right. Of Coltrane's practice regimen, the jazz and culture critic Gerald Early rather bluntly states, "Such obsession does not suggest a very balanced or integrated personality."[27]

While the Miles Davis Sextet of 1958 and 1959 produced some of the finest and most enduring recorded music in the history of jazz, as it progressed Coltrane's tenure with the band was marked by a growing restlessness. This is the group that in 1959 produced the ground breaking modally-based album *Kind of Blue*, to say nothing of the 1958 classic *Milestones.* Yet like his band-mate Bill Evans, Coltrane was clearly stretching toward his own, more personal explorations. During the period of just over two years he was with Davis, Coltrane collaborated on recordings with Kenny Burrell, Wilbur Harden, and Milt Jackson. He also played on any number of other sessions, recorded a small armful of records as a bandleader for Prestige Records, and released his landmark record *Giant Steps* on Atlantic. He agreed to remain with Davis for a month-long European tour in the spring of 1960, but this was to be his last stint with band. And though he was a member of the group, he was increasingly less a *part* of it, as the reviews in

26. Coltrane with DeMicheal, "Coltrane on Coltrane," 68.
27. Early, "Ode to John Coltrane," 376.

the French jazz magazine *Jazz Hot* would suggest. Effectively, John Coltrane had already moved on.

The closing date of the European tour took place in Stuttgart, West Germany on April 10, 1960. Just six days later Coltrane was on a shared bill at New York's Town Hall, and by early May he was leading a quartet and playing regular engagements in and around New York City. With the addition of the pianist McCoy Tyner in late May or early June of 1960, this working group began its evolution toward becoming what is known as "the classic quartet." By October the band, which by then included drummer Elvin Jones, was in the studio to record material that would eventually be released as the Atlantic albums *My Favorite Things* (1961), *Coltrane's Sound* (1961), and *Coltrane Plays the Blues* (1962).

In April 1961, Coltrane signed with Impulse Records, the label that would go on to release some of his most challenging and boundary-expanding records. The contract with Impulse was not only attractive financially; it also gave Coltrane considerable artistic control, right down to the album packaging. His years with Impulse can be roughly divided into two periods: the records leading up to *A Love Supreme* (January 1965), and those that followed. In a very real sense *A Love Supreme* was the hinge on which the two periods turned.

While the opening few years of his tenure with Impulse included several highly accessible and commercially successful projects—*Ballads*, *Duke Ellington and John Coltrane*, and *John Coltrane and Johnny Hartman*, all released in 1963—several of his early releases for the label did offer serious challenges to listeners. For one thing, early in 1961 he added reed player Eric Dolphy to the group as a fifth member, which resulted in critics such as *Down Beat's* John Tynan labeling their music as "anti-jazz."[28] Following on the heels of their first Impulse release—the 1961 big band experiment of *Africa/Brass*, the arrangements for which were done by Dolphy—came *Live at the Village Vanguard*, with its use of twin basses, the presence of Dolphy's various reed instruments, and the highly controversial sixteen-minute, piano-less jam, "Chasin' the Trane."

April 1962 brought two changes that would solidify Coltrane's classic quartet. Eric Dolphy moved on to pursue other work and was not replaced, and Jimmy Garrison came on board as

28. Woideck, *Coltrane Companion*, 232.

the permanent bass player. Garrison had played alongside Reggie Workman on *Live at the Village Vanguard*, and was the lone bass player on "Chasin' the Trane." For a number of reasons, this combination worked in a way that previous ones had not, leading Lewis Porter to conclude that, "Each of them—not Coltrane alone—deserves credit for some of the most moving and exciting group creations ever recorded."[29]

The first two years that the quartet worked together set the musical stage for what was to come with *A Love Supreme*. At the same time, Coltrane was going through a series of personal challenges that would set the spiritual and emotional stage for that landmark recording. In the liner notes to *A Love Supreme*, Coltrane writes of having experienced, "a period of irresolution . . . a phase which was contradictory to the pledge and away from the esteemed path." In a 1966 interview with the writer Frank Kofsky, Coltrane refers to the early 1960s as having been a time when he "went through quite a few changes, you know, like the home life—*everything* . . ."[30] Here, I agree with Porter's suggestion that the "period of irresolution" is very much tied to a domestic crisis; or more accurately, domestic *crises*, because there were actually a series of events that really shook the foundation of his home life. For all that he loved and relied on Naima—and these comments will be significantly expanded in chapter 5 of this book—Coltrane was not faithful to her. A brief affair that took place around the time of his 1957 battles with his addictions resulted in the birth of a baby girl, Sheila Coltrane. Evidently the child and her mother continued to have contact with John and Naima, which would have undoubtedly caused some real strain in the marriage (and probably doubly so since Naima and John were unable to have children of their own).

In *Chasin' the Trane*, J. C. Thomas provides excerpts from the diary of "Trane's Lady," an unnamed woman with whom Coltrane had an ongoing affair. The first entry is from the day the two met in May 1960, and within a month of this meeting they had become lovers.[31] While the excerpts Thomas provides do not make it entirely clear just how often the two saw each other, it does appear

29. Porter, *John Coltrane*, 201.
30. Kofsky, "Interview with John Coltrane," 303.
31. J. C. Thomas, *Chasin' the Trane*, 137–39.

that they were together on a relatively regular basis over the course of several years. The journal excerpts also indicate that on several occasions Coltrane spoke of ending the affair, only to resume it again. In one particularly striking entry from October 1961, the woman records that he said to her, "Are you a Christian? Because if you're not, we're through."[32] In an entry from November 1963 she mentions that Coltrane told her that he had left Naima and was living with Alice McLeod, who he would go on to marry on October 20, 1965. The final entry in these journals is from May 1966, when the woman records, "We decided to end the affair then and there."[33] This date is not only after his wedding to Alice, it is well after the births of his and Alice's first two children, John William Jr. (August 26, 1964) and Ravi John (August 6, 1965). It is also fully two years after the recording of *A Love Supreme*.

So we're left here with an interesting picture. On the one hand there is Coltrane's acknowledgment of his "period of irresolution," which seems tied to the collapse of his marriage and to all that was involved in that, and on the other hand there is this material that suggests his affair continued well into the period in which he said that he had found "resolution"; and "Resolution" is actually the title of the second movement of *A Love Supreme*. In that 1966 interview with Frank Kofsky, Coltrane follows up his comments about the collapse of life as he had known it by saying, "But it was a hell of a test for me, and coming out if it, it's just like I always heard, man: when you go through these crises and you come through them or come out of them, you're definitely stronger, you know, in a great sense."[34] And it is clear that he had done some other work to mend relationships and get his life back in perspective. For instance, *Down Beat* writer Don DeMichael refers to a letter of apology he received from Coltrane. It seems that due to the harsh criticism he had received from many of the jazz critics, at some point in the midst of his time of "irresolution" he had decided to simply shut them out and refuse all communication, even with those whom he considered friends. Though unaware Coltrane had made such a decision, DeMichael was at some point the recipient of a very hostile cold shoulder from the musician. "Later in 1964,

32. Ibid., 145.
33. Ibid., 163.
34. Kofsky, "Interview with John Coltrane," 303.

John sent me a letter asking me to forgive him. He said he'd lost God before and had just now found God again."[35]

Still, if the unnamed woman's timelines are to be believed, he was still a long way from integrating his desires and resolving the complexities of his relational and sexual self. Again, I will be revisiting these issues in chapter 5, but for now, allowing for the complexities of Coltrane's life, and allowing that he might yet have been making a serious mess of some things, it must be affirmed that A Love Supreme stands as one of the most engaging and influential jazz albums of all time. Outside of sacred and choral music, it is also one of the most unapologetically theological jazz recordings ever made.

Further, it is the only album for which John Coltrane made such detailed and formal preparation. Certainly there was much room for improvisation and collective group work, but even before the quartet set foot in the studio he had a very strong sense of its movement, flow, and end point. And in terms of being a spiritual and/or theological work, it really marked a new beginning. In a 1966 interview for Newsweek, he expounds upon his renewed vision for his life and music. "My goal is to live the truly religious life and express it in my music. If you live it, when you play there's no problem because the music is just part of the whole thing. To be a musician is really something. It goes very, very deep. My music is the spiritual expression of what I am—my faith, my knowledge, my being . . ."[36] The music that he would make to express his faith, knowledge and being was intensely challenging; music that would lose him many of his early fans, and cause even his friends in the jazz fraternity to wonder at his decisions. It is music that still stirs the critical pot, as is evident in the writings of people such as Stanley Crouch. In a piece from 2002 titled "Coltrane De-Railed," Crouch asks, "What could have led one of the intellectual giants—one of the great bluesmen, one of the most original swingers and a master of the ballad—into an arena so emotionally narrow and so far removed from his roots and his accomplishments?"[37] The twin contentions that this later music is both emotionally narrow—and by this I suspect Crouch means that he hears only anger and

35. J. C. Thomas, Chasin' the Trane, 182.
36. Porter, John Coltrane, 232.
37. Crouch, "Coltrane De-Railed," 214.

intensity in the playing—and far removed from Coltrane's roots are ones with which I greatly disagree, and part of what I will be attempting to illustrate in the second part of this book is the degree to which Coltrane is deeply and passionately tied to his roots. But Crouch is certainly not alone in his assessment.

In a well-known 1966 interview, the white Marxist writer and journalist Frank Kofsky attempts several times to engage Coltrane in conversation about Black Nationalist ideas and ideals.[38] Again and again Kofsky tries to steer things toward a discussion of the significance of Malcolm X, and while Coltrane does say that he was "*quite* impressed" by a public address he had attended, he gives his interviewer very little beyond that. During the course of the interview, Kofsky raises what he clearly thinks are socially significant topics, including the new black music (of which Coltrane remarks "it makes no difference to me one way or another what it's called"), the Vietnam War, the relative indifference of American audiences to the avant-garde, and the fact that while many jazz musicians are black, most of the club owners are white. On this latter issue, all Coltrane offers is the rather benign, "Yeah, well, this could be, Frank, this could be. I don't know." When Kofsky attempts to press him further by asking, "How do you think conditions are going to be improved for the musicians?" Coltrane responds by talking about "self-help," and how musicians will need to "work out their own problems in this area." That the interview went on to be published by Kofksy in his book, *Black Nationalism and the Revolution in Music* is all but astonishing, given how disinterested his subject was in engaging anything even approaching revolutionary Black Nationalism.

As Salim Washington observes, the music of the classic John Coltrane Quartet "modeled an ethos more in line with King's ethic of love and social democracy than it did the separatist ideology of Elijah Muhammad," and that it "perfectly exemplified in music the yearning for egalitarian social arrangements in the body politic."[39] Regardless of what Kofsky, Leroi Jones / Amiri Baraka, and others might have made of the revolutionary and political character of Coltrane's music, he himself apparently was simply not interested in going there. His own sense of his quest was that

38. Kofsky, "Interview with John Coltrane," 281f.
39. Washington, "'Don't Let the Devil,'" 140.

it was spiritual and musical, and his connection to African culture and identity was fueled entirely by a positive interest in what such explorations might have to contribute to a common good. Further, when his playing was described as angry—and for many listeners this also meant revolutionary—Coltrane would often protest that he obviously was not communicating with sufficient clarity.

What John Coltrane did communicate with great consistency and integrity was his burning passion for religious truth and spiritual exploration. During the final two-and-a-half years of his life he spent a remarkable amount of time in the recording studio, in search of the sound that could best express his spiritual vision. He had clearly begun to tire of the nightclub scene, remarking in his interview with Kofsky that he felt his current musical explorations demanded something other than a forty-minute set in a room filled with potential distractions for audience and musicians alike.[40] The sheer volume of recorded material meant that alongside of the records released on Impulse—generally three a year—there was sufficient material on the shelf to fill a fairly steady series of posthumous releases.

As was often the case with jazz recordings, the albums were not necessarily released in the order in which they were recorded either. For instance, material that made its way onto *Kulu Se Mama* (1967) and *Transition* (1970) was recorded in May and June 1965, prior to the June 28 session that would produce the highly controversial record *Ascension*. Had listeners had the opportunity to first wrestle with a piece such as the twenty-one minute "Suite" from *Transition*, perhaps *Ascension* wouldn't have been quite so shocking. With the quartet augmented by two trumpets, four saxophones, and an extra bass, the sound was bound to be big. The fact that *Ascension* is a collective group improvisation that on a first listening tends to sound completely unstructured and even wildly chaotic explains why it was summarily dismissed, not only by many of the critics, but also by some of Coltrane's most supportive fans. Many fellow musicians questioned both the worth of the album and the wisdom of incorporating so many young and struggling avant-garde musicians. According to Ben Ratliff, Coltrane's friend and former band mate Jimmy Heath referred to these large format groups as being Coltrane's "antipoverty bands,"

40. Kofsky, "Interview with John Coltrane," 288–89.

which gave to struggling musicians a place and a profile on the jazz scene, even at the cost of alienating his audience.[41]

Even Bob Mathieu's five-star review in *Down Beat*, in which he describes *Ascension* as "possibly the most powerful human sound ever recorded," does not gloss over the challenging nature of this record. Making a distinction between the manufactured record and the actual studio event, Mathieu suggests that in the case of *Ascension*, "The music does not transcend the event. In fact, the music *is* the event, and since there is no way of reproducing (i.e., reliving) the event except by doing it again, the music is in essence non-recordable." Mathieu adds that in cases where, "the listener is informed enough to be able to imagine what it was really like when this event took place, then the record may have meaning," but beyond that qualifying "may," he assures potential listeners only of the power of the sound. "Meanwhile, it is useful to regard this album as a documentation of a particular space of history. As such, it is wonderful—because the history is. If you want immersion in the sounds of these men, if you want their cries to pierce you, if you want a record of the enormity and truth of their strength, here it is."[42]

I have to confess, it took me a long time to acquire a taste for *Ascension*, and while I think Lewis Porter is right in calling the work "thrilling," it still isn't something I listen to more than just occasionally. *Ascension* requires—no, *demands*—that the listener pay attention, and that takes some real work. But more on that in chapter 8.

Though Coltrane never returned to recording with so large an ensemble, the pattern of adding musicians to fill out his sonic explorations seemed set. For both McCoy Tyner and Elvin Jones, this was not particularly good news. The addition of Pharoah Sanders on saxophone and Rashied Ali on drums led to the departure first of Tyner and then Jones; each alleging that he could no longer hear himself play. Prior to their departures, though, this expanded group recorded *Meditations*, a five-part extended suite that I consider to be second only to *A Love Supreme* in its theological significance.

Just two months prior to the *Meditations* session, however, a different experiment with an expanded line-up recorded *Om*, an

41. Ratliff, *Coltrane,* 158.

42. Mathieu, "'Ascension,'" 25.

album I consider to be the least successful of Coltrane's attempts to pray with sound. Not released until 1968, the album consists of just one piece, "Om," which begins and ends with chanted excerpts from the Hindu *Bhagavad-Gita*. The twenty-nine-minute piece is marked by an unfocussed screeching shrillness that offers the listener almost nothing by way of an anchored point of entry. The use of the Hindu text feels as if it comes without any proper context; rather than drawing on his "mother tongue" of religious faith as he does on *A Love Supreme* and *Meditations*, here Coltrane uses a religious text with which he has a merely passing and theoretical engagement. In the liner notes Coltrane is quoted as saying that, "'Om' means the first vibration—that sound, that spirit, which set everything else into being," and one can see how, in his search for a music that could be truly prayer, he might have found this an attractive idea. It is true that Coltrane had been studying various religious and esoteric texts, and in typical 1960s fashion he was open to everything from eastern mysticism to numerology, astrology, and even the scientific speculations of Albert Einstein, but "Om" doesn't seem to draw on any of those threads in a particularly meaningful or coherent way.

It is known that during this time Coltrane was actively experimenting with LSD, and it could well be that "Om" was recorded under the influence of this hallucinogenic drug. It can be hard to imagine how someone who fought so hard to overcome alcohol and heroin addictions—and offered such a powerful statement on the grace he experienced in the midst of his struggles—could turn around and begin using another drug. As Nisenson suggests, however, much has to do with the social context in which Coltrane was living. "The use of LSD, especially before it was made illegal, was not seen as a way of simply getting high, but rather a viable method of attaining spiritual ecstasy and gaining personal, religious, and even social insight. When Timothy Leary and Allen Ginsburg decided to save the world through acid, jazz musicians, including Dizzy Gillespie, Charles Mingus, and Roland Kirk, were among the first cultural figures they turned on."[43] He goes on to relate that Miles Davis had once told him, "Coltrane died from taking too much LSD," which Nisenson interprets as meaning Coltrane's music "died" or degraded in the midst of a psychedelic

43. Nisenson, *Ascension*, 165–66.

haze. I think Porter's insight here is important; that it could well have been Coltrane's use of LSD that led him to ignore the signs of his deteriorating health, such that by the time he did seek medical help for what turned out to be liver cancer, it was too late for treatment. I also appreciate Porter's contention that Coltrane's playing "is perfectly coherent on all his late recordings—in fact, incredibly so."[44] However even if his playing on *Om* is coherent, because it is lacking in any real musical and/or theological center, as a whole the project is anything but.

The final live dates on which McCoy Tyner and Elvin Jones both played took place the week of November 15–21, 1965 at the Jazz Workshop in Boston, and in early 1966 Rashied Ali took over the role as the main drummer (though often augmented by a second drummer or percussionist), while Coltrane's soon-to-be wife Alice assumed the role of pianist. The only recording by the new quintet that was released during Coltrane's life was *Live at the Village Vanguard Again!*, recorded in May 1966 and released in November that same year.

In live performances this quintet often incorporated other players as well, at times performing with as many as eight or nine musicians. While critics such as Stanley Crouch view this opening of the bandstand to younger and less seasoned musicians as being a fatal error—he refers to them as avant-garde "army ants" eating away at the body of Coltrane's music[45]—others have embraced it as a bold experiment in democracy. There is any number of reviews available of these often-infamous performances, notably from the "Titans of the Tenor" concert at New York's Lincoln Center in February 1966, but to be fair, even the classic quartet (with the addition of the controversial sax player Archie Shepp) caused no less a stir when it appeared at Chicago's Downbeat Jazz Festival in August 1965. The only sense that a friend of mine could make of that Chicago concert—and he says it finally came together for him the next day as he rode a Greyhound bus home, staring out across endless cornfields—was to understand the music as a "wailing and pleading to the heavens" and as Coltrane's "singing to God . . . singing something that only God, at that time, could really hear."[46]

44. Porter, *John Coltrane*, 266.

45. Burns, *Ken Burns' Jazz*.

46. Snyder, "Coltrane in the Corn Fields," para. 10.

Some might have heard Coltrane "singing to God" in this later music, while others heard only noise and fury. The noted Indian musician Ravi Shankar heard the evolving sextet during its November 1965 run at the Village Gate in New York, and later reflected, "I was much impressed, but one thing distressed me. There was a turbulence in the music that gave me a negative feeling at times . . . I could not understand it."[47] The jury was very much out, and for Coltrane part of what would have been most difficult was the fact that he was effectively losing touch with much of his black audience. This wasn't particularly unique to Coltrane, however, for as the black jazz critic A.B. Spellman once observed, "The reality is that it was Greenwich Village which heard the evolution of the New, not Harlem."[48]

It is worth noting that at the time that he was pressing into such adventurous and controversial musical terrain, Coltrane's domestic life was probably as stable and as settled as it had been since the days in High Point before his father and grandparents died. His relationship with Alice was by all accounts a very good one, and the fact that she was a very capable pianist, who understood the life of the musician, would have been a great thing for him. Happy in their Long Island home, with three children born in under four years, they seemed to have carved out a life together as friends, musicians, and lovers. In Alice's own words, "It was like God uniting two souls together."[49]

I will pick up the last section of the story of Coltrane's life in my epilogue, so for now it is time to move to my reflections on specific pieces of his music, and consider how each might help to unpack or enact particular theological themes. Because each reflection will have pieces of Coltrane's story woven in and through it, it just makes sense to wait until the end of the book to draw the many strands together in a consideration of his final days, his death, and his legacy.

47. J. C. Thomas, *Chasin' the Trane*, 199–200.

48. Sandke, *Dark and the Light Folks Meet*, 30.

49. J. C. Thomas, *Chasin' the Trane*, 172.

"My Favorite Things"

On Improvisation, Part 1

As jazz improviser you never quite know what it going to happen and that is the exhilarating part of it. You are so invested in being in the moment at that moment, and to reacting and listening to what is going on around you, and to say something that is meaningful and direct and that will exclaim or caress or strut or whatever.

You are doing this in the moment to express things that vocally you couldn't. And you have to have supreme confidence in your ability to do that, or it won't come off at all. That act of improvisation is a supreme act of faith, because you really don't know what is going to happen.

—Jimmy Greene

The jazz tradition can speak to our theological tradition . . . jazz is a kind of music that specializes in new songs. In fact, some songs are so new that you will never hear them again in quite the same way. Even when there is an established tune with melody, harmony, and rhythm, the music always sounds new.

—William Carter, "Singing a New Song"

For a musician known as a pioneer, an innovator, and a leader in the jazz avant-garde, John Coltrane's signature song is an entirely unlikely one. By some accounts, between 1960 and 1967 he performed the song some 2,000 times, and in the various recorded versions it is easy to hear the song evolve and be stretched *almost* to the breaking point. When in 1966 he was asked if he ever tired of playing it, Coltrane replied that he didn't, "because once you go into the solos, it's wide open for any kind of creation you can get going."[1] Who would predict that a Broadway show tune from the very white-bread musical *The Sound of Music* would have found this parallel life through Coltrane's soprano saxophone? Yet that is exactly what happened with the Rodgers and Hammerstein song, "My Favorite Things."

There is this moment in James Baldwin's classic short story, "Sonny's Blues," when the young jazz pianist Sonny suddenly finds himself able to open up, to find his own voice, and to make the song he is playing his own. "Sonny's fingers filled the air with life, his life,"[2] Baldwin writes. And the song that the bandleader calls to spur Sonny to make that move is "Am I Blue?," a 1929 song by two white songwriters working for a music publisher on New York's Tin Pan Alley. Initially a hit for Ethel Waters, over the years the song has been recorded countless times and has been featured in any number of Hollywood movies. It is as unlikely a vehicle for self-discovery and transformative sonic exploration as "My Favorite Things."

"Sonny's Blues" provides an important path into this exploration of the theme of improvisation and how it might function theologically. The story is certainly about Sonny and his older brother, the unnamed narrator of the story, but as is so often true of James Baldwin's fiction, it is also very much about its author. Baldwin could hardly be labeled a Christian, much less a Christian writer, at least not if one insists on maintaining a tight link between institutional church membership and Christian identity. His own story is told in his highly personal essays and writings—notably *The Fire Next Time* and *Nobody Knows My Name*—and less directly in his fiction—particularly *Go Tell It On the Mountain* and *The Amen Corner*.

Born in 1924, Baldwin was raised in a strict church home in Harlem. As he tells the story, his stepfather, who was a lay preacher in the family's church, was a violent and angry man, unwilling to accept his son's interest in reading and writing. At the age of fourteen, Baldwin had a powerfully unsettling charismatic experience in an independent holiness church, which launched

1. Liner notes to *Live at the Village Vanguard Again!*
2. Baldwin, "Sonny's Blues," 47.

him into three-year period as a teenaged preacher. Aware that his charismatic experience had contained something both very real and almost unbearably painful—"the anguish that filled me cannot be described"[3]—Baldwin did everything in his power to respond in faith. However, he remained quite profoundly troubled; troubled by questions about what had actually happened to him in that holiness church; troubled by the way in which he was using his own growing reputation as a young preacher to best his father; troubled, too, by the hypocrisy he was seeing in the culture of Harlem preachers and church leaders. After three years he walked away from the church, and effectively left behind anything close to pride or even comfort in his self-identity as an African-American. Baldwin eventually left the United States for Europe, and ultimately ended up in Switzerland. It was in the Swiss Alps, listening to the blues-based jazz records of Bessie Smith, that he began to make his return home. "It was Bessie Smith, through her tone and her cadence, who helped me to dig back to the way I myself must have spoken when I was a pickaninny, and to remember the things I had heard and seen and felt. I had buried them very deep. I had never listened to Bessie Smith in America (in the same way that, for years, I would not touch watermelon), but in Europe she helped to reconcile me to being a 'nigger.'"[4]

Baldwin found himself able to return home to his own country, though he did not remain in the United States permanently, choosing instead to return to Europe for the latter part of his life. More significantly, he was able to reclaim a sense of his own self as a black man, something of which he would never let go. In James Cone's view, "[Baldwin] can tell you what the faith is. Baldwin left the church in order to stay within that spirituality."[5] And it is true that while he never did return to the church, in a very real sense James Baldwin did return to Christianity, if only to spend the rest of his life wrestling in the shadows with doubt and with God.

In its own way, "Sonny's Blues" tells that story. As it opens, the unnamed narrator discloses that he has just learned that his younger brother Sonny has been arrested for dealing heroin. As the pages unfold we discover how estranged the two brothers have

3. Baldwin, *The Fire Next Time*, 45.

4. Baldwin, *Nobody Knows My Name*, 5.

5. Cone, "Cross and the Lynching Tree."

become, and how much pain each has been living with. As James Tachach notes, the story is shot through with themes from the parable of the prodigal son, though in this case we get an inside view of the elder brother in all of his complexities.[6] In this version, the elder brother has tried to do right by his inheritance. He has gone to school, gotten married, secured a teaching job, and arranged for what he thought was going to be decent family housing in a subsidized complex in Harlem. He'd been loyal to his parents, and during the time when his mother was approaching her death, he had been the one to receive a painful family secret about his own father's "lost brother"; a story that was now his to carry. He'd even promised his mother that he would watch out for Sonny; that he would be his "brother's keeper." Yet, as the two brothers talk on the day following their mother's funeral, it is clear that this older brother has no idea how to keep the promise he has made. Sonny, it seems, intends to be a musician, and a jazz musician at that.

> "Are you *serious*?"
> "Hell, yes, I'm serious."
> He looked more helpless than ever, and annoyed, and deeply hurt.
> I suggested, helpfully: "You mean—like Louis Armstrong?"
> His face closed as though I'd struck him. "No. I'm not talking about none of that old-time, down home crap."
> "Well, look, Sonny, I'm sorry, don't get mad. I just don't altogether get it, that's all. Name somebody—you know, a jazz musician you admire."
> "Bird."[7]

The younger brother—still in high school at this point—is looking to follow Charlie Parker and to situate himself within bebop and its attendant subculture. According to Cornel West, bebop marks "the grand break with American mainstream music, especially imitated and co-opted Afro-American popular music."[8] "Through their technical facility and musical virtuosity, bebop jazz musicians expressed the heightened tensions, frustrated aspirations, and repressed emotions of an aggressive yet apprehensive Afro-American."[9] Sonny's

6. Tachach, "The Biblical Foundation," 109f.

7. Baldwin, "Sonny's Blues," 31.

8. West, "On Afro-American Popular Music," 178.

9. Ibid., 179.

disdain for Armstrong's "old-time, down home crap" serves to signal his deeper frustrations and barely repressed emotions. After dropping out of school and alienating what is left of his family, Sonny escapes Harlem by joining the navy. His return to New York is hardly the stuff of a returning prodigal. Instead, he takes a room in Greenwich Village and begins to immerse himself in the life he considers to be his future. The one attempt by the older brother to mend the division is a failure:

> So I got mad and then he got mad, and then I told him that he might just as well be dead as far as I was concerned. Then he pushed me to the door and the other people looked on as though nothing were happening, and he slammed the door behind me. I stood in the hallway, staring at the door. I heard somebody laugh in the room and then the tears came to my eyes. I started down the steps, whistling to keep from crying, I kept whistling to myself. *You going to need me, baby, one of these cold, rainy days.*[10]

Sonny does manage to immerse himself deeply in the bebop subculture; too deeply, in fact, for he ultimately buys into the myth that heroin is the key to freedom and creativity. He is arrested and jailed for trafficking, and to his older brother it is proof that the young man is as good as dead. It is at this point that the world of the older brother also begins to unravel. His dreams of a settled life in Harlem are interrupted by the realization that though the buildings are new, the streets and the stories are the same. And as he wrestles to come to terms with that truth, his two-year-old daughter is stricken with polio and dies. It is the death of this child—fittingly named Grace—that finally lets him drop his resentment and write to Sonny in jail. It is the beginning of their grace-tinged, though still uneasy, reconciliation.

When Sonny is released from jail his brother takes him in, and together they attempt to make at least some sense of the world that is urban black America. Still, there remains between them a kind of wall. Both of them know that Sonny is always at risk of falling back into using heroin, and in the mind of the older brother, Sonny's aspirations as a jazz musician are clearly part of the problem. On the night that Sonny invites his brother to accompany

10. Baldwin, "Sonny's Blues," 36–37.

him to the jazz club where he will mark his return to music, the tension is palpable.

At first Sonny is tentative on the bandstand, having been away from the piano for over a year. As the set comes to its close, the bandleader calls "Am I Blue?," the song that finally frees the young man to really play; the song that will "get Sonny in the water."

> Listen, Creole seemed to be saying, listen. Now these are Sonny's blues. He made the little black man on the drums know it, and the bright brown man on the horn. Creole wasn't trying any longer to get Sonny in the water. He was wishing him Godspeed. Then he stepped back, very slowly, filling the air with the immense suggestion that Sonny speak for himself.
>
> Then they all gathered around Sonny and Sonny played. Every now and again one of them seemed to say, amen. Sonny's fingers filled the air with life, his life. But that life contained so many others. And Sonny went all the way back, he really began with the spare, flat statement of the opening phrase of the song. Then he began to make it his. It was very beautiful because it wasn't hurried and it was no longer a lament. I seemed to hear with what burning he had made it his, with what burning we had yet to make it ours, how we could cease lamenting. Freedom lurked around us and I understood, at last, that he could help us to be free if we would listen, that we would never be free until we did. Yet there was no battle in his face now. I heard what he had gone through, and would continue to go through until he came to rest in earth. He had made it his: that long line, of which we knew only Mama and Daddy. And he was giving it back, as everything must be given back, so that, passing through death, it can live forever.[11]

It is not as if everything is instantly put right—"the world waited outside, as hungry as a tiger"—but more that "Sonny went all the way back . . . [and] began to make it his," and in so doing he opened the possibility that the older brother and everyone else who bore witness to his act of defiant beauty "could cease lamenting" and claim a new vision for themselves. It is something of a wordless parallel to the move made in so many of the Psalms of lament, when sorrow and complaint shift toward praise and doxology. In writing of that shift, Walter Brueggemann suggests that

11. Ibid., 47.

while we can only speculate as to how this move is actually made, "What we do know, both from the *structure of the text* and *our own experience*, is that grievance addressed to an authorized partner does free us."[12] And in the case of Sonny, the "authorized partner" is that collection of people who have gathered around him to hear him play his blues, play his truth. The story closes with the older brother sending drinks to the bandstand. "He didn't seem to notice it, but just before they started playing again, he sipped from it and looked toward me, and nodded. Then he put it back on top of the piano. For me, then, as they began to play again, it glowed and shook above my brother's head like the very cup of trembling."[13]

The image of the cup of trembling is drawn from Isaiah 51:17–23, where it stands as a symbol of God's judgment against a morally and religiously compromised Jerusalem. Or at least it stands *first* as a symbol of judgment, but then it is transformed into a sign of forgiveness and new hope:

> "See, I have taken from your hand the cup of staggering;
> you shall drink no more from the bowl of my wrath.
> And I will put it into the hand of your tormentors . . ."
> (Isa 51:22b–23a)

"The glowing glass on the piano above Sonny, his personal cup of trembling," writes James Tachach, "has become, in effect, a shining halo above Sonny's head; his sinning and suffering and redemption, in some way, have sainted Sonny."[14] Rather than knowing only separation and division, Sonny has learned to play his blues from that deeper place in his wounded soul, and through those highly personal improvisations he is able to offer a taste of a deeper freedom, both to his brother and to the others who would hear him play.

I have to say that I am made nervous by Tachach's suggestion that in and through his struggles Sonny has been "sainted." I would hope that Tachach is not suggesting that Sonny has reached some place of personal holiness, in the sense that he has managed to put his brokenness entirely behind him. To make that claim would actually cut against the grain of both Baldwin's story and of the parable that so obviously informs it. And as is true in the

12. Brueggemann, *Spirituality of the Psalms*, 37.

13. Baldwin, "Sonny's Blues," 48.

14. Tachach, "The Biblical Foundation," 117.

biblical parable, this story is clearly about *two* brothers, each of whom is, in his own way, a prodigal. What Baldwin unveils here is the image that is left hanging in the biblical parable, that of the older brother coming to grips with his own lostness and need for reconciliation. Baldwin's insistence on telling a layered family story (and it is notable that the band is also described in familial terms) makes what I think is a very important point. As is true of the blues, where one musician may be the writer and singer yet the people together share in the song, so too with the improvisational work Sonny does with the song that Creole calls for him. "The blues," says James Cone, "are a transformation of black life through the sheer power of song,"[15] and for those minutes in the club, that is what Sonny manages to accomplish simply by letting go into the music. Further, for all of his ambivalence about Harlem and what it symbolizes, the older brother hears something in those improvisations that allows him to reach a place of making peace, not only with his brother, but also within himself.

But again, I need to point out that "Am I Blue?" is not really a conventional blues song. This leads Richard Albert to ask, "Is it possible that in 'Sonny's Blues' [Baldwin] is indicating that tradition is very important, but that change is also important (and probably inevitable) and that it builds on tradition, which is never fully erased but continues to be an integral part of the whole?"[16] That question marks a good place to begin to think about John Coltrane's improvisational engagement with the tradition, and how that worked itself out in a piece of music so seemingly safe and domesticated as "My Favorite Things."

When John Coltrane recorded "My Favorite Things" in October 1960, the song was not nearly so well known as it would become in 1966 when the film version of *The Sound of Music* was released. In fact, because an edited version of the thirteen-and-a-half minute song became a radio hit, many people unfamiliar with the Broadway musical assumed that the song was a Coltrane original. "I wish I had written it," he told one journalist, and then added, "'My Favorite Things' is my favorite piece of everything we've recorded; I don't think I'd like to redo it in any other way, although all the other records I've done could be improved by a

15. Cone, *Spirituals and the Blues*, 105.
16. Albert, "The Jazz-Blues Motif," 179.

few details."[17] A fascinating comment, given that over the years he would effectively remake the song many, many times.

His original recording is a wonderful arrangement, which takes a very sing-able show tune and transforms it into an extended exploration in modal jazz. Partly because he uses a soprano saxophone and partly because of the way the piece is arranged around just two chords, the feel is decidedly Eastern in character. Lewis Porter suggests that the way in which Coltrane extends the two chords across the whole piece effectively, "extends the list of good things ('raindrops on roses') that help one overcome the bad ('when the dog bites'), and he dramatizes this opposition by lengthening the time span of minor versus major."[18] Of course the words are not actually sung, and it is impossible to know if Coltrane even paid attention to the lyrics while preparing this arrangement. But for anyone familiar with the words—and when 1966 rolled around, tens of millions would become very familiar with it—the impact remains.

John Coltrane makes the song his own, which is precisely what Sonny does with "Am I Blue?" It would be foolish to try to push too far the comparisons between Baldwin's short story and Coltrane's life narrative, because aside from Coltrane and Sonny both being young black musicians who had to face down heroin addiction, their experiences were very different. For Coltrane there was no older brother, no pushback from his family when he began to pursue jazz, and there seems to have been no ambivalence concerning his identity as a black man. While the brothers in Baldwin's story are busily working through the complexities of having grown up in Harlem, Coltrane spent his formative years in small town North Carolina. Different stories.

And yet, this business of finding a voice in and through improvisation; of taking a piece of music that is not necessarily or narrowly a part of the tradition and being able to resituate it in the unfolding and renewing tradition? And in doing that, finding something like freedom?

I think that words and phrases like "resituate" and "unfolding and renewing tradition" are extremely important not only for jazz improvisation, but also for the church and theology. It is part of

17. Postif, "John Coltrane: An Interview," 133.
18. Porter, *John Coltrane*, 182.

what Richard Albert suspects Baldwin is attempting to say with "Sonny's Blues," which is why Albert raises the idea that change (which he calls "probably inevitable") can build on tradition in a way that never fully erases it. It is the age-old distinction between freedom *from* and freedom *for*; freedom from constraint, as opposed to freedom for creativity, for life, for love. A freedom *for* assumes a starting point and parameters, and while the parameters or boundaries might be stretched to the point of breaking, they never quite do. Instead there is a recapitulation of things known, in a way both utterly new and utterly liberating. Raw freedom *from* constraint offers no such liberty, but instead little more than an oftentimes-debilitating license that is no freedom at all.

The accusation often leveled at the free jazz movement, which is birthed at least partly through the sonic experiments of John Coltrane, is that it is rootless, shapeless, and without anything resembling the parameters that make for true jazz. And while in later chapters I will seek to show that Coltrane's forays into free jazz—or at least his more successful ones—are in fact both rooted and boundaried—it is not an altogether unfair criticism of some of the music that is offered in the name of "free." This is the stuff of St. Paul at his radical and invigorating best, as in his Epistle to the Romans, wherein he ironically recasts questions of true freedom in the terms of slavery.

> When you were slaves of sin, you were free in regard to righteousness. So what advantage did you then get from the things of which you now are ashamed? The end of those things is death. But now that you have been freed from sin and enslaved to God, the advantage you get is sanctification. The end is eternal life. For the wages of sin is death, but the free gift of God is eternal life in Christ Jesus our Lord. (Rom 6:20–23)

Yes, Paul writes of having been "freed *from* sin," yet this is framed in terms of being "enslaved to God" for the sake of being sanctified and gifted with eternal life, which marks the greatest of all freedoms. "For freedom Christ has set us free," writes Paul in his letter to the Galatians. "Stand firm, therefore, and do not submit again to a yoke of slavery" (Gal 5:1). Do not, in other words, forsake this true freedom—characterized in the tradition of the *Book of Common*

Prayer as life lived for a God "whose service is perfect freedom"—for the sake of mere license. Or as stated in the First Epistle of Peter,

> He himself bore our sins in his body on the cross, so that, free from sins, we might live for righteousness; by his wounds you have been healed. For you were going astray like sheep, but now you have returned to the shepherd and guardian of your souls. (1 Pet 2:24–25)

Christ is the guardian of our souls, who has both healed us and freed us through the cross. Such freedom is anything but unbound-aried or unconstrained, and that for the good of our own souls.

In the African-American church tradition, perhaps the single most significant biblical narrative is that of the exodus from Egypt. It is not hard to imagine why this story had such resonance for the slave church, or why it continued to hold such importance through the era of segregation, the civil rights movement, and right up to the present day.

> Then the Lord said, "I have observed the misery of my people who are in Egypt; I have heard their cry on account of their taskmasters. Indeed, I know their sufferings, and I have come down to deliver them from the Egyptians, and to bring them up out of that land to a good and broad land, a land flowing with milk and honey . . ." (Exod 3:7–8a)

The image of Moses standing in the royal Egyptian court and ut-tering the message from this liberating Lord that Pharaoh must "Let my people go" was taken up in "Go Down Moses," one of the great liberation songs of the slave church. Originating in the mid-1800s, the first published version of the song was released in 1872 by the Fisk Jubilee Singers, with the following as the opening verse:

> When Israel was in Egypt's land: Let my people go,
> Oppress'd so hard they could not stand: Let my people go.
> Go down, Moses,
> Way down in Egypt land,
> Tell old Pharaoh,
> Let my people go.

With Egypt and the Pharaoh also signifying the slave master—and later the racist and segregationist society—and Israel standing for the African-American community, the song gave voice both to the community's dream of freedom and to its confidence that God would indeed be faithful. In that context, for Moses to "go down" to confront the Pharaoh was doubtless an acknowledgment that the further *down* the Mississippi one traveled the worse the conditions generally became. To be freed from slavery—and later from the oppressive Jim Crow south—generally meant going *up* to the cities of the north and even to Canada. Among other things, the hearing of the biblical story in such terms is a significant improvisational move.

Yet the story of the exodus doesn't end at the moment that the freed slaves cross the Red Sea; quite the contrary. The story of Israel's forty-year sojourn in the wilderness of Sinai is critical to the larger narrative, for it is in the desert that the freed slaves must learn to become a community. At the heart of that learning is the giving of the *torah*, the observance of which was to be the way in which this people would be formed in covenant relationship with its God. Here again is this idea of constrained freedom, as opposed to raw freedom from all constraints. Such a freedom is not an easy thing to learn, and particularly not after so many years in slavery, which is why it takes forty years and the passing of an entire generation before the community is ready to enter its promised land. Even Moses is not permitted to cross the Jordan into this new land, though unlike the others he is permitted to ascend Mount Nebo and from that vantage point to see across to the other side. It is an image that Martin Luther King, Jr. invoked—and improvised—in the closing paragraph of what turned out to be his final speech:

> Well, I don't know what will happen now. We've got some difficult days ahead. But it doesn't matter with me now. Because I've been to the mountaintop. And I don't mind. Like anybody, I would like to live a long life. Longevity has its place. But I'm not concerned about that now. I just want to do God's will. And He's allowed me to go up to the mountain. And I've looked over. And I've seen the promised land. I may not get there with you. But I want you to know tonight, that we, as a people, will get to the promised land. And I'm happy, tonight. I'm not worried about anything. I'm not fearing any man. Mine eyes have seen the glory of the coming of the Lord.[19]

19. Martin Luther King, Jr. "I've Been to the Mountaintop," delivered April 3, 1968, Mason Temple, Memphis, Tennessee.

Seen through this lens, freedom is a responsibility, a commitment, and a long struggle in which the only sure thing is the faithfulness of God.

In terms of how this plays out in music, Jeremy Begbie observes that, "Improvisation provides a powerful enactment of the truth that our freedom is enabled to flourish only by engaging with and negotiating constraints."[20] As I noted in chapter one, Begbie categorizes such constraints as being either musical—in jazz, such things as meter and harmonic sequence—or occasional—for instance the physical space, as well as the presence and participation both of other musicians and of an audience.[21] Plainly stated, Begbie sees constraint as being very good news in jazz, which is why he is ultimately highly suspicious of the avant-garde and free movements. In his view, the freedom to improvise, even in the most adventurous of ways, assumes a clear set of constraints or boundaries, including a starting point within the tradition. "[I]mprovisation reminds us powerfully of the futility of searching for a tradition-free environment of creativity. Traditional jazz falls to bits without interacting deeply with tradition. There can be no *tabula rasa*, no producing which is not a re-producing."[22]

One of the most dazzling images of improvisational jazz as being *liberated* through constraint—as being an expression of "freedom *for*"—was offered to me by the Canadian singer-songwriter Steve Bell. Bell's musical formation took place first in the Baptist church and then in the Western Canadian roots and folk traditions. A gifted musician and songwriter, he would not claim to have any deep familiarity with jazz, nor would he claim any particular abilities or gifts as an adept improviser. He tells the story of the moment when jazz and improvisation suddenly made sense to him. He was working alongside the pianist Mike Janzen, proofreading scored arrangements of a set of his songs that Janzen had prepared. Two days of this tedious work had left the two of them feeling more than just a bit tired and giddy, and so when the pianist began to play "lounge lizard" versions of Bell's songs, the two could hardly contain themselves. And then it happened. Bell writes of how Janzen's demeanor suddenly changed, and instead

20. Begbie, *Theology, Music and Time*, 199.
21. Ibid., 205–210.
22. Ibid., 217.

of merely playing around with the songs he was suddenly playing one of them. Differently. Deeply.

> It was like a ball suddenly bounced in front of him and he was helpless but to chase it. I was mesmerized to hear my simple song flame out and become something almost entirely "other" but because I knew the song so intimately, no matter how "outside" the improvisation became, my ear never lost reference to the melody and structure Mike's imagination was leaping off of. And that's when I suddenly saw it—the burning bush of Moses in the Sinai desert; a desert vast, rugged and barren but for this curious sight. I could see the solitary Moses standing motionless, staggered completely by what he saw. I could see the glory of the blaze, ferociously surging skyward creating dizzying heat waves against the pale blue. Interior to the fire, obscured by flame but not lost to sight, was the bush itself with its sturdy centre stem, black branches like a menorah and green leaves fluttering furiously in the energy. It remained entirely intact and unconsumed yet absolutely on fire.[23]

Here is jazz as the burning bush, which sometimes flames so brightly that it is all but impossible to see the unconsumed melodic core that remains intact at its center. It is an extraordinary image, in part because it pictures how the root and the parameters remain intact, allowing the improvisation to reach such a pitch that it seems to all but consume the center. And it isn't just the melodic center of a particular piece of music that remains intact; it is the rooted tradition itself, which is at once set alight and yet still somehow there.

And that is what I hear going on in "My Favorite Things," as the Coltrane quartet strikes an improvisational match and sets the song alight. Because they performed it so often over the years, they became increasingly creative in the ways in which they chose to kindle the fire. In fact, because there are a number of recorded versions available, it is easy to get a sense of how differently that bush could burn. I'm going to limit myself to three versions: the original 1960 studio version; a live version from 1965, on the DVD *John Coltrane Live in '60, '61 & '65*; and finally another live version, this one from the 1966 record, *Live at the Village Vanguard Again!*

23. Bell, e-mail correspondence.

1. The 1960 studio version was released in 1961 by Atlantic Records on the album, *My Favorite Things*. On this version, the song runs for just over thirteen-and-a-half minutes, during which the listener really never has a sense that the melody is too, too far from sight. Coltrane's solos do explore and push at the melodic constraints, but in a way that is gently exhilarating. And there is a kind of meditative, almost chant-like quality in the approach of the rhythm section. This arrangement does swing, yet in a way that is almost subdued. This probably has much to do with the fairly understated playing of both Tyner at his piano and Jones on the drums—and this changes dramatically on later recordings—but it is also due to the arrangement itself, with its simple two-chord structure and space for extended vamping. In his 1961 review for *HiFi/Stereo* magazine, Nat Hentoff characterizes the song as being "sinuous, too long, but generally effective."[24] Had he only known how the song would unfold over the ensuing years.

2. By August 1965, the classic Coltrane quartet had been working together for several years, and had performed the song countless times. Though also released by two smaller labels in CD format, the best way to experience the 1965 recording is on the 2007 DVD release, from which one really gets a sense of both the intensity of the later improvisations and of the interaction between the four musicians.

   The song begins with Coltrane counting in the band by stamping his foot on the stage, but as soon as he begins to play he backs away from the microphone to adjust his soprano saxophone, which has gone out of tune due to the chill evening air. Tyner takes hold, and begins to set up the vamp, preparing for Coltrane to return to the microphone to resume the melody. Within the first twenty seconds of his statement of the melody, Coltrane moves into the highest registers of his horn, giving the first indication of where things might be headed. His opening statement and solo last for just over three minutes, at which point he steps to the back of the stage to allow the others in the band to take up their own explorations. If Tyner and Jones were understated on the original 1960 recording, that is anything but the case here. Along with bass player Jimmy Garrison, they push, stretch, and press the

24. Hentoff, "My Favorite Things," 230.

boundaries of "My Favorite Things" to the point where its resemblance to the original show tune is almost imperceptible. But the tune is there. In the midst of the flames, it is very much still there.

Tyner's playing is powerful and exhilarating, his left hand sometimes pounding down on the piano keys from six and eight inches above. Jones, too, is a powerhouse, with steam rising from the top of his head and sweat pouring down his face; all passion and intensity, yet with an extraordinary touch to his playing. And then there is the almost athletic strength of Jimmy Garrison's bass playing, somehow keeping it all from flying apart. When, after a nearly ten-minute absence from the stage Coltrane returns to his microphone, you wonder if he might just restate the melody and give everyone a well-deserved rest. Not a chance.

Instead he steps up to the microphone, closes his eyes, and sets out on his eight-minute solo. Coltrane states and restates the melody at various points—sometimes in just the tiniest of glimpses—and then launches into these brilliant runs, swirls, and sonic explorations. Sometimes he stands absolutely still, appearing utterly focused and in the moment, and at other times, with his body rocking and swaying, he seems caught up in a kind of ecstasy, his horn speaking in tongues. It is exquisite, from beginning to end.

Or at least it is to me. Others will find that these improvisations stretch things beyond the breaking point; as instances in which the constraints of which Begbie writes have been transgressed. Frankly, though, Begbie's reticence to deal with much jazz after 1960 due to what he calls "the upheavals of jazz"[25]—and here he names Coltrane along with Cecil Taylor and Ornette Coleman as notable examples—suggests to me that he is working with a rather narrow sense of the constraints of the tradition. Practically speaking, as soon as the experimentation of the 1960s get underway Begbie seems convinced that things were no longer sufficiently constrained by the jazz tradition, and so it all began to unravel. The clear implication of this is that whatever theological wisdom might have been enacted in Coltrane's earlier improvisational excursions—and I suspect Begbie would be relatively at home with the 1960 version of "My Favorite Things"—it was pretty much all over and done by the time of the 1965 recording.

25. Begbie, *Theology, Music and Time*, 200, n77.

Of course, Begbie is not the only one to draw specific lines as to when jazz has crossed the tradition's acceptable boundaries. As I detailed in chapter one, Hans Rookmaaker believes that the line was crossed with the advent of bebop, which to his ear, "tries to break down the laws of structure which apply to melody, and not only search for the unconventional, but also for the irrational, for elements that demonstrate the freedom of the individual."[26] And he is not using the phrase "freedom of the individual" in any positive sense, but rather as a cipher for individualistic license. "Love does not govern here," Roomaaker writes. "Everyone tries to outplay the other, even in the very matter of irrationality."[27]

It is not only the theologians and philosophers of the church who struggle with the question of where the lines—the boundaries and constraints—might be drawn. As I've noted, the jazz critic Stanley Crouch is more than a little derisive of the merit of Coltrane's late work. Crouch enthusiastically embraces the work of the classic quartet, highlighting *Coltrane, Crescent*, and *A Love Supreme*, commenting that, "Few ensembles have ever made such lasting music."[28] Yet he completely dismisses *Ascension* (recorded in 1965 and released in early 1966) and everything that follows as being only so much noise. In fact, as I pointed out earlier, Crouch's main reason for finding this later music so objectionable is that he sees Coltrane as having lost all sense of being rooted in the blues. But again, not unlike Rookmaaker, many jazz critics in the 1940s had drawn that line at bebop, arguing that it didn't make sense or didn't swing in the manner of traditional jazz, or that it was individualistic, competitive, and aggressive.

3. Now to a version of the song that surely embodies a transgression of the constraints . . . and quite intentionally so. This is a version recorded live in May 1966, and released later that year on *Live at the Village Vanguard Again!* Gone are McCoy Tyner and Elvin Jones, replaced by Alice Coltrane on piano and Rashied Ali on drums, with Emanuel Rahim on percussion and Pharoah Sanders on flute, tenor sax, and percussion. This is now fully into the

---

26. Rookmaaker, *New Orleans Jazz*, 275.
27. Ibid., 275.
28. Crouch, "Titan of the Blues," 115.

period of Coltrane's career of which Crouch, Begbie, and others are so very critical.

This version of "My Favorite Things" opens with a six-minute bass solo, in which Jimmy Garrison plucks and strums at his instrument, sometimes playing it in a style reminiscent of Spanish flamenco guitar. Not merely an impressive display of technique, the imaginative solo is marked by real emotional depth; it must have been quite something to experience live. From the audience's point of view, it may also have been the most accessible point of entry into this version of the song.

Following Garrison's solo, the piece itself gets underway . . . more or less. For the better part of three minutes, Alice Coltrane bangs out chords on the piano, Ali and the percussionists (including Sanders as well as Rahim) build a wall of their own sound, Garrison works his bass furiously, while Coltrane solos over top of it all without ever actually playing the melody. Coltrane does pick up the melody at around the beginning of the third minute, and it remains recognizably intact in his improvisations for the next three and a half minutes. During this time, Alice Coltrane's work at the piano even sounds reminiscent of that of Tyner, though because of the volume of the percussion it is rather lost in the mix. When Sanders enters with his tenor sax around the seven-minute mark, he plays with what were at the time his characteristic honks, growls, and squalls, never actually setting out anything resembling a melody. For all of five seconds around the thirteen-minute mark, the familiar melody surfaces once more, only to be submerged beneath what Nat Hentoff describes in the liner notes as, "A ferocious, spiraling dialogue between Sanders and Coltrane." I actually find a considerable sense of relief when just before the fifteen-minute mark Coltrane takes over as the lone horn. Not that his solo here is any less stretching. It is just that there seems to be so much more coherence and order to his playing than there is to that of Sanders. Coltrane had told Hentoff that part of what drew him to Sanders' playing was that, "Pharoah is constantly trying to get more and more deeply into the human foundations of music," which in turn led Hentoff to reflect that "Sanders' solo here is acutely, turbulently, compellingly personal." Well, maybe.

The briefest hint of the melody surfaces again just prior to the eighteen-minute mark, and then thirty seconds later Coltrane's horn brings it back into full view. The piece closes with Sanders on flute, weaving remarkably beautiful and even tuneful lines in and through Coltrane's soprano, making for a decidedly more melodic and even lovely ending than a listener might have predicted five minutes earlier.

So, big banging chords on the piano, enough percussion to sometimes bury the other instruments, two horns playing with ferocious intensity (and regardless of whether you appreciate Sanders' playing or find him to be nowhere near Coltrane's league, he is ferocious . . .), and a bass player trying vainly to be heard as an anchor for the whole thing. Is this a searching improvisational take on the song Coltrane had made famous? A failed experiment? A barrage of sound? Or a radical experiment in pressing the edges of music?

The answer, of course, will depend on who you ask. When the album was released, the writer Frank Kofsky proclaimed, "This just might be the greatest work of art ever produced in this country—not to mention the greatest selection of jazz music to get set down on wax."[29] Eric Nisenson, meanwhile, says that Coltrane's playing on the record, "touches dark emotions, ranging from foreboding to a certain weariness." With all the confidence in the world, Nisenson then claims that, "He was telling intimates that he thought his best music was long behind him."[30] And I don't want to even think what Stanley Crouch would say.

For me, the answer is yes, on all counts. I do think it is a searching improvisational take on the song, but it is also something of a failed experiment. Part of its failure has to do with it being a barrage of sound, which is not an accident. It is, however, unbalanced, such that all of that percussion buries the bass and threatens to do the same to the piano. I must also admit I'm not a fan of Pharoah Sanders at this stage of his development. I'd so much rather hear John Coltrane.

But simply because an arrangement or a recording pushes hard against the edges of the conventions doesn't mean that it should therefore be dismissed from the jazz canon. Even if I were convinced that Coltrane's later explorations were taking the music down a blind alley and straight toward a brick wall—an idea

29. Ratliff, *Coltrane*, 170–71.
30. Nisenson, *Ascension*, 208–9.

explored in Ratliff's *Coltrane: The Story of a Sound*—it doesn't mean that it can all just be swept away as unacceptable. I understand part of the value of Coltrane's later experiments to be located in the way that they did stretch the tradition, and maybe at points even broke outside of the tradition entirely. Rather than seeing the tradition as simply "the way it once was" or as today's *status quo*, to view it as organic and fluid allows a good deal more room for experimentation. To understand the tradition as something at once rooted and dynamic is to acknowledge its capacity for innovation. Time will tell if such innovations become part of the organic whole, or if they simply play a temporary role in one particular time and context. Time *and* reception by musicians and listeners (and to a lesser degree by critics) will be the test of the place in the tradition of particular artists, recordings, and even genres within jazz.

Personally, I don't think that this 1966 version has stood the test of time and been received in the way that the versions from 1960 and 1965 have—Porter doesn't even *mention* it in his exhaustive survey—but that doesn't mean it shouldn't have been performed, recorded, and released. I see real parallels here to the manner in which the theological tradition moves, develops, and unfolds.

The church has a decidedly longer view of things than the hundred or so years that jazz has been recognized as a distinct music, so the Christian tradition does have some experience navigating questions of innovation and tradition. We also have a rather patchy history when it comes to successfully making room for innovation; I think here of the divisive controversies of the ancient church, to say nothing of the violence that accompanied the Reformation and the splintering of Protestantism into countless denominations and sects. Yet, we also have at least some idea as to how theological and liturgical innovations can be given room on board the ship without necessarily turning it in a whole new direction or sinking it to the bottom of the sea. I think here, for instance, of the work of someone such as the New Testament scholar and theologian Rudolph Bultmann, with whom I have deep, deep theological differences. He was a true innovator, and yet in so many ways faithful to the tradition that shaped him. Were his great project of "demythologizing" the Bible the thing that had turned the ship in an entirely new direction, to my mind we would be in serious trouble indeed.

But it didn't. Instead, Bultmann's project faithfully raised very important and timely questions with which the tradition needed to wrestle. Ninety years after the publication of *Jesus Christ and Mythology* you would be hard pressed to find a thoroughly Bultmannian scholar currently at work, yet in both North America and Europe you'd also be hard pressed to find a decent theologian or biblical scholar who hasn't had to contend with Bultmann's contribution, if only by having to answer the questions he raised. To have pushed Rudolph Bultmann off the ship in 1920 would not only have deprived the tradition of the chance to engage the issues that he raised, it would also have been doing violence to the church itself. There is always a kind of violence involved in the act of defining who is, or is not, acceptable.

In "Sonny's Blues" what makes it possible for the two brothers to each find the peace that they crave is Sonny's willingness to let go and to risk wading out into the deep waters of improvisational music. Both Sonny and his older brother will discover—even if only fleetingly—that they are at ease with their own selves and that their reconciliation has been sealed. Even if at this point no formal words of reconciliation have been spoken between them, reconciliation has still been won. For this to happen, Sonny had to trust himself, but also the musicians with whom he is playing, as well as the audience (most especially his brother) before which he stands in naked vulnerability. He finds the courage to trust, and so he risks. And though he successfully makes it into the deep waters, he could well have failed, for such is the nature of risk. As the pianist Jim McNeely suggests, "Improvisation is an act of faith."[31]

Just as "Am I Blue?" was not a particularly likely song to spark what turns out to be a soul-transforming moment in the life of Baldwin's fictional character, "My Favorite Things" was hardly an obvious choice for John Coltrane. That it became so central to his work as a boundary-stretching musical innovator and a tireless spiritual seeker is truly remarkable, yet as Coltrane continued to draw new sounds and new ideas from the song, he essentially enacted something about the nature of true freedom. In my reading of things, even that which might be seen as a misfire, or perhaps as succeeding in only a limited or provisional way, need not be dismissed out of hand. Such freedom, claims Begbie, "liberates us for

31. Carter, "Singing a New Song," 43.

a life of joyful (not anxious) restlessness, a perilous 'emptying of our hands' for the sake of music of limitless interest and variety, in the knowledge that failure has in a sense already been accounted for and future error will in some manner be taken up. To discover that the risk 'was worth it' generates more trust, which in turn generates more fruitful risk-taking—such is Christian liberty."[32]

32. Begbie, *Theology, Music and Time*, 245.

"Naima" and "Wise One"

Love, Brokenness, and the Movement toward Peace

Some years ago I went into a period of depression and almost gave up. I thank God for enabling me to pull out of it. My wife Nita [Naima] was a great help to me, also. She and daughter, Toni have made my life far happier.

—John Coltrane, 1958 interview

[T]hat was a funny time—a period in my life, because I went through quite a few changes, you know, like the home life— everything, man, I just went through so many—everything I was doing [slaps hands] did this . . . Everything, everything I was doing [slaps hands] hit like that.

—John Coltrane, 1966 interview

Over the spring of 1959, John Coltrane took a quartet into the studio on three different occasions to record the tracks for what would be released in January 1960 as *Giant Steps*, his breakthrough album as a leader. Evidently unhappy with the results of a session in March, for the two May sessions he used a different drummer and pianist, and with the exception of just one track they recorded everything he needed for the album. Again using a different drummer and pianist, that one additional track was eventually recorded in early December 1959, just in time to be included on *Giant Steps*. That final song was "Naima," written and titled for his wife Juanita Naima "Nita" Coltrane.

"Naima" is one of three songs on *Giant Steps* titled for family members, with "Syeeda's Song Flute" named for Coltrane's step-daughter, and "Cousin Mary" for his cousin Mary Alexander. To these three family songs can be added "Mr. P.C." named for Paul Chambers, Coltrane's friend and bass player on the album. Taken together, one gets the picture that the value of close relationships was very much on the musician's mind that year, so much so that Mary Alexander even referred to *Giant Steps* as "the family album."

It wasn't the first song that Coltrane named for Naima, and it certainly wouldn't be the last one dedicated to her. The first song he wrote for Naima was "Nita," which he recorded in 1956 while working as a session player with the Paul Chambers Sextet. The recording of "Nita," which was released on the 1956 *Whims of Chambers* record, took place just shy of the date of their first anniversary, and the title probably stands as a simple expression of his affection. Coltrane chose never to record the song again.

However "Naima" certainly was recorded again, and released on *The Complete Copenhagen Concert* (1961), *Live in Paris* (1965), *Live at the Village Vanguard Again!* (1966), and *The Complete 1961 Village Vanguard Recordings* (1997), among other albums. In several contexts Coltrane referred to it as being the favorite of all of his own compositions, and he continued to return to it as a standard for live performance. But he also spoke of his desire to write a second piece for her, and there is some consensus that "Wise One" from the 1964 *Crescent* album is that song.[1]

In listening first to "Naima" and then to "Wise One," it is not hard to sense that a story is being told in the background. This is particularly so when you listen to these songs against the backdrop of all that was unfolding in their lives and marriage. Even a review of the basic timeline has to give the listener pause. The two were married in October 1955, and in the spring of 1957 with Naima's support, Coltrane was able to face down his addictions and experience what he later identified as his "great spiritual awakening."[2] For a marriage, which at that point was less than two years old, a change so pivotal as recovery from a serious addiction would have had the potential to permanently make or break the relationship. That Naima's support was widely recognized as being so

1. Porter, *John Coltrane*, 96, 156, 232.
2. Liner notes to *A Love Supreme*.

very crucial to Coltrane during this transitional period would seem to weight things in the direction of this being a marriage-making time. However, at some point very close to his recovery from his addictions, Coltrane had the extramarital affair that resulted in the birth of a baby girl, Sheila Coltrane. While Lewis Porter observes that, "Naima appears to have handled the situation with grace and understanding,"[3] there is little doubt that the marriage would have been strained by his very serious breach of trust. This breach was all the more complicated by the fact that John and Naima were unable to have children of their own. In real terms, this means that by the time of the 1959 recording of "Naima," the Coltrane's marriage had been not only reshaped through his struggles to overcome his addictions, but also pressed into a deep crisis through his infidelity.

What's more, sometime near the end of May 1960, just months after the January release of *Giant Steps*, Coltrane again became involved in an affair, this time with an anonymous woman identified only as "Trane's Lady" in J. C. Thomas's 1975 biography, *Chasin' the Trane*. This is a relationship that would continue for at least three years, and while it is impossible to determine whether or not Naima knew of the affair, even if it did remain hidden it clearly would have deeply compromised the marriage. In the late summer of 1963, John and Naima finally separated, though contrary to what one might assume, he did not leave his marriage in order to join the anonymous woman. In fact, within months of the separation Coltrane was living with the musician Alice McLeod. In April 1964, less than a year after the collapse of his first marriage, Coltrane recorded the haunting and lovely "Wise One." Eighteen months later his divorce from Naima was finalized, allowing him to marry Alice, with whom he already had two children.

An additional complexity in these timelines comes with the dates of the excerpts from the journals of "Trane's Lady," published in Thomas's book. Part of what makes this complicated is that it is impossible to know if the anonymous woman's original journal included other entries related to the affair. As I noted in chapter three, a journal entry from November 1963 indicates that Coltrane told the woman that he had left his marriage to Naima and was living with Alice McLeod, giving every indication that this affair

3. Porter, *John Coltrane*, 270.

had reached its end. However, the final excerpt that Thomas includes in his book is from May 1966, in which the woman records, "We decided to end the affair then and there."[4]

The most obvious way to read all of this is to conclude that John Coltrane slept around. Quite frankly, in the working musician's world of nightclubs, extended road trips and adoring fans, sexual license is often a part of the picture, and so Coltrane may have simply been falling in line with that lifestyle. Even if you read the May 1966 journal excerpt as representing the woman's final acknowledgment that the affair was well and truly over, and that it had been since 1963—and I do think that this is a legitimate way of reading it, in that the 1966 meeting appears to have been a case of her tracking him down while he was touring—Coltrane was clearly anything but faithful in his marriage to Naima. I'm not particularly interested in glossing over that fact or rationalizing it in any way. However, it is important to offer some reflection on the social, cultural, and *theological* milieu in which John Coltrane was formed, and how utterly different it is from my own.

When asked which three wishes he would most like to have granted, Coltrane replied:

1. To have an inexhaustible freshness in my music. I'm stale right now.

2. Immunity from sickness of ill health.

3. Three times the sexual power I have now. And something else too: more natural love for people. You can add that on to the other. [5]

The question was one asked of hundreds of musicians by the Baroness Pannonica de Koenigswarter (née Rothschild), a very wealthy and notoriously generous Manhattan-based patron of the jazz scene. Koenigswarter began her collection of wishes in 1961, but unfortunately didn't attach any dates to the answers she received, so it is not possible to know precisely the point at which Coltrane made his three wishes. Because Koenigswarter only began her project in 1961, Coltrane's answers clearly date to a time after his marriage to Naima had already begun to falter. In fact, he might have done his interview after he'd already initiated his relationship with Alice, as the Baroness also recorded her wishes.

4. J. C. Thomas, *Chasin' the Trane*, 137–39.

5. Koenigswarter, *Three Wishes*, 61.

Not only is it rather telling that he wished that his sexual power be tripled, it is quite striking that Coltrane so easily rolled this together with the additional wish for "more natural love for people." Here, I find the perspective of James Cone to be quite illuminating. Cone insists that because it was the *bodies* of black slaves that were held in bondage, black American culture has, in a very particular way, refused to separate body from spirit. And extending well past the end of slavery, Cone sees this as connected to the ongoing experience of racial oppression:

> Indeed, for black people, existence is a form of celebration. It is joy, love, and sex. It is hugging, kissing, and feeling. People cannot love physically and spiritually (the two cannot be separated!) until they have been up against the edge of life, experiencing the hurt and pain of existence. They cannot appreciate the feel and touch of life nor express the beauty of giving themselves to each other in community, in love, and in sex until they know and experience the brokenness of existence as disclosed in human oppression. People who have not been oppressed physically cannot know the power inherent in bodily expressions of love. That is why white Western culture makes a sharp distinction between the spirit and the body, the divine and the human, the sacred and the secular. White oppressors do not know how to come to terms with the essential spiritual function of the human body. But for black people the body is sacred, and they know how to use it in the expression of love.[6]

Cone further contends that even within the church, "most blacks only verbalized the distinction between the 'sacred' and 'profane' and found themselves unable to follow white Christianity's rejection of the body."[7]

In his powerful and challenging 1962 essay *The Fire Next Time*, James Baldwin sounds many of the same chords. Having already characterized America as an "Anglo-Teutonic, antisexual country"[8] at an earlier point in the essay, Baldwin claims that white Americans "are terrified of sensuality and do not any longer understand it." "The word 'sensual' is not intended to bring to mind quivering dusky maidens or priapic black studs. I am referring to

6. Cone, *Spirituals and the Blues*, 114.
7. Ibid., 117.
8. Baldwin, *The Fire Next Time*, 45.

something much simpler and much less fanciful. To be sensual, I think, is to respect and rejoice in the force of life, of life itself, and to be *present* in all that one does, from the effort of loving to the breaking of bread."[9]

Now I need to be clear that I do not mean any of this to be taken as a justification for Coltrane's marital infidelity, as if to suggest that, "this is what black people do." Rather, I hear in both Cone and Baldwin an insistence that the sensual and sexual are very much a part of what it means to be human, and that black culture has a very particular grip on that reality. In the case of Coltrane's third wish, the ease with which he linked "more natural love for people" to increased sexual power actually suggests to me that at some level he might have been aware that within his own self a line dividing body from soul was emerging; that perhaps his emotional remoteness, his difficulties in his marriage, and his sexual infidelities were all arising precisely because he was struggling to be sensual in Baldwin's sense; to be truly present in all that he did.

Of course, this is based on speculation, and I have really begun to take a perilous step away from theological or even pastoral reflections and toward the terrain of the psychotherapist. That is always a risky move, even if the person with whom you are dealing is very much alive and engaged with you in some searching conversation. It is all the more perilous when dealing with someone who has died, so let me simply point to that which is demonstrably clear, namely that not only did John Coltrane's marriage fail, he also failed his marriage. And it is for precisely that reason that I am so taken by what he managed to say about Naima in these two pieces of music.

In both the March and the May, 1959 *Giant Steps* sessions, versions of "Naima" were recorded. The version from the March session was eventually released as a bonus track on various albums, while the tape from the May session is missing and presumed lost. That he recorded it yet again in December of that year, in the context of sessions for a whole other album, indicates just how badly he wanted it included as part of *Giant Steps*. And not just any version of the song either, but one with which he could be truly happy. Even more importantly, he may have been trying to

9. Ibid., 61–62.

produce a version of the song that he could, in all confidence, offer to Naima. The cynic might be tempted to wonder if this isn't the recorded version of the flowers brought home by the sheepish husband to try to make up for some failing, and who knows? Maybe at some level, "Naima" was an apology. But you have to listen to it before making that judgment, and listen knowing what they had been through by this point in their marriage.

"Naima" is a lovely, slow, and emotionally rich ballad. Jimmy Cobb's brushwork on his drums almost sounds lazy, even though he's keeping time in his typically flawless way. Paul Chambers' bass works in and out between the voices of Coltrane's saxophone and Wynton Kelly's piano, at times sounding like an answering voice to theirs, and at others times like a heartbeat. Kelly's piano is lovely, and just sufficiently adventurous to really catch the listener's attention without shifting the song's overall mood. Coltrane is subdued and almost melancholic in his playing; almost, but never quite. Right at the very end of the four-and-a-half minute piece there is a hint that he might be ready to let the reins out a little more, but instead he brings it to a quite gorgeous ending in which he somehow soars without really changing his tempo or volume.

Lewis Porter characterizes "Naima" as a "serene, exotic tribute to his wife," and then adds that "It is typical of Coltrane that his slow pieces do not sound like 'ballads' at all—there is no touch of that 'Oh baby, I miss you' feeling. 'Naima' is more like a hymn."[10] Porter is certainly right in identifying the song's serenity, though I hear it as being not so much exotic as it is quite frankly sensual. By that I don't mean that it is particularly charged with erotic or sexual energy, and I believe Porter is bang on in saying that it is utterly without any of the "Oh baby" sentiment that often comes through in some of the more stereotypically sultry late-night jazz ballads. Yet "Naima" is at a very real level quite deeply sensual, in a way that could only come from one who understands not only the tenderness, but also the fragility and vulnerability of intimacy. This is the sensuality voiced by a lover to his beloved, whose body and soul he has touched. And wounded. It is a sensuality touched by sorrow.

10. Porter, *John Coltrane*, 156.

In the liner notes for *Giant Steps*, Nat Hentoff includes Coltrane's own brief description of the song, and then offers a comment that is more telling than he imagines:

> The tender "Naima"—an Arabic name—is also the name of John's wife. "The tune is built," Coltrane notes, "on suspended chords over an E-flat pedal tone on the outside. On the inside—the channel—the chords are suspended over a B-flat pedal tone." Here again is demonstrated Coltrane's more than ordinary melodic imagination as a composer and the deeply emotional strength of all his work, writing and playing. There is a "cry"—not at all necessarily a despairing one—in the work of the best of the jazz players. It represents a man's being in thorough contact with his feelings, and being able to let them out, and that "cry" Coltrane certainly has.

Hentoff has heard the cry of a man who is in touch with his emotional life, and who understands, at least at this moment, the depths of the hurt that he has caused. By rights, Naima shouldn't have stayed with him. Though he did not share her faith as a Muslim, she was prepared to accept his searching spirituality and to join her life to his in marriage. She lived with his addictions for the first year-and-a-half of their marriage, and then saw him through his withdrawal. He declared this to have precipitated his spiritual awakening, and by all accounts Naima's steadying presence through all of his ups and downs was a big part of what made that even possible. Add to this the affair that produced a child, while their own marriage had to endure two miscarriages. Of all of this, John Coltrane would have been acutely aware, and so he offered to her a lovely and sensual song as his gift of gratitude and of hope for a new beginning. Or maybe it was just an apology, and his way to try to make amends. Perhaps it was some combination of all of these, and more. The fact is he did have another affair, which began less than half a year after he recorded the version of "Naima" that landed on *Giant Steps*. Whatever he hoped or thought the song was saying to his wife about his love for her, it wasn't long before things were again going off track. Whatever his hopes and intentions were for the future of the marriage, it might have been that sufficient damage had already been done, such that it was beyond repair. It would also appear that he might not have been quite as thoroughly attuned to his feelings as Hentoff had assumed. Perhaps in his emotional detachment and remoteness—and again and again this is something on which even his friends remarked—he was simply too vulnerable to the unconditional adoration offered by a devoted female fan. The uphill climb required to truly reconcile and rebuild a marriage with Naima was quite possibly too steep, however much he might have wanted it. The musician Yusef Lateef—who together with his wife had shared a friendship with Naima and John—recounted that on the day Coltrane told him of the marriage's demise and spoke of all that had gone wrong, he ended by saying very clearly that he still loved her.[11]

As I mentioned in chapter three, Coltrane's reflections in the liner notes of A Love Supreme include a confession that he hadn't always managed to order his life in accordance with his great "spiritual awakening." "As time and events moved on, a period of irresolution did prevail. I entered into a phase which was contradictory to the pledge and away from the esteemed path." This sense of having been caught in a space in which his choices and patterns were not in alignment with what he knew to be right and true—"the righteous path" is what he calls it in those same liner notes—is not unlike what Paul writes in his letter to the Romans: "I do not understand my own actions. For I do not do what I want, but I do the very thing I hate." (Rom 7:15) "Wretched man that I am!" Paul continues several verses later. "Who will rescue me from this body of death?" And without hesitation, he answers his own question: "Thanks be to God through Jesus Christ our Lord!" (Rom 24–25a) Again, it is not hard to see parallels in Coltrane's understanding of his own "rescue," experienced as a spiritual re-awakening, given "through the unerring and merciful hand of God," as he says in his notes to A Love Supreme. While certainly not articulated with any great theological or poetic sophistication, his closing words in those liner notes do actually manage to say something quite significant. Framed almost as a benediction pronounced over his listening audience, Coltrane writes, "May we never forget that in the sunshine of our lives, through the storm and after the rain—it is all with God—in all ways and forever. ALL PRAISE TO GOD." Much as I wish that he had found a phrase more eloquent than "in the sunshine of our lives," his insight here is substantial. Both in the light of grace he experienced in his

11. Brown, "Conversation with Yusef Lateef," 195.

awakening, as well through those years in which he'd let his life dis-integrate, he had not been abandoned. "Where can I go from your spirit?" asks the writer of Psalm 139,

> Or where can I flee from your presence?
> If I ascend to heaven, you are there;
> if I make my bed in Sheol, you are there. (Ps 139:7–8)

> If I say, 'Surely the darkness shall cover me,
> and the light around me become night.'
> even the darkness is not dark to you;
> the night is as bright as the day,
> for darkness is as light to you. (Ps 139:11–12)

I read in Coltrane's phrase, "after the rain," a recognition that something has indeed passed, and that there is no going back to the place he had been before the storm. His movement is forward, and if he is going to make peace with himself, with his own actions, and—insofar as it might have been possible—with his estranged wife, it would not be by attempting to patch things up. The storm has done its damage, yet after its passing there is still work to be done. It is precisely this conviction that I hear voiced in his composition, "Wise One."

"Wise One" was recorded in April, 1964 and released in July of that same year on the album *Crescent*. Up to this point in his recording career, Coltrane's sound had often been characterized as angry or restless, and some of his harsher critics even called his music "anti-jazz." That the critic Martin Williams could then remark on *Crescent*'s "moments of contemplation" and "relative serenity"[12] really does say something about the mood and energy that is behind this album. Writing nearly thirty years after the album's release, Ashley Kahn suggests that with *Crescent*, "Coltrane seemed to have found a stylistic resting point."[13] It is the last album before the recording of *A Love Supreme*, with which it actually shares much in common, including that sense of being at a resting point. "The underlying intensity was in no way diminished, but there was a notable lack of explicit struggle in the sound,"[14] Kahn continues, and I think he is absolutely on target. Here Coltrane's sound does come without any sense of struggling to press forward

12. Kahn, *A Love Supreme*, 79.
13. Ibid.
14. Ibid.

for a new sound, a new idea, or a new expression. Not that it is in any way a tame record, as Coltrane is typically unafraid to make some serious and challenging explorations on his horn. He also gives what amounts to a feature song to each of the other members of his quartet, and each very much rises to the challenge. There's plenty to be heard on this record. As Kahn points out, it just doesn't happen to include "explicit struggle."

I have to say that "Wise One" is simply lovely. It is in no way sentimental, and like the rest of the record it isn't particularly tame. Coltrane does stretch out a bit on his solo in the middle of the piece, even heading for the upper registers that he just won't go near on "Naima." At the beginning of the third minute, the piece sets out into four-and-a-half minutes of mid-tempo Afro-Latin swing featuring some very fine work by McCoy Tyner, as well as some of Coltrane's adventurous work on his saxophone. But the impression that is most lasting comes from the opening three minutes and the closing minute-and-a-half. When Kahn identifies the song's "prayer-like mood,"[15] he is really referring to those two sections. The same is true of Nat Hentoff's comments in the album's liner notes, in which he refers to "the quality of utterly unabashed delicacy and intimacy which are reflected in the way he sketches the portrait of the Wise One." And it does sound like a portrait; it is somehow very visual, almost as if written to accompany just the right film or series of images.

It is also one of the three pieces on this record that Coltrane said he based on poems he had written.[16] There is no way of knowing anything about the poem that lies behind "Wise One," though it is hard not to imagine it as something that spoke to the wise woman who had accompanied him through so much, and from whom he was now separated. By this point, they weren't merely separated. Their marriage was over and done, and Coltrane was already building a new marriage and a new family. At the date of the recording of "Wise One," John and Alice had been living together for close to half a year, and she was already pregnant with the child who would be born just a month after *Crescent* was released. If "Naima" could be interpreted as a love song intended to help rekindle a romance, or as a peace offering to try to make amends,

15. Kahn, *House that Trane Built*, 119.
16. Delorme and Lenissois, "Coltrane, Star of Antibes," 244.

"Wise One" can only be a gift. I hear it as a moving tribute, a word of thanks, a request for forgiveness, and an acknowledgment of the wisdom that Naima embodied even during the times that he himself had not. It is a statement of what it might actually look like—or sound like—to make the move from betrayal and division to forgiveness and reconciliation. In the album liner notes, Coltrane is quoted as saying, "The main thing a musician would like to do is to give a picture to the listener of the many wonderful things he knows of and senses in the universe." All that informed the creation of "Wise One" is among those wonderful things.

But I'm not trying to kid myself here. During the course of his first marriage John Coltrane acted deceptively, and he truly hurt the person he loved. There's no question that it was a two-way street—marriages always are—and as Lewis Porter speculates, as an outsider to the music world Naima probably wasn't particularly able to cope with her husband's lifestyle, much less his fame.[17] And for all I know the affair with the unnamed woman did continue well into Coltrane's marriage with Alice, as her journal excerpts might indicate. Again, this is pure speculation, though I'd want to say that regardless of the actual shape of his personal struggles, Coltrane still managed to offer real wisdom and insight in both of these pieces, and to my hearing particularly in "Wise One." Without falling into anything even resembling sentimentality, "Wise One" speaks poignantly of the woman he had loved, but ultimately failed. Such truthful tones are particularly substantial. If Jeremy Begbie is even close to right in his characterization of much contemporary Christian and devotional music as "atrociously harmless" on account of its unwillingness to look in to "the world's dissonance" and the "clanking distortions and contradictions of human rebellion,"[18] Coltrane can be accused of no such avoidance. With "Wise One," I hear John Coltrane looking directly at the shape of his life and choices, and then playing his tribute to his "Wise One" right *through* those realities and contradictions, anticipating a deeper way of making peace with the woman he both loved and betrayed.

I had the opportunity to speak with Loren Schoenberg, the Director of the National Jazz Museum in Harlem, regarding the

17. Porter, *John Coltrane*, 270.
18. Begbie, *Resounding Truth*, 260.

way in which John Coltrane has been refashioned into the iconic and saintly figure of "Trane." Schoenberg's initial comment was, "I think all great music is in a sense spiritual," and then he added, "There's this feeling that Coltrane and his work almost became beyond criticism." He suggested, for instance, that jazz students are almost never prepared to state that there is music by Coltrane that they don't like. "I'm making a deeper point here, that Coltrane in a sense became beyond criticism, and I think that is really too bad. No one should like everything that any artist ever did. You just can't."[19] Something very similar surfaced in a conversation I shared with Lewis Porter in which he admitted, "For me, it revolves around a myth more than it revolves around reality. They're all impressed that he was a drug addict, and that he got over it. That always impresses people. That's why this Sheila Coltrane thing is interesting, because they don't want to know about this . . . He is just as great as they think he is, and just as spiritual and just as profound, but he is still a human being, who could make mistakes."[20] Some of his devotees simply don't want to know about the child conceived in his affair of the late 1950s. The addiction recovery story is just wonderful . . . but only so long as he stays good and recovered, and doesn't get himself into any trouble. It is a bit like the appeal of conversion stories in many church traditions; the best stories are the ones told by the people who come with the grittiest and messiest stories of life before their conversion, but Lord help them if things come apart after they've been born again. It is funny how we do that to people. We desperately want Mother Teresa to be the person we believe we couldn't possibly be, so that when her personal diaries are published, complete with entries that indicate she suffered with doubt and despair, the publisher and editor come under fire from some quarters for ostensibly undermining the public perception of this saintly woman. And she *was* saintly, even if she did have bouts of despair. I have an acquaintance who had been a devotee of the writings of Thomas Merton, yet on the day that he discovered that Merton had engaged in a late-life intimate affair, my friend immediately rid himself of his collection of Merton's books. People have had similar reactions upon finding out that Henri Noewen not only struggled with depression, but

19. Schoenberg, personal interview.
20. Porter, personal interview.

also came to identify himself as a gay man, albeit one committed to priestly celibacy. In so many cases, people just don't want to know that their own iconic heroes are as complicated as anyone else, and maybe even more so thanks to the pressure of being an icon-in-the-making.

So why aren't we prepared to acknowledge the humanity and fallen nature of those who have impressed us, or moved us, or shaped us? And from a Christian theological perspective, why would we be even vaguely surprised that some of the people who are gifted by God to say and do extraordinarily important things are also flawed? In the case of many of them, they could easily be judged failures right from the start, which is part of why they're called by God in the first place. Has no one in the church ever read the stories of the Bible, with its losers and shysters and little ones and lost sheep, who end up being the very hinges upon which the great narrative turns? Aside from Jesus of Nazareth, find me a biblical character who isn't marked by any number of flaws . . . and even Jesus needed parents to teach him and form him, and the occasional opinionated woman to keep him on his toes. Frankly, the theological wisdom and personal insight John Coltrane manages to speak through his horn is made even more significant when you realize it is being offered both out of the mess of his life and in search of something that might help him pull at least a few of the pieces together.

In *Finding Beauty in a Broken World*, Terry Tempest Williams explores the notion that beauty is often given us in unexpected ways and places. Williams writes of learning to take broken pieces of tile and glass and use them in the creation of mosaics, and also of learning something of the beauty of a memorial to the victims of the Rwandan massacre made entirely of human bones and skulls. Williams takes the art of mosaic making that she learned in Ravenna, Italy, and works alongside survivors of the Rwandan genocide to create a memorial, made quite literally from the shards of war. "Shards of glass," she writes, "can cut and wound or magnify vision. Mosaic celebrates brokenness and the beauty of being brought together."[21] Such beauty is not merely given, but requires of us fresh imagination and maybe a willingness to get our hands dirty. "Finding beauty in a broken world becomes more

21. Terry Tempest Williams, *Finding Beauty in a Broken World*, 385.

than the art of assemblage," she continues. "It is the work of daring contemplation that inspires action."[22]

The 1966 entry in the journal of "Trane's Lady" aside, there is nothing to suggest that John and Alice Coltrane's marriage was anything but stable and life giving, and there is certainly nothing to suggest that he involved himself in any further marital infidelities. The two not only lived and parented together, they also recorded and toured together, which at the most basic level may have provided him the kind of wife and partner he most needed in order to stay constant and faithful. It is interesting, though, that their relationship blossomed at precisely the same time as he was moving toward the recording of *A Love Supreme* and all that follows. His attention was turning increasingly to questions of God, prayer, and spiritual truth, and his search and spirituality were primarily carried out through his music. Of their relationship, Alice once observed, "We were both traveling in a particular spiritual direction, John and myself. So it seemed only natural for us to join forces. It was like God uniting two souls together. I think John could have just as easily married another woman, though. Not myself and not because I was a musician. But any woman who had the particular attributes or qualities to help him fulfill his life mission as God wanted him to."[23] While she claimed that he could have "just as easily married another woman," Alice Coltrane also believed that their marriage was in fact caught up in the shared quest for God. As implied by Baldwin and Cone, there has been a powerful tendency in Eurocentric theological traditions to draw too firm a line between *eros* and *agape*—between sensual and erotic love on the one hand, and self-giving or unconditional love on the other—as is exemplified in the work of Anders Nygren in his two-volume work from the 1930s, *Eros and Agape*. Yet there have always been other Christian theological voices, both ancient and modern, speaking in critique of the firmness of that line. Among the more notable twentieth-century writers in this regard are Paul Evdokimov, Charles Williams, and the current Archbishop of Canterbury, Rowan Williams. This project has been picked up and carried forward in fresh ways by Eugene Rogers, who writes, "Sexual desire is a bodily manifestation of my desire to be wanted, which

22. Ibid.
23. Kernodle, "Freedom is a Constant Struggle," 81.

is finally satisfied only by God's desire for me."[24] For Rogers, eros and agape are not in conflict one with the other, for in fact, "The love by which God loves human beings is eros, if eros is a love that yearns for union with the other, yearns for the flesh of the other, is made vulnerable and passionate for the other."[25] It is simply not necessary to reject eros for the sake of some higher spiritual calling—and some do live sensually and in this sense erotically within a celibate vocation—because in and through the sensual and erotic we encounter something of what it means to stand in a tradition that says, "The Word became flesh and dwelt among us." In short, John Coltrane's most searching spiritual and theological work happened during those years in which his deepest longings for both a passionate, erotic relationship *and* a stable family life were finally met. His music about God cannot be disconnected from his life as a lover, husband, and father.

As I've already mentioned, John Coltrane continued to play the song "Naima" through to the end of his life. There is a good example of where his quartet went with the song on the Jazz Icons DVD *John Coltrane Live in '60, '61 & '65*. Recorded live in Belgium in 1965, this version is far more open and searching than the *Giant Steps* original, and Coltrane is certainly not shy of really cutting loose on his saxophone. A more experimental live version appears on the 1966 album *Live at the Village Vanguard Again!*, with Coltrane pushing his innovations even further, and Pharoah Sanders offering up a tempestuous extended solo filled with honks, squawks, and squeals. It is an understatement to say that the critics were divided on the merits of this particular version, but of course that was true of all of the work of Coltrane's late career ensemble. Notably, Alice Coltrane is the pianist on this version of "Naima."

"Wise One," however, was not recorded again after its appearance on *Crescent*, and I can find no indication that it ever found a place as part of Coltrane's performance repertoire. It seems that while "Naima" could be appreciated as a great song, well suited for ongoing exploration, Coltrane needed for that recording of "Wise One" to stand on its own as a unique and singular statement. To adapt it or improvise from it might have meant risking a perceived change in its stated meaning. And it just might be that

24. Rogers, Jr. *Sexuality and the Christian Body*, 83.
25. Ibid., 225.

John Coltrane was not prepared to see that happen. Yet again, this is just a matter of speculation.

What is not speculation, though, is that at Coltrane's funeral his body was draped with a dashiki made by Naima in the days following the news of his death. Evidently she too had reached a place of being able to make peace after the rain.

6

"Alabama"

Lament

The bombing of the Sixteenth Street Baptist Church in Birmingham is but a single manifestation of this crisis, although somehow more than typical. It is fitting to begin with Birmingham as there is something about the violation of childhood (and perhaps of worship) and what can be called without exaggeration an attendant reaction of horror that best introduces this decade of radical questioning.

—James C. Hall, *Mercy, Mercy Me*

It is a striking piece of music. If anyone wants to begin to understand how Coltrane could inspire so much awe so quickly, the reason is probably inside "Alabama." The incantational tumult he could raise in a long improvisation, the steel-trap knowledge of harmony, the writing—that's all very impressive. But "Alabama" is also an accurate psychological portrait of a time, a complicated mood that nobody else could render so well.

—Ben Ratliff, *Coltrane*

At 10:22 on the morning of Sunday September 15, 1963, Robert "Dynamite Bob" Chambliss detonated a charge of dynamite in Birmingham's Sixteenth Street Baptist Church, wounding several church members and killing four young girls. Three of the girls were fourteen years old, and the fourth only eleven. Though Chambliss and three associates underwent an FBI investigation, in the end he was issued only a small fine and sentenced to a six-month jail sentence for possession of a box of over a hundred sticks of dynamite.

On November 18, 1963 John Coltrane took his quartet into the studio and recorded "Alabama," his haunting lament for all that was lost—and all that was signified—in the violence of that morning in Birmingham. As recalled by Coltrane's friend, the bass player Art Davis, "He was very conscious of what was happening when those girls were murdered in the bombing in Alabama. He was incensed—we talked about that. And for this to happen in a House of God and people were there worshipping God and for people to bomb a church like that, he said, 'That's reprehensible. I'm livid with the hate that can happen in this country.'"[1] What was recorded that day and released in January 1964 as one of two studio tracks on the *Live at Birdland* album doesn't strike the listener as being particularly angry, though for a brief section near the end of the piece the quartet does cry out with an impassioned intensity. No, as a statement "Alabama" is mournful and melancholic, yet filled with dignity and a firm resolve. In his album liner notes LeRoi Jones / Amiri Baraka describes the piece as having "a slow delicate introspective sadness" which is "almost hopelessness, except for Elvin [Jones], rising in the background like something out of nature." *Almost* hopeless, in the same way that the deepest of the blues and the deepest of the biblical laments sing out the experience of lostness as a way of telling the truth, and so of somehow keeping hope alive. To be mute in the midst of sorrow, that is hopelessness. "How could we sing the Lord's song in a foreign land?," asks the author of Psalm 137. In the midst of this exilic nightmare, after we've experienced so much loss and so much violence, what could we possibly have to sing about? Yet the sorrow is expressed—can only be expressed—precisely by giving it voice in a freshly written psalm of lament.

I hear the psalms of lament in "Alabama," and I also hear what W. E. B. Du Bois calls the "Sorrow Songs," the spirituals of the slave church. In his classic book *The Souls of Black Folks*, Du Bois writes with a steady and at times melancholic resolve about the songs that tell, "in word and music of trouble and exile, of strife and hiding; they grope toward some unseen power and sigh for

1. Brown, "In His Own Words," 25.

rest in the End."[2] And though they sing of the sorrows of a whole people, these songs are anything but hopeless. "Through all the sorrow of the Sorrow Songs there breathes a hope—a faith in the ultimate justice of things. The minor cadences of despair change often to triumph and calm confidence. Sometimes it is faith in life, sometimes a faith in death, sometimes assurance of boundless justice in some fair world beyond. But whichever it is, the meaning is always clear: that sometime, somewhere, men will judge men by their souls not by their skins."[3] In "Alabama" the "minor cadences" are clearly there, and while it might not quite be triumph that is sounded, there is a calmness and steadfastness that speaks to the possibility of a different future. Yet, before there can be anything like a hopeful new dream in which "men will judge men by their souls not by their skins," there must first be expressions of deep loss and sorrow.

"Alabama" opens with what Ratliff describes as "almost a classical recitation."[4] For the opening minute and twenty seconds of the piece—which is just over five minutes long—McCoy Tyner allows his hands to all but tremble on the piano keys as he repeats again and again the single chord on which this opening section is built. It is against that backdrop that Coltrane offers what sounds as much like a spoken recitation as it does a melody. Through this opening section, he plays much lower on his horn than is usual for him, and with a subdued and mournful gentleness. You can almost picture him with his head bowed before the coffins of those four young girls; it is *that* kind of gentleness.

At 1:24, this opening section begins to be drawn to its close, and for the first time we hear Elvin Jones, as he taps ever so lightly on a cymbal, offering what amounts to a twenty-second musical "amen," "so be it," "rest in peace." A medium tempo blues begins, and for just a single minute the piece even swings a bit. But just a bit, and just for that minute. And then for just a very few seconds there is silence before the piece returns to the sonic space it had inhabited in its opening section. This time Tyner is a bit further back in the mix, and it is Jimmy Garrison's heartfelt bass and Jones'

2. Du Bois, *Souls of Black Folks*, 247.

3. Ibid., 251.

4. Ratliff, *Coltrane*, 86.

very subdued drumming that you most hear working alongside Coltrane's horn in his restatement of the opening theme.

It is in its final forty seconds that "Alabama" moves into a place where Jones can cut loose on the drums and Coltrane can finally let his saxophone really wail. In the background you can hear one of the band members vocalizing, as if to give a human voice to the pain expressed in what has just been played. Yet rather than taking his wailing horn up to the next level as his audience had come to expect, Coltrane instead just finds that deeply melancholic note again and stays there. The other musicians allow the sound of their instruments to fade toward silence, and "Alabama" is brought to its close.

So, here is the movement of the piece in summary: from a gentle sadness and sorrow, to "amen," to that *almost* swinging blues, back to the gentle sadness (though now stated a bit differently, and by all four instruments), to a cry of . . . a cry of what? Protest? Agony? Resilience? Hope? As I hear it and will seek to set out in the next few pages, I think at least all four are present. And of course that cry folds into yet another statement of sorrow, giving it both the first and the last word in the piece. Still, I'm convinced that if the work of lament and the work of the blues are being done, the sorrow of the opening is different from that of the close.

I believe that the brief swing into the blues that lies at the heart of this piece is not incidental, and so I need to state very clearly that alongside the psalms of lament and the spirituals or Sorrow Songs, I also hear the blues, and I hear them loud and clear. The blues tradition is literally present in that single minute in the middle of "Alabama," but not only there. I understand Coltrane to have drawn his quartet into playing that brief blues section as his way of saying that they are at that point engaging in a longer and deeper story, and it is a story from the tradition in which they were all rooted. As jazz players their music was rooted in the blues, but if we take seriously the insights of James Cone, it goes much deeper than just the roots of the music. As black Americans their lives simply were intertwined with the blues tradition. "The thing that goes into the blues is the experience of being black in a white racist society. It is that peculiar feeling that makes you know that there is something seriously wrong with the society, even though you may not possess the intellectual or political power to do anything about it. No black person can escape the blues, because the blues are an inherent part of black existence in America."[5] "The blues," Cone writes, "are about black life and the sheer earth and gut capacity to survive in an extreme situation of oppression."[6] And that isn't narrowly tied to the lyrics of the blues—which likely as not are earthy or sexually charged or blasphemous or some combination of the three—nor even to specific songs offered by the blues men and women. It is more connected to the stubborn insistence that life and freedom can be found, regardless of how the class-bound and racist society might be configuring things.

Here I would want to draw attention to the work of Adam Gussow in his book, *Seems Like Murder Here: Southern Violence and the Blues Tradition*. Gussow sees a powerful correlation between the emergence of blues music in the 1890s and what he describes as "an unprecedented increase in lynching, which had suddenly been reinvented by white folk as a spectator sport."[7] As Gussow observes, it is not that lynchings and other racially-based acts of violence were the actual subject of blues songs—in fact, it was not until the 1920s and 1930s that some blues men and women began singing what he calls "coded lynching blues" songs—but rather, "that black southerners evolved blues song as a way of speaking back to, and maintaining psychic health in the face of, an ongoing threat of lynching."[8] The blues speak of life in spite of death, freedom in spite of captivity, hope in spite of sorrow, personal and communal resilience in spite of the ever-present threat of violence. And at least occasionally, this "in spite of" can come across as being quite thoroughly and unapologetically spiteful.

Certainly for black jazz musicians (and here we need to recall the discussions from chapter two, on the contested story of the development of this music), the bringing forward of the blues as part of the creation of jazz implied a fresh extension and expression of the old resilience embodied in the tradition. To play a blues with a jazz quartet in a downtown New York club in 1963 remained a way of saying, "we are here, freely doing this thing we do, even if many of us are still being crushed in most places in this country."

5. Cone, *Spirituals and the Blues*, 103.
6. Ibid., 97.
7. Gussow, *Seems Like Murder Here*, 2.
8. Ibid., xii.

It strikes me that in turning to the blues as the heart of "Alabama," John Coltrane was declaring himself a bluesman, and his response to the Birmingham bombing was a deep blues offered on behalf of that besieged community. To again pick up on Gussow's work, how better to respond to an act of racial violence than with the blues? And the fact that on "Alabama" it actually swings a bit is not at odds with how the blues tended to do its often coded and socially subversive work. Here, Cornel West is helpful. "Rhythmic singing, swaying, dancing, preaching, talking, and walking—all features of black life—are weapons of struggle and survival. They not only release pressures and desperation, they also constitute bonds of solidarity and sources for individuality."[9] To swing the blues in the midst of an agonizing lament is a statement of this kind of struggle and survival; of refusing to be bent low by the weight of the sorrow, and to find a unique and individual voice with which to speak of a deeper hope.

Writing in 2011 as a white middle-class Canadian, I can only say that I hope I have absorbed enough from the work of people like James Cone, Cornel West, Jon Michael Spencer, W. E. B. Du Bois, and even LeRoi Jones / Amiri Baraka, to be able to write the preceding paragraphs with at least a small measure of integrity and understanding.

Let me back us up to something Du Bois wrote regarding the central message of the Sorrow Songs; "that sometime, somewhere, men will judge men by their souls not by their skins." This sentiment is echoed in the speech delivered from the steps of the Lincoln Memorial by Martin Luther King, Jr. some sixty years after the publication of *The Souls of Black Folks*. In that speech King famously proclaimed his great dream for America, including his hope that, "my four little children will one day live in a nation where they will not be judged by the color of their skin but by the content of their character." This brings us to something that has been raised again and again in relation to "Alabama," namely whether or not Coltrane based the recitation-like sections of the piece on a speech by King, and perhaps even on the eulogy King preached at the funeral for the young victims of the Birmingham bombing. While Coltrane himself is not on record as having said anything that would indicate this, several writers and Coltrane biographers take it for

9. West, "Subversive Joy and Revolutionary Patience," 162.

granted. Lewis Porter, however, is not convinced. When I asked him if he thought that Coltrane could have been "reading" with his saxophone in the way he so clearly does on the "Psalm" section of *A Love Supreme*, Porter replied that he didn't believe so. "I don't think he's doing that on 'Alabama,' because the melodic line in 'Alabama' doesn't strike me as being as recitative and chant-oriented as the one on 'Psalm' [from *A Love Supreme*]. And I don't believe he was referring to Martin Luther's speech, only because people have combed through every speech Martin Luther King gave . . . and they haven't found anything that remotely fits."[10] Given that Porter is widely recognized for publishing the first detailed outline of how Coltrane actually played the written text of his prayer/poem on "Psalm," his opinion is one to be respected. And in our conversation, Porter also added that he does think Coltrane was doing a recitation on "Attaining," a piece recorded in 1965 and released *on Sun Ship* in 1971. "That one sounds like 'Psalm,'" he commented, "It sounds like a recitation. It doesn't sound like a melody."

However, according to Ashley Kahn, the recitation theory was at least partly confirmed by McCoy Tyner in a personal interview for the 2002 book *A Love Supreme: The Story of John Coltrane's Signature Album*. In that interview, Tyner evidently told Kahn that the song was based on one of King's speeches. "The song 'Alabama' came from a speech. John said there was a Martin Luther King speech about the four girls getting killed in Alabama. It was in the newspaper—a printed medium. And so John took the rhythmic patterns of his speech and came up with 'Alabama.' "[11] Yet when I asked Tyner about this matter, he replied that while it would have been in keeping with Coltrane's concerns of the day, "I really can't be sure of that." He then added that while Coltrane had not been a particularly political man—"he was really all about the music; we all were"—the events of the early 1960s had deeply impacted all of them, and had called for some response. "Many people in the North weren't all that aware of how bad things really were, in terms of the awful racism," he said, adding that what people like King had done was so very, very necessary. "We changed for the better because of that."[12]

10. Porter, personal interview.
11. Kahn, *A Love Supreme*, 79.
12. Tyner, telephone interview.

Clearly that doesn't solve the question of whether or not "Alabama" was built around a recitation, much less a recitation of one of King's speeches. Perhaps it is just best to recognize that there is something of a vocal quality to those sections of the piece, and that they do their work of wordlessly articulating the sorrow connected to those events. To this can be added McCoy Tyner's firm conviction that, in collaboration with his quartet, John Coltrane needed to respond to the awful reality people in the South were living through, and that King's vision was an important part of that. If on "Alabama" Coltrane was actually influenced by one of King's speeches, it may have been simply in terms of borrowing from its "rhythmic patterns" or even in picking up on the cadences of sorrow conveyed by a written text. For someone schooled in the black church—and specifically someone who felt that he could speak most powerfully and clearly through his saxophone—wordless articulation is hardly without meaning or weight. As Paul writes in his Letter to the Romans, "we do not know how to pray as we ought, but that very Spirit intercedes with sighs too deep for words" (Rom 8:26b). Such sighing might lie at the heart of the lament for those children in Birmingham.

I can only know the blues and the spirituals second-hand and from across a significant cultural gap. Closer to my own mother tongue of faith are the Psalms, which I have read and prayed daily for years. As the rock musician Bono observes, the Psalms are not entirely different from the blues. In his introduction to *The Pocket Canon Psalms*, Bono writes,

> Before David could fulfill the prophecy and become the king of Israel, he had to take quite a beating. He was forced into exile and ended up in a cave in some no-name border town facing the collapse of his ego and abandonment by God. But this is where the soap opera got interesting. This is where David was said to have composed his first psalm—a blues. That's what a lot of the psalms feel like to me, the blues. Man shouting at God—"My God, my God, why hast thou forsaken me? Why art thou so far from helping me?"[13]

In drawing our attention to these opening lines of Psalm 22, Bono is pressing us toward one of the key theological issues raised by the Psalms, namely theodicy; the existential problem of the presence of

13. Bono, "Introduction," ix.

evil and suffering in a world believed to be under the providential care of a supposedly just God. Though some would disagree, Jon Michael Spencer understands the blues tradition to be shot through with questions of theodicy. In *Blues and Evil*, Spencer writes of what he sees as being a "discourse of 'theodicy' in the blues—provisional answers to the question of how an all-knowing and all-powerful good God permitted evil and suffering to exist in God's created world."[14] The blues men and women offered answers that discounted or rejected some of those held by many within the church—for instance that suffering might be necessary for redemption or as a way of instructing believers in preparation for salvation—though according to Spencer they did include what he calls "a reap what you sow theodicy." Having stepped outside of the church in which they had been formed, the blues men and women were still very much haunted by theological concerns, and by a fear that their hard luck and personal misfortune was their due.

In this sense, Spencer argues, "Suffering was justifiable to them for reasons of divine retribution";[15] they were simply reaping what they had sown through hard living and the free decision to live outside of the shelter of the church. However, when it comes to the suffering of a whole people through the systemic evil of racism, Spencer is extremely clear: "What was never manifested in the blues was the use of the 'reap' theodicy to explain evil heaped upon black people for their alleged crime of being black."[16]

Similarly in the Psalm tradition, when in the face of suffering or abandonment "provisional answers" are uttered to the heavens, there is never a sense that God is rejecting or punishing Israel for the crime of being Israel. Israel might have fallen into corruption or faithlessness, and so for a time God is angry or even apparently absent, but the claim that these Psalms place on God is that God *must* remember Israel, for Israel is the chosen and beloved. All to say that in both the Psalms and the blues the answer to the problem of suffering is never one that suggests that God has rejected this race or this people simply on account of their being this particular race or people. And the same must be said for the spirituals, in their thoroughgoing rejection of slavery. "The basic

14. Spencer, *Blues and Evil*, 68–69.
15. Ibid., 81.
16. Ibid.

idea of the spirituals is that slavery contradicts God; it is a denial of God's will," writes Cone. "To be enslaved is to be declared *nobody,* and that form of existence contradicts God's creation of people to be God's children."[17]

So when the writers of the Psalms give voice to suffering and loss, be that as individuals or on behalf of the community, it is assumed that the pain is not arbitrary and that in addressing God things can be set right. The first step in "setting right" is achieved in the very act of crying out, of finding a voice with which to speak truthfully and openly about the pain and the loss and the bewilderment—"*Why* have you abandoned me?"—even to the very throne of heaven.

Biblical scholars have attempted to categorize the Psalms in any number of ways, though for our purposes here the model proposed by Walter Brueggemann is particularly helpful. Brueggemann suggests that the Psalms can be viewed in terms of three general types: psalms of safe orientation, psalms of painful disorientation, and psalms of surprising new orientation.[18] Within each broad category falls any number of subcategories, though here I am really just interested in his category of painful disorientation, which includes both the laments and the psalms of complaint. Lament may be voiced over some transgression, or, as in the case of Psalm 22, over a seemingly meaningless experience of suffering and loss. They can be voiced by an individual or framed as community songs. These psalms are at times marked by a deep sense of penitence, though often they declare the innocence of the writer, and cry out in protest that things must be set right. In fact almost without exception, laments culminate in a resolute and even challenging cry to God to *do* something. Still, before the cry for God to act is voiced, the deep truth of the pain of disorientation is told: "*This* is what I/we are living with." The truth is told, and it is told with tears, be those the guilty tears of the penitent, or the heart-wrenching tears of victims of injustice or of meaningless violence.

From the shedding of tears these psalms often move next to a statement reminding God that the person or community in pain in fact belongs to God, and has for generations. This is an appeal to the tradition, and the voice of the writer begins to become more

17. Cone, *Spirituals and the Blues,* 33.
18. Brueggemann, *Spirituality of the Psalms,* 8–13.

firm. "Remember us, and remember the promises you made to our ancestors," is one move in this appeal, but so is, "and you don't want people to think that the enemy is stronger than you, do you Lord?" Figuratively speaking, the writer's head has been raised, and there is a firmness to the set of the jaw.

That firmness doesn't necessarily last. There can follow another cry of helplessness and agony, or perhaps even a loud call for justice to be done and retribution meted out. After all, the writers of the Psalms are not following a formula or template, so there are great variations in how the various laments unfold. But they are shaped by a common theological, spiritual, and even liturgical imagination, which almost inevitably carries them from plea to praise. That praise may take the form of a bold affirmation that God will act, or it might be the quietest "amen," yet with the notable exception of Psalm 88—which ends, "You have caused friend and neighbor to shun me; my companions are in darkness"—it marks a belief that in telling of the pain and loss of disorientation, the movement toward the grace of reorientation has already begun.

Don Saliers suggests that in the unfolding and ongoing tradition of music produced from within African-American culture one can discern a parallel movement from lament to doxology. It is clearly present in the spirituals and in the gospel music that developed from them, but also in the blues and jazz, in rhythm and blues and in soul, and even in rap and hip-hop. "This is an exemplification of the spirituality we see in the Psalms, now transposed to urban musical forms," Saliers observes. "It is not accidental that the sensibility and emotional range of the Psalms shows up."[19]

In the case of John Coltrane's "Alabama," I believe that Saliers is right on track. The piece moves first from its opening statement of sorrow-filled lament to the blues; to a "heads-up and jaws-set" appeal to the tradition. The very playing of that blues is a statement that this is a people actively refusing "to accept the absurdity of white society,"[20] and at the same time it is a declaration that in being thus rooted there will be a way forward. And yet those raised heads drop just a little, as the piece returns to once again voice lament. This time, though, there are more voices and

19. Saliers, telephone interview.
20. Cone, *Spirituals and the Blues*, 105.

more intensity in the playing. And this time it leads toward that cry of protest, which is sufficiently impassioned and sufficiently determined to allow for the transition to a closing "Amen." There is a way forward.

Now, it is impossible to ever know whether or not Coltrane was at all aware of the psalm-like qualities that I see as so characterizing this piece of music. I would argue, though, that given his foundation in a church tradition in which the Psalms would have been read and the spirituals sung, and given his formation in a musical world that paid deep attention and even homage to the blues, it is not at all surprising that this was his way of telling the painful truth about what was really going on. Growing up in the South, he would have been immersed in a world shaped by the Bible and preaching, by the music of both church and neighborhood, and by the persistent racism that hung heavy in the air. Is it any wonder Coltrane knew how to offer up his lament?

Back to my conversation with McCoy Tyner. You'll recall he suggested that through the protests and laments and confrontations and bold dreams that made for the civil rights movement of the 1960s, "We changed for the better." From that statement, Tyner went on to add that as far as he is concerned, "we live in the best nation in the world." Not that McCoy Tyner would be so naïve as to claim that there aren't still problems and very pressing issues, but rather that in having experienced that movement away from lamentable and horrific violence and racism, something very hope-filled could be said about the nation he calls home.

With Robert Chambliss found "not guilty" in the original trial, the case remained dormant until 1970, when Bill Baxley was elected the attorney general of Alabama. After reviewing the original FBI files on the case, Baxley had the matter reopened and in November 1977 Robert Chambliss was once again tried for the church bombing. He was found guilty on four counts of murder, and sentenced to life in prison, where he died October 29, 1985. By 2000, sufficient evidence had surfaced to clearly connect the bombing to the so-called "Cahaba Boys," a Ku Klux Klan splinter group. Along with Chambliss, three other men were implicated in the crime, and the two who were still alive at the time were arrested. Thomas Blanton and Bobby Cherry were both convicted of murder, and sentenced to life imprisonment.

Now clearly I am not suggesting that the creation of a single piece of jazz music led to this legal turnaround. However, insofar as it participated in the stubborn resilience of the blues, and insofar as it gave voice to psalmic and God-haunted lament, "Alabama" was indeed a part of what made it possible for an oppressed people to keep pressing ahead for those elusive things called justice and freedom. And as a nation found its own version of truth challenged by the civil rights movement, the truth-telling sorrow of lament could give way to something new. As the Psalmist sings,

> "Weeping may linger for the night,
> but joy comes with the morning." (Ps 30:5)

7

"A Love Supreme"

Grace

Is it mere accident that *A Love Supreme* (1964)—the masterpiece of the greatest musical artist of our time and the grand exemplar of twentieth-century black spirituality, John Coltrane—is cast in the form of prayer? The slave authors of the spirituals . . . and John Coltrane all engaged in a Keatsian "soul-making" in that they courageously confronted the darkness in and of modernity with artistic integrity and genuine spirituality.

—Cornel West, "The Spirituals as Lyrical Poetry"

In the verse dedication accompanying *A Love Supreme*, Coltrane returns again and again to the assertion that "No matter what . . . it is God." This "no matter what" very precisely addresses the reasons that divinity *cannot* be delimited by the concerns of harmony alone, the reasons that the divine must necessarily include the dissonant.

—Michael Bruce McDonald, "Traning the Nineties"

You can't do better than *A Love Supreme*. You can do different, but you can't do better. His work stands alone.

—Jimmy Greene

Of all the chapters in my book, this one on *A Love Supreme* was easily the most difficult to begin. In fact, I actually left this chapter to the very end of my work, with some sense that when the time came to start writing it I had better have done as much preliminary work as possible. That has partly to do with the fact that so much has been written about this album, including both a full chapter in Lewis Porter's *John Coltrane: His Life and Music* and an entire book by Ashley Kahn. For all that I have listened to this record over the years, and for all that I've read and reread Coltrane's liner notes and prayer/poem, I was quite deeply aware of all that I didn't know about this particular work. And I still am.

It makes little sense to try to replicate Kahn's book or to summarize Porter's careful musical analysis of the four-part suite. I will offer a brief and fairly personal sketch of the suite's structure, freely acknowledging the debt I owe to Porter on this count. I will also draw on Kahn's research and insight, and I commend both his and Porter's books to anyone who wants to further explore this music.

So many have written or spoken passionately about the importance of *A Love Supreme* that it can be challenging to remember that not everyone in the jazz world is all that enthusiastic about this record. Kahn's book is filled with quotes from musicians from both the jazz and rock music genres, for whom the record was influential, even transformational. As noted in one of the quotes with which this chapter opens, Cornel West calls it, "the masterpiece of the greatest musical artist of our time and the grand exemplar of twentieth-century black spirituality." The theologian William Edgar suggests that, "It is doubtful that any jazz recording has ever matched the spiritual power of this musical gift,"[1] while long-time radio host and jazz aficionado Eric D. Jackson says that it, "spoke to a hunger I had inside." "I knew that even if I was disillusioned with the actions of the members of the church, Trane helped me to remember that there is a God of the universe."[2]

However, others have begged to differ. At the time and in spite of its commercial success, at least some of the critics were unsure what to make of *A Love Supreme*. Joe Goldberg opens his review for *HiFi/Stereo Review* by suggesting, "John Coltrane has made it very difficult to discuss this disc with any objectivity," and goes on to highlight the "almost embarrassingly open and fervent" spiritual tone of the record's liner notes.[3] After acknowledging that it is ultimately a "good record," Goldberg advises the potential purchaser that he or she "might enjoy the music without need of

1. Edgar, "A Love Supreme," 5.
2. Eric Jackson, "Somebody Please Say, 'Amen!,'" 175.
3. Goldberg, "A Love Supreme," 233.

the philosophy that accompanies it."[4] In a kind of reverse fashion, the jazz writer Ekkehard Jost is also attuned to the impact of the accompanying written text: "It is doubtful whether the same piece, under a different title and without Coltrane's religious confession on the record jacket, would have attracted the kind of attention it ultimately did."[5] Jost is far more interested in the place of *A Love Supreme* in Coltrane's movement toward free jazz, and so acknowledges that, "the influence it had, as the manifestation of a new, spiritual attitude, on many young musicians in the New York free jazz circle, cannot be overlooked."[6]

And then there is work of the culture critic Gerald Early, who though quite willing to recognize Coltrane's technical abilities as a musician, is unforgiving in his view of this album, and especially of its liner notes: "[Coltrane's] thinking in this realm seemed positively banal, a kind of pantheistic muddle of God is the universe and truth is the sum total of all religions."[7] Further, Early is deeply concerned that Coltrane has been uncritically and unhelpfully embraced by the African-American intellectual culture, largely because the musician fit its need for a rather enigmatic, and apparently thoroughly "regenerated" black artist. "Probably the very simplistic and sincere nature of his beliefs—their anti-intellectual thrust, if you will, that refused to consider what a religion actually required its adherents to believe or how religion structured history—gave those beliefs a greater profundity and a greater resonance with the black intellectual public than they deserved; this, coupled with the fact that as a result of a conversion of sorts, Coltrane cleaned up his life—in short, resurrected or regenerated himself—made him an ideal hero for intellectual and literary types."[8] I will revisit Early's essay in some detail in my closing chapter, but for now suffice it to say that *A Love Supreme* does have its detractors, in spite of the fact that it is one of the most influential—and most written about—albums in jazz history.

It is, however, worth picking up on the issue of Coltrane's conversion or regeneration, as it is so very central to the album as a

4. Ibid., 234.

5. Jost, *Free Jazz*, 32.

6. Ibid.

7. Early, "Ode to John Coltrane," 376.

8. Ibid., 377.

whole. As I made clear in chapter three, a good deal of the mythic figure of "Trane" is connected to the actual experiences John Coltrane had in confronting his addictions. As summarized by James Hall, "Whatever the truth about his conversion—and all such tales tend, of course, toward the mythic—Coltrane begins around 1957 to shape (or have shaped for him) his identity as a 'seeker.'"[9] That, at least, is where it begins. In his liner notes to *A Love Supreme*, Coltrane writes that, "During the year 1957, I experienced, by the grace of God, a spiritual awakening which was to lead me to a richer, fuller, more productive life." This is an obvious reference to his overcoming of his addictions to alcohol and heroin, which as I've already suggested may have been far less of a dramatic "Damascus Road" kind of conversion than is often assumed by many of his biographers. In a sense, both Hall—in arguing that "all such tales tend . . . toward the mythic"—and Early—in his more cynical view of how Coltrane's regeneration led to his cultural canonization—support my own reading of his struggles with addiction as being not so much mystical as they were work-a-day, yet no less liberating or grace-filled.

In his liner notes Coltrane writes that in response to his spiritual awakening, "I humbly asked to be given the means and privilege to make others happy through music. I feel this has been granted through His grace. ALL PRAISE TO GOD." Several things are worth noting here. Firstly, that he says he asked to be able to make others merely "happy" through his music would seem to reflect a somewhat underdeveloped theology. Secondly, his use of the upper case for this phrase, ALL PRAISE TO GOD, as well as for various other words, phrases, and sentences in these liner notes, do suggest that Coltrane was anything but sophisticated as a writer. Finally, and more positively, that his response to an act of grace is to ask to be enabled to then pass something on to others, and that insofar as that happened it was itself by grace, suggests that at least at an intuitive level he had integrated some things of considerable spiritual and theological depth.

Coltrane also acknowledges that even after his initial awakening he was still vulnerable. "As time and events moved on, a period of irresolution did prevail. I entered into a phase which was contradictory to the pledge and away from the esteemed path."

9. Hall, *Mercy, Mercy Me*, 128.

As I've already suggested, it is entirely likely that this "irresolution" had to do with a marriage increasingly compromised by his infidelities. A quick review of the dates already set out in chapter three is useful here in establishing the end of his "period of irresolution." According to the excerpts from the diaries of "Trane's Lady," it was in November 1963 that Coltrane disclosed to her that he had separated from Naima and was already living with Alice McLeod. The sessions for *A Love Supreme* took place just over a year later, on December 9 and 10, 1964, by which time he and Alice McLeod already had a child together, John William Jr., born on August 26, 1964. A second child, Ravi John, was born on August 6, 1965, a little over two months prior to their October 20, 1965 wedding. If one brackets off that final entry from May, 1966 in the anonymous woman's diary—"We decided to end the affair then and there"—seeing it as her final acceptance that the affair had long been over, then it is quite clear that the "irresolution" was very much tied to his settling down with Alice and beginning a family with her. In fact, even if in 1966 Coltrane did again become briefly involved with the anonymous woman, the basic picture remains. Sometime over the summer and fall of 1963, John Coltrane finally faced down the contradictions in his own life, committed himself to a life shared with Alice McLeod, and rededicated himself to his spiritual path. As he writes in his liner notes to *A Love Supreme*, "thankfully, now and again through the unerring and merciful hand of God, I do perceive and have been duly re-informed of His OMNIPOTENCE, and of our need for, and dependence on Him."

Hall reads in these liner notes what he calls, "A special concern for the individual's flawed nature," observing that, "At some level, Coltrane's grand theme—here and elsewhere—is sin."[10] In an extended section written in upper case letters, Coltrane proclaims, "NO MATTER WHAT . . . IT IS WITH GOD. HE IS GRACIOUS AND MERCIFUL. HIS WAY IS IN LOVE, THROUGH WHICH WE ALL ARE. IT IS TRULY—A LOVE SUPREME—." There is an almost palpable sense of having been forgiven, and of being offered the opportunity of a new or renewed beginning. I have little doubt that this was all tied to the grace he experienced in the establishment of a new relationship and the beginnings of family.

10. Ibid., 136.

In was in the family's home in Dix Hills, Long Island, that *A Love Supreme* evidently had its beginnings. In a 2001 interview with Ashley Kahn, Alice Coltrane offered her own very personal memory of how things unfolded.

> It was late summer, or early fall [of 1964], because the weather was nice at the time in New York. There was an unoccupied area up there where we hardly ever went, sometimes a family member would visit [and] would stay there. John would go up there, take little portions of food every now and then, spending his time pondering over the music he heard within himself.
>
> It was like Moses coming down from the mountain, it was so beautiful. He walked down and there was that joy, that peace in his face, tranquility. So I said, "Tell me everything, we didn't see you really for four or five days . . ." He said, "This is the first time that I have received all of the music for what I want to record, in a suite. This is the first time I have everything, everything ready.[11]

Given that this interview took place more than thirty-five years after the recording of *A Love Supreme*, it is probably wise to read her memories alongside of those of others involved in the project. It is entirely possible that Alice Coltrane's emphasis on "the music he heard within himself" and his having "received all of the music" with "everything ready," is at least in part a reflection both of her own experiences as a composer and of her highly personal spiritual beliefs.

In a 1965 interview, John Coltrane spoke of the dynamic that existed in his classic quartet, stating that, "There is a perfect musical communion between us that doesn't take human values into account. Even in the case of *A Love Supreme*, without discussion, I don't go any further than to set the layout of the work."[12] This description of how the music was created is borne out by McCoy Tyner, in a 2001 interview with Kahn. "In the case of *A Love Supreme*, it was actually songs, but the structure itself was very limited. A simple melody line, and not too stretched out." "We'd been playing together for so long at that point," Tyner continues, "that the band had a sound, so it wasn't like we were stuck in a situation where we were tied down to these chords. In other words, you could

11. Kahn, *A Love Supreme*, xv.
12. Delrome and Lenissois, "Coltrane, Star of Antibes," 246.

do what you wanted, keeping the form in mind. That's what *A Love Supreme* was about."[13] It is also instructive to note that according to Tyner, prior to the recording the quartet had begun to play some of the music from the suite in the clubs. "By the time we got into the studio, we didn't know exactly what was going to happen but we were very familiar with what we felt we had to do. I think that's why John liked to play the songs for a while, open them up. The more familiar you get with it, the more interesting places you can go with the song."[14]

This takes us back to the matter of improvisation, and how chemistry and trust figure so prominently in the creation of this music. As Elvin Jones writes in his forward to Kahn's book, "It was a band that gave me the freedom to explore the music, that invited innovation. We weren't playing by any rules—they weren't there."[15] Yet Jones by no means downplays Coltrane's place as the suite's primary creative—and compositional—force. "John deserves all the recognition—all the credit—for what *A Love Supreme* became. It was his music, his technique, his philosophy of sound, his liner notes."[16]

What emerges is a picture of a visionary artist, bringing to his trusted band the layout of a four-part suite, inspired by his own inner spiritual life. In terms of the suite's overall inspiration, Alice Coltrane's memory of her husband's clarity and peacefulness is surely right. As Tyner points out, there were certainly melodies and what he calls "form," and as will become quite evident when we come to a consideration of "Part 4—Psalm," Coltrane had a very clear and careful plan in mind. Still, parts of the suite were "work-shopped" in the clubs in preparation for the recording, presumably giving the quartet time and space to explore and expand its possibilities.

A Love Supreme consists of four movements or parts: "Acknowledgment," "Resolution," "Pursuance," and "Psalm." There is a definite movement at work here, which Porter characterizes as, "a kind of pilgrim's progress, in which the pilgrim acknowledges the divine, resolves to pursue it, searches, and, eventually, celebrates

13. Kahn, *A Love Supreme*, 92.
14. Ibid., 94.
15. Ibid., ix.
16. Ibid., ix–x.

what has been attained in song."[17] In his biography, John Fraim attempts to track what he calls Coltrane's personal "steps to spiritual enlightenment" with reference to the four parts of the suite. "One could argue that they define the periods in his life after the rebirth experienced in 1957. In 1957 he 'acknowledged' the presence of God and made a 'resolution' to 'pursue' the path which would move him closer to God. Viewed this way, the years after 1957 were years of pursuance of a technique and style, and of fellow travelers along the path to enlightenment." In Fraim's view, it is with the creation of *A Love Supreme* that, "these years of pursuance come to an end [and] the final period of 'psalm' begins."[18]

There are, however, real problems with Fraim's approach. Fraim hangs everything on the 1957 "rebirth experience," completely ignoring Coltrane's own comments about his "period of irresolution." Fraim's picture leaves little room for anything resembling struggle, failure, or suffering in the years after 1957, yet Coltrane is quite clear that he had lived in a way "contradictory to the pledge and away from the esteemed path." As Emmett G. Price III points out, Coltrane actually experienced two spiritual awakenings, one in 1957 and one in 1964, which together, "greatly inspired him to realize the importance of the spiritual ethos and led him to define much of his playing as prayer."[19]

In contrast to interpretations such as Fraim's, James Hall understands Coltrane to be offering anything but a narrative of his own victorious and progressive spiritual enlightenment. Rather he suggests that, "In speaking the language of human limitation—of personal and cultural ruins—Coltrane does participate in a fairly focused challenge to myths of progress and the denial of death. *A Love Supreme* can be experienced as a substantive and even unrelenting jeremiad. He reminds the reader/listener that he has been to the precipice and come back."[20] Quite fully aware of the musician's struggles and "irresolution," Hall wonders if in shaping *A Love Supreme* Coltrane might have been inspired by Howard Thurman's 1963 work, *Disciplines of the Spirit*, "a book organized in a strikingly similar way to Coltrane's suite: 'Commitment, Growing

17. Porter, *John Coltrane*, 232.
18. Fraim, *Spirit Catcher*, 160.
19. Price, "Spiritual Ethos in Black Music," 160.
20. Hall, *Mercy, Mercy Me*, 137.

in Wisdom, Suffering, Prayer, Reconciliation.'"[21] Thurman, after all, was a very influential African-American theologian, educator, and civil rights leader, and his book was in wide circulation at precisely the time Coltrane was beginning his preparations for *A Love Supreme*. And Thurman's view that suffering occurs in the midst of the spiritual life, and that it must be confronted in prayer before there can be any real reconciliation or restoration, would have had strong resonance with the arc of Coltrane's own spiritual path. Further, in my hearing of the suite, struggle and suffering are addressed not in the opening movement, but in the third movement, "Part 3—Pursuance."

"Part 1—Acknowledgement" opens with the sounding of a gong, something entirely unexpected on a jazz recording of the day. Not only does this signal that *A Love Supreme* is not a conventional jazz album, it also stands as a call to prayer. According to Kahn, Alice Coltrane once characterized "Acknowledgement" as a statement that "the doors are opening and the service is beginning,"[22] which is very much in line with the sounding of that gong. Within thirty seconds, a four-note bass line emerges, serving as the movement's mantra-like theme. Coltrane's explorations over the course of "Acknowledgement" are searching, though the bass ostinato is never far from view. As the movement shifts into its closing minute-and-a-half, however, something both quite unexpected and entirely fitting happens; for thirty seconds and in unison with the bass, Coltrane chants the words "a love supreme." Porter's take on the impact of this chanting is perceptive. "He brilliantly executed a reverse development, saving the exposition—or perhaps 'revelation' would be a better word in this case—for the end. He's telling us that God is everywhere—in every register, in every key—and he's showing us that you have to discover religious belief. You can't just hit someone on the head by chanting right at the outset—the listener has to experience the process and then the listener is ready to hear the chant."[23]

The first movement ends with a brief bass solo, which folds more or less seamlessly into the opening of "Part 2—Resolution." This second movement shifts quickly into full gear. A twenty-four

21. Ibid., 141.
22. "Episode 24," *The Traneumentary*.
23. Porter, *John Coltrane*, 242.

bar song with a conventional chorus structure and chord progression, for the entirety of its seven and a half minutes "Resolution" simply swings, accounting for why of all the movements in *A Love Supreme*, this one is the most covered by other musicians. Coltrane's playing has a fiery intensity, and occasionally he soars into those upper registers, where his sax becomes scorching hot. Yet "Resolution" in no way speaks of being in a struggle or of losing sight of the spiritual pathway. It is more a pilgrim's traveling song, executed with a sense that the most important thing is to resolve to keep moving along this path, because the path is really going somewhere.

It is in "Part 3—Pursuance" that I hear things begin to get murky, troubled, perhaps sidetracked. Though at heart "Pursuance" is a twelve-bar blues, it opens with a fairly tempestuous drum solo by Elvin Jones, signaling that a new phase has been entered. Jones batters his kit for a minute and a half, and even as the others enter, the drummer's fury continues for a further twenty-five seconds before settling into a more evenly swinging groove. Until the 4:16 mark, it is McCoy Tyner's piano that drives things forward, with his characteristically powerful left hand building tension until Coltrane enters to take it all up a notch. His solo ranges all over his horn, at times screeching into the highest registers, as if to cry out in agony. At the same time, the fury returns to Jones's drumming, which becomes the lone voice on the track again at 7:16. At 7:46 the reins are turned over to Jimmy Garrison, whose bass solo slows everything down to a kind of deep melancholy. For just under three minutes, he strums chords and explores single note runs up and down his instrument, slowly taking "Pursuance" to its gentle end, at which point it shifts seamlessly into the closing movement.

My real question about "Pursuance" has to do with who is the one in pursuit? In Porter's brief summary, it is the seeker or pilgrim who is in search of the divine, and much the same is true for Fraim in his suggestion that in 1957 Coltrane began "to 'pursue' the path which would move him closer to God." Yet, in his album liner notes, Coltrane seems fairly clear that it was only by grace that he was returned to his spiritual path: "Through the unerring and merciful hand of God, I do perceive and have been duly reinformed of His OMNIPOTENCE, and of our need for, and dependence on Him." The "period of his irresolution" was not something he could bring to an end on his own. Instead, in the midst of that time of wandering lostness, he needed to be pursued by something like the "hound of heaven" of Francis Thompson's 1909 poem of that name—"Ah, fondest, blindest, weakest, / I am He Whom thou seekest!" This is not by any means a painless process, which is what "Pursuance" speaks to in Jones's furious percussion and Coltrane's sometimes screeching work on his horn. To be brought back to what he calls "the righteous path" can be an experience not unlike the refiner's fire and fullers' soap of the prophet Malachi (3:2). I will return to these themes shortly, but it is important first to look briefly at what is worked out in "Part 4—Psalm."

In his liner notes, Coltrane writes that, "the fourth and last part is a musical narration of the theme, 'A Love Supreme' which is written in the context; it is entitled 'PSALM.'" *A Love Supreme* includes not only Coltrane's liner notes, which are framed as a letter to the listener, but also an extended prayer/poem bearing the same title as the record. While in a 1965 CODA magazine review of the album, Doug Pringle did make note of the fact that on "Psalm" Coltrane is actually playing, note for syllable, the text of the poem, it was really not until the publication of Lewis Porter's 1999 Coltrane biography that this was widely recognized. As Porter points out, not only is he playing a musical recitation of the text, "his playing beautifully expresses the meaning of the words—serene on the word 'beautiful,' shouting out 'He always will be.'"[24]

Just as the piece had opened with the unconventional choice of a gong, this closing section finds Jones playing an equally unconventional instrument, the tympani. Along with Garrison and Tyner, Jones works to provide a kind of sonic bed over which Coltrane carefully and meditatively plays his recitation. The text of the prayer is an extended expression of thanks—for peace, for deliverance from fear and weakness, for grace and mercy—punctuated by the repetition of the phrase "Thank you God." Regarding the repetition of this phrase, Porter makes an interesting connection to the black preaching tradition. "These words are associated with a formula characterized by a minor third or fifth descending to the tonic, resembling formulas used by black preachers for such phrases as 'Yes, He did' and 'Oh, Lord.' Coltrane uses this formula

---

24. Ibid., 246.

almost every time the words 'Thank You God' appear."[25] Besides being an act of thanksgiving, the prayer is also a gentle cry for continued help, an affirmation that "all paths lead to God," and a statement of faith that, "God will wash away all our tears." Coltrane readily confesses that, "No road is any easy one, but they all go back to God," and then expands this by writing, "God breathes through us so completely . . . so gently we hardly feel it . . . yet, it is our everything." It is a place of knowing that even at his lowest point, when the road seemed all but impassable, he was not abandoned. With the Psalmist he rhetorically asks, "Where can I go from your spirit? Or where can I flee from your presence?" (Ps 139:7). There is nowhere in which God has not been present, for, "even the darkness is not dark to you; the night is as bright as the day, for darkness is as light to you" (Ps 139:11).

For Kahn, "The feel, the effect that it has is almost like you're peeking in on someone's private prayer session; and it is meant to feel that way."[26] And on this count, he is surely right.

In summary, I hear—and read—*A Love Supreme* in terms of a spiritual path that moves from an opening acknowledgement of the abiding presence of God, through a picture of the steadfast pilgrim seeker striving to walk the road faithfully, to a strong statement of the reality of the seeker's failing. With that admission of failure comes an equally strong statement that the failed seeker has been pursued all along by the very God from whom he has drifted. This experience of being pursued is one of considerable turmoil, fear, and perhaps even suffering, yet once caught by God the realization is made: there is nothing to fear, and there never was. The peace and joy that come through having been caught up in the grace of God are affirmed in the closing movement, with its almost tearful repetition of "thank you God."

This is not a denial of suffering or of the consequences of having strayed far from the path. Contrary to the altogether linear readings offered by John Fraim and Bill Cole, among others—which have Coltrane launching into a heightened spiritual awareness in 1957 and never really stumbling or looking back—Coltrane's own statement is rather more searching and transparent. There is, I believe, a fairly robust spiritual theology at work here, voiced most

25. Ibid., 247.

26. "Episode 24," *The Traneumentary.*

articulately through the music and supplemented by the admittedly less sophisticated written text. It is also one with very real resonance with his deeper roots and identity as a child of the black church and culture.

For rather obvious reasons, the reality of struggle and suffering is anything but ignored in the tradition of the spirituals. They come out of the slave church, and are given further shape in light of the violence and racism of the Jim Crow south. W. E. B. Du Bois calls them the "Sorrow Songs," and includes titles such as "Nobody Knows the Trouble I've Seen" and "My Way's Cloudy" in his list of "ten master songs," all of which, "tell in word and music of trouble and exile, of strife and hiding; they grope toward some unseen power and sigh for the rest of the End."[27] In this tradition, if occasionally God might allow suffering in order to test, strengthen, or discipline his people, there is little doubt that the only source of evil is the devil. And though it is not set out explicitly, it is assumed that all too often this devil has a white face.

Similarly, in the blues suffering is anything but denied. As I outlined in chapter one, it is the view of Jon Michael Spencer that suffering was understood by many of the blues men and women as being God's punishment for their having strayed far from the faith of the church. In this tradition, too, the devil is likely to have a white face, but what the unrepentant blues singer suffers is still very much of his or her own making. Further, Spencer points to a corresponding tradition of seeing the repentant blues musician as being the returning prodigal son or daughter, who having confessed his or her sin has been received home by grace.[28]

It is not out of line to read Coltrane's own life narrative in light of these traditions in black culture and music. In 1957, he confronted the self-destructive character of his addictions, and with the support of his wife returned to the home of his mother to set himself straight. Even avoiding the more melodramatic readings of these events, it is clear that he confronted his addictions with a kind of stubborn determination, in the midst of which he was awakened to the presence and grace of God. This first great "spiritual awakening" seems to have been both healing and hope-filled, and there is no indication that he was again seriously troubled

27. Du Bois, *Souls of Black Folks*, 247.
28. Spencer, *Blues and Evil*, 77–81.

by alcohol or heroin. Yet, by his own admission he fell from "the esteemed path," and so like the repentant prodigal blues singer, he again places himself at the mercy of the One from whom he'd strayed. In this case, there would have been a painful confrontation with the hurt he'd caused both Naima and his step-daughter Saeeda, and with the damage he'd done to the integrity of his own self. To his surprise, as he made his turn he discovered that he had not been abandoned by God at all; he was met by the "love supreme," which had been pursuing him all along. Not incidentally, part of the grace with which he was met was embodied in the person of Alice McLeod, with whom he would go on to create a very new and very different kind of marriage and life.

This second spiritual awakening seems a purifying one, in a way that his experience of 1957 had not been. Judging from what he says in a 1964 letter to *Down Beat* magazine's editor Don DeMicheal—"He said he'd lost God before and had just now found God again"[29]—Coltrane moved into a period of his life in which he was able to embrace God's transforming grace in a way that he'd been unwilling or unable to do in the late 1950s. In *The Blackwell Guide to Theology and Popular Culture,* Kelton Cobb turns to a distinction made by William James in his 1902 classic *The Varieties of Religious Experience,* as a way of thinking about the ways in which faith is lived and practiced. James works with the categories of "once-born healthy-minded souls" and "twice-born sick souls," and one might assume that in his use of the terms "healthy-minded" and "sick" James is indicating that he sees the former as a better path than the latter. As summarized by Cobb, the once-born "embrace the world into which they were born, and persist in their belief that the God who oversees it is trustworthy."[30] Notable examples offered are Walt Whitman and Ralph Waldo Emerson, along with the liberal Christianity of his day. Of James's category of the "twice-born sick soul," Cobb offers the following: "Sadness, dread, despair, and melancholy overtake the sick soul. But what impressed James was the testimony of those who, like Leo Tolstoy and John Bunyan, had transcended these dark nights of the soul and, without denying the reality of the causes of their despair, had found a way to reaffirm their faith. James calls those who have undergone such anguish

29. J. C. Thomas, *Chasin' the Trane,* 182.
30. Cobb, *Blackwell Guide to Theology and Popular Culture,* 15.

and come out the other side, confident of the goodness of existence and the meaningfulness of life, 'the twice-born.'"[31] It is precisely this kind of faith that I hear informing *A Love Supreme*, as well as *Meditations*, "Attaining," and other material from Coltrane's later period. It is "a faith sobered by the awful grace of God,"[32] which brings a famous musician to his knees uttering the three-fold "ELATION—ELEGANCE—EXALTATON—All from God" in his prayer/poem.

Probably no modern theologian has written so starkly and so personally about suffering and the "awful grace of God" as Dorothee Soelle. Soelle claims that she came to these concerns very young, and that as an adolescent she recognized a deep desire to know more about Jesus, "the tortured one who did not become a nihilist."[33] Significantly, for Soelle there is a direct link between suffering and love: "It is not God who makes us suffer. But love has its price."[34] Yet, it was in the midst of living into such a love that she encountered the potential depths of its price, when without any warning her husband left their marriage. The collapse of the marriage was for her very much a death. "For me the experience of dying had the effect of tearing to shreds a whole design of life. Everything I had built and hoped for, believed and wanted, had been dashed to pieces. It was as though one who was very, very dear to me had been taken away by death."[35] Yet for Soelle, this death was marked by something almost worse than grief, and so she writes, "One cannot escape the sense of guilt, of having forgotten or failed to do something, of having made a dreadful mistake that could not be soothed and calmed by some kind of belief in fate."[36] She writes of her three years of being wracked by grief, guilt, and even suicidal thoughts, until finally coming to a place of being able to make a strange kind of peace within herself. Her own peace came ultimately by making peace with her God. She writes of being recalled to the biblical statement, "My grace is sufficient for you" (2 Cor 12:9), but also of discovering that in some very real sense the death of her marriage had become a most painful occasion

31. Ibid., 15–16.
32. Ibid., 22.
33. Soelle, *Memoir of a Radical Christian*, 12.
34. Soelle, "The Cross," 109.
35. Soelle, *Death by Bread Alone*, 31.
36. Ibid.

of grace. And she is not entirely prepared to let God off the hook for his role in this death. "He slapped me in the face, knocked me to the ground," she writes. "That was not the kind of death I had wanted. It was an entirely different kind of death. Gradually it began to dawn on me that people who believe limp somewhat, as Jacob limped after wrestling with God on the shore of the Jabbok. All of them have died at one time or another."[37] Soelle's spiritual awakening—or is it a resurrection?—is made possible through the dark night of the soul that was the death of her marriage. On the other side of her own Jabbok, in a manner not unlike that of John Coltrane, she realizes that she has been pursued all along by the God who is willing to take her to the ground and wound her for the sake of bringing her home. It is a troubling picture in many respects, if we take her to mean that God dealt a death blow to the Soelle marriage in order that she be spiritually tested and seasoned. She herself is somewhat agnostic on the matter, and willing to live with that sense of unknowing. As surely as she writes, "What I do know is that pain is a part of life because pain is a part of love," without any hesitation she adds a most startling and bold statement: "I do not wish to have a God free of pain, for I could not trust such a God."[38] Like Coltrane, she is one of James's "twice-born," able to come through soul-sickness and an almost unbearable anguish into a place of foundational trust.

Though often treated as the high point or even the end point of Coltrane's work, it is probably best to see *A Love Supreme* as both a pivotal step in his musical explorations and as a resting place—a moment of blessing—along his road. Over the years that followed the creation of *A Love Supreme*, Coltrane's sound became increasingly free and searching, with many people taking note of the intense determination with which he seemed to be playing. Coltrane himself spoke of his need to "just get *it* out,"[39] and of, "going all the way, as deep as you can . . . right down to the crux."[40] As Michael Bruce McDonald observes, in the prayer/poem "A Love Supreme" Coltrane keeps returning to a basic assertion that, "No matter what . . . it is God." For McDonald, "This 'no matter

37. Ibid., 33.

38. Soelle, *Memoir of a Radical Christian*, 77.

39. Ratliff, *Coltrane*, 170.

40. Liner notes to *Live at the Village Vanguard Again!*

what' very precisely addresses the reasons that divinity *cannot* be delimited by the concerns of harmony alone, the reasons that the divine must necessarily include the dissonant."[41] The search was to continue, and it would take him into a place of facing that divine dissonance, finding in it the very grace—the awful grace—he'd discovered in being pursued by God. His search would take him into some very rich theological and musical territory, but also down at least a couple of blind alleys. That, too, is part of the risk.

For the most part, *A Love Supreme* was left to stand on its own, as a singular recorded statement. It was performed and recorded live in its entirety on only one occasion, in July of 1965 at the Festival Mondial du Jazz Antibes in France. Released in 2002 as part of the Deluxe Edition of *A Love Supreme*, this is a considerably longer and freer version than the original, and is marked by the notable absence of both the opening gong and Coltrane's spoken word chant. Also on the Deluxe Edition are alternative takes of both "Acknowledgment" and "Resolution," recorded on December 10, 1964 and incorporating two additional musicians: Art Davis on bass, and Archie Shepp on tenor saxophone. Again, the spoken chant is absent, and on the whole the feel is less focused and reflective. It would seem that the quartet's version from December 9, 1964 would ultimately stand alone. Perhaps the one live performance that might have caught the reflective and prayerful nature of the suite was offered on April 24, 1966 at a concert held at St. Gregory's School Hall in Brooklyn. Organized by the musician Cal Massey as a way to raise funds for a neighborhood playground, the quartet of John and Alice Coltrane, Elvin Jones, and Jimmy Garrison performed a version of "Acknowledgement" that day, during the course of which Coltrane read his prayer/poem in its entirety. No recording of the concert was made, so only the three hundred people who were in attendance will ever know how it sounded. However, according to Massey the reading elicited a tremendous positive response, with the audience chanting "a love supreme" as Coltrane read.[42] Sixteen months later, Cal Massey would read that same prayer aloud at John Coltrane's funeral.

41. McDonald, "Traning the Nineties," 278.

42. Kahn, *A Love Supreme*, 191.

8

"Ascension"

On Improvisation, part 2

> This is possibly the most powerful human sound ever recorded.
>
> —Bill Mathieu, *Down Beat*

> To begin at the beginning, a caveat for the casual listener. Be advised that this record cannot be loved or understood in one sitting . . . it's like Wagner—it begins on a plane at which most performances end and builds to a higher plane than the average listener considers comfortable.
>
> —A. B. Spellman, liner notes to *Ascension*

> [Coltrane's] latter day religiosity, exemplified in turgid suites such as *A Love Supreme* and *Ascension* that set up pretension as a way of life; that willful and hideous distortion of tone that offered squeals, squeaks, Bronx cheers and throttled slate-pencil noises for serious consideration—all this, and more, ensure that, for me at any rate, when Coltrane's records go back on the shelf they will stay there.
>
> —Philip Larkin

While John Coltrane would press the boundaries of music even further on some of his later work, no other recording demanded of his audience an answer to the question, "are you prepared to go with me *this* far?" Even more significantly, *Ascension* effectively asked that same question of the three other members of his quartet. On June 28, 1965, with an additional seven musicians augmenting the established and seasoned quartet, two takes of the intense and unrelenting forty-minute piece were recorded. Between the two, Coltrane evidently looked to his tired drummer and asked if he was prepared to record that second take. Though Elvin Jones did agree, when it was finished he apparently threw his snare drum at the studio wall, effectively announcing that this recording date was done. Six months later Jones left the band.

As A. B. Spellman writes in the liner notes, "it is not intended that *Ascension* will be background music for polite dinner conversation," and as I describe in chapter nine of this book, my first attempt at listening to the album was aborted after all of ten minutes. Then again, as Jimmy Greene said to me, aside from an album like *Ballads*, "You have to pay attention to Coltrane's records; you can't just have that music playing and have a conversation."[1] Coltrane's music consistently requires the listener to really pay attention; otherwise it does become distracting or even irritating. For *Ascension* to make any sense at all, the listener has to really attend to it, and as I discovered even that won't be enough if you've not acquired some capacity to hear what is going on.

In an age where we have become increasingly "consumers" of music, Don Saliers fears that we too easily "think that hearing is something quite passive."[2] We need only press a button or flick a switch, and we're provided a background soundtrack to whatever we might happen to be doing. The radio and record player gave way first to sophisticated home and car stereos, and then to the iPod and its various imitators. Digital downloads brought easy access not only to full albums, but also to the individual tracks, meaning that for many people the personalized "playlist"—or even the random shuffle—has eclipsed the album as the preferred way to organize music. Combine this with the availability of satellite radio and of twenty-four hour streaming music stations on both television and online, and for most consumers of music, the very idea of buying and then really *listening* to an album is all but obsolete.

This makes finding a way in to a recording such as *Ascension* all the more daunting. The music critic Gary Giddens recalls that when it was first released the *Ascension* record was given very focused attention in many of the college dorms of the day. Giddens recalls

1. Greene, personal interview.
2. Saliers, *Music and Theology*, 67.

groups of students gathering to listen by the hour to records both old and new, choosing very carefully which records to play, and in what order. Echoing the sentiments of Saliers, Giddens concludes, "That kind of deeper listening experience has disappeared."[3]

In order to be able to hear a record such as *Ascension*, (or even to do justice to more accessible projects such as *A Love Supreme*) we need to do some of that "deeper listening," or to develop what Saliers calls "listening practices." "Because music has power to speak and to reveal more than the mere organization of sound, we ask: what can music require and even demand of us as hearers?"[4] And this, I think, is a particularly important question for a piece such as "Ascension," in which many first-time listeners will not hear even that "mere organization of sound," but instead something closer to random, cacophonous noise.

So my advice would be that if you have never actually listened to *Ascension*, now would be a good time to put this book down and go find a recording. And I'd actually suggest that you *not* download it, because in doing that you would be missing out on the packaging with its evocative cover and Spellman's liner notes. You really do need to read Spellman's comments prior to launching into a deep listening of the album, as they provide a very helpful set of entry points into what you will be attempting to hear. Chances are that the copy of *Ascension* you lay your hands on will include both of the takes from that day in the studio, and the one you should listen to is "Edition II" as that was Coltrane's preferred take. This is where Spellman's notes do hit a bit of a glitch, in that the version that Impulse Records originally released was the day's first take, and so that was the one Spellman had in hand when he was writing his notes. It doesn't really change the force of his text, though it does mean that the sequence of soloists he lists does not line up with Edition II. It was only after the album was pressed and in circulation that Coltrane realized the mistake and notified his record label. Impulse quickly ran another pressing, and from that point on all of the vinyl versions were of Edition II. For the sake of clarity—and to give a bit of help to giving it a deeper listening—the order of soloists on Edition II is John Coltrane (tenor), Dewey Johnson (trumpet), Pharoah Sanders (tenor), Freddie Hubbard (trumpet),

3. Kahn, *The House that Trane Built*, 137.
4. Saliers, *Music and Theology*, 67.

Marion Brown (alto), Archie Shepp (tenor), John Tchicai (alto), Mc-Coy Tyner (piano), Art Davis and Jimmy Garrison (basses). I'd tell you to put on the album, and then sit back and relax . . . but when it comes to *Ascension* the "relax" part is really not the point. Even if you do know the album, it wouldn't be such a bad thing to give it another listening. And in the interest of fairness, that is precisely what I am going to do before writing another word.

Some of you may now be resenting the fact that I had you spend good money on such a thing, while others might be ready to dig in for a second listen. There might even be a few wondering what all the fuss was about. Had I launched you in at about the thirty-minute mark, what you would have heard was McCoy Tyner's very fine, thoroughly accessible piano solo, set against the hard-driving rhythm section of Elvin Jones and the two bass players. You could even tap your foot in time at that point. Tyner's section transitions into a two-and-a-half-minute duet by the two bass players, which is downright subdued, even if it is not entirely what one thinks of as jazz. Depending on who is playing, even the solo sections by the various trumpet and sax players can be quite accessible. I'm thinking here of the section featuring the trumpeter Freddie Hubbard, which begins shortly after the fifteen-and-a-half-minute mark. Then again, Hubbard's section is bookended by those of Pharoah Sanders and Marion Brown, neither of whom play anything that could be labeled as "accessible," and that may be part of the reason Hubbard sounds so very fine . . . or so very tame, depending on your perspective.

And perspective does have a lot to do with how it is heard. In what appears to be the only interview in which Coltrane discusses the *Ascension* album, Frank Kofsky calls it "a beautiful record," adding that it is "probably the one record I've had to listen to the most number of times to get everything that is on it."[5] Kofsky is a politically radical writer, quite deeply committed to what he understands to be the social and political significance of free jazz and the avant-garde. Given how enthused his interviewer is about the recording, it is interesting to read that Coltrane laughed and commented that he was "so doggone busy" and "worried to death" that he "couldn't really enjoy the date."[6]

---

5. Kofsky, "Interview with John Coltrane," 285.
6. Ibid.

Given how unsuccessful I was in my first attempt at listening to *Ascension*, I find it fascinating to now be able to hear how carefully structured the piece really is. Basically, it begins with an opening statement that quickly moves into a full group improvisation, and then for the next thirty minutes it alternates between two to three minute solo sections and the slightly shorter group improvisations. These group improvisation sections are in free time, while the solo sections generally have a fairly steady beat that then folds back into the free sections. As Marion Brown offers in the liner notes, "Spontaneity was the thing. Trane had obviously thought a lot about what he wanted to do, but he wrote most of it out in the studio. Then he told everybody what he wanted: he played this line and he said that everybody would play that line in the ensembles. Then he said he wanted *crescendi* and *decrescendi* after every solo. We ran through some things together, and then we got into it." So yes, spontaneity might well have been "the thing," but it was a spontaneity made possible by the structure that Coltrane had clearly thought through. To revisit the insights of Jeremy Begbie outlined in chapter one and revisited in chapter four, we are again dealing with the relationship of improvisation to a set of constraints, even if in Begbie's view a piece such as "Ascension" isn't even close to being sufficiently constrained. And yes, in the studio that day the constraints were rather loose, as is clear from Archie Shepp's remarks in the album liner notes, regarding the way in which the piece was set up. "The ensemble passages were based on chords, but these chords were optional. What Trane did was to relate or juxtapose tonally centered ideas and atonal elements, along with melodic and non-melodic elements. In those descending chords there is a definite tonal center, like a B flat minor. But there are different roads to that center." Optional chords, and different roads to the center . . . that pretty much sums up what it is that gives the piece its free blowing anything-is-possible quality, in spite of the fact that it is neither unstructured nor nearly so chaotic and cacophonous as I had once believed.

But let me to return to that picture of Elvin Jones throwing his snare drum against the wall. There were probably a number of things at work at that moment, not the least of which would have been his sheer physical exhaustion. And because Jones was known to have had a sometimes fiery and even volatile temperament, it wouldn't have been an altogether surprising way for him to definitively state that that he was all done for the day. Yet, the fact that he was just six months away from permanently leaving the band does suggest that there was more to it than just his exhaustion. As Coltrane's experiments in expanding the group progressed, one of the complaints voiced by both Jones and McCoy Tyner was that they could no longer hear themselves play. For Jones, this would become particularly acute when Coltrane added Rashied Ali as a second drummer. Though he is the lone drummer on the *Ascension* album, Jones was certainly pressed to play extremely hard to be heard through the high volume generated by the five saxophones and two trumpets. Yet it wasn't just the issue of volume that pressed on both Jones and Tyner, it was also Coltrane's movement away from building his music around a steady beat. As Lewis Porter sums it up, "Despite their innovations, they were not 'free jazz' players."[7]

Which raises one more very important issue. For musicians of the caliber and experience of McCoy Tyner and Elvin Jones, some of the players who were called on to record on projects like *Ascension* simply would not have measured up. In a 1977 interview, the trombone player Curtis Fuller—who had played on the 1958 sessions for *Blue Train*—spoke of what was informing Coltrane at this stage of his explorations:

> Coltrane had a lot of young musicians playing with him at the time *Ascension* was recorded. One reason was because of his kindness, another reason was the music had reached this particular level at this time. But Coltrane did not call anything too difficult for them to play. It was a series of sounds he wanted or a series of 'avant-garde' sounds. He knew their task was not difficult. He also knew he could embarrass them if he wanted to, but this was not the way Coltrane worked. Therefore, you must consider that a lot of these young musicians never jammed on tunes like "Lazy Bird."[8]

Drawn increasingly to explorations in sound, Coltrane quite willingly made room for these players who were *all* about sound, even if they were not able to play at the level of the classic quartet. Which is why, of course, it signaled the end of the quartet.

Though Fuller's reference to Coltrane's "kindness" might make it sound as if he was basically too nice to say no to these players, there

7. Porter, *John Coltrane*, 266.
8. Grey, *Acknowledgment*, 99–100.

is something significant signaled by that comment. One reading of the move to incorporate these younger and less seasoned players is offered by Ekkehard Jost in *Free Jazz,* where he suggests that whether or not he was fully aware of it, Coltrane was effectively taking a stand. "Coltrane declared his loyalty to a new generation of free-jazz musicians, for whom he had already become a kind of father figure in the mid-Sixties. His backing of musicians like Archie Shepp and Pharoah Sanders (he helped them get jobs and recording dates) gives the collective improvisations in *Ascension* a social import."[9] More than simply giving the project a "social import," it may be that Coltrane was drawing deeply on the tradition in which he had been formed. In his article "You Have to Be Invited," Leonard Brown offers a reflection on how music was learned and passed on in the cultural world in which Coltrane was raised. Focusing on the blues and jazz—which he characterizes as being "created by black musicians to meet the needs of their people and community"—Brown writes that, "These were oral and aural traditions passed on through mentoring and apprenticeship. Consequently, the musicians had the responsibility of determining to whom, when, and where this knowledge would be passed. There were no 'jazz studies' programs at this time. The musicians were the keepers of musical knowledge and controlled its dissemination."[10] As the title of Brown's essay suggests, the aspiring musician had to pay his or her dues in what he calls the "conservatory of the community," exhibiting not only a strong ability to play, but also a readiness to be both immersed in the tradition and to do the hard work it would take to become a part of that tradition. As Brown describes the process of a young musician being drawn into the living tradition, he emphasizes the centrality of the aspiring player's *feeling,* of the "sincerity and conviction of the sound."[11]

Something Brown doesn't really deal with in his brief essay is just how ruthlessly demanding this paying of dues could be, particularly at the point that an aspiring musician took the great risk of attempting to become a recognized member of the scene. For an unknown or untested musician to walk into a club with an instrument or to ask to sit in on the drums or piano was to declare that

9. Jost, *Free Jazz,* 96.
10. Brown, "You Have to Be Invited," 4.
11. Ibid., 6–7.

he or she was ready to be tested; something the established players were not at all shy to oblige. If a musician could pass muster and impress both the band and the audience, there would be a place on the bandstand another night. If not, it meant heading back to the endless listening and practicing and struggling to measure up.

And then there were the famous "cutting sessions," which were the jazz musicians' version of the African-American tradition of verbal sparring referred to as "playing the dozens." As was true of "the dozens," cutting sessions could be ruthless. "This musical action on the New York battlefield was the cutting session, and the expression was an appropriate one. When a musician picked up his instrument, his intention was to outperform the other man. No quarter was given or expected, and the wound to a musician's ego and reputation could be as deep as a cut."[12] In other words, this jazz world was not always an easy or kind one to navigate.

In his taking such a deep interest in younger and increasingly less conventional players, Coltrane appears to be both standing very much within the tradition, yet at the same time disregarding it. He was very interested in drawing in these younger players and supporting their work, but he was also quite prepared to learn from what they were doing and how they were playing, and he said as much on several occasions. Brown's "conservatory of the community" takes on the shape of a cooperative or artists' collective, with the master now prepared to sit right alongside the students. This is vividly demonstrated on *Ascension*, for while Coltrane did set the parameters and determine the shape of the recording, each musician was given a solo of similar duration and all were invited to participate in the creation of the whole. With his reputation for marathon solos of upward of forty and forty-five minutes, it is particularly significant that on this project Coltrane restricts himself to a single solo of just over two and a half minutes.

And while he did invite the various participants, in at least one case that invitation evidently took place by sheer coincidence. On the day that Coltrane called Archie Shepp with his invitation, the alto player Marion Brown happened to be visiting at Shepp's home.

12. Stewart, "The Cutting Sessions," 387. According to the veteran bass player Bill Crow, while some musicians were fiercely competitive, most of the musicians saw it all as being more of a friendly competition. "The cutting sessions were like 'I can jump over this stick,' you know? 'Can you jump over this stick? Let's put this stick a little higher.'" From a personal interview with Bill Crow.

After accepting the invitation to be a part of the recording, Shepp suggested that Coltrane might want to speak with Brown, and after a brief conversation he too was invited to come on board.[13]

Coltrane took a lot of heat for what was sometimes perceived as his uncritical acceptance of these younger players, these "avant-garde army ants," as Stanley Crouch deemed them.[14] Many fans and critics just could not understand why he insisted on not only making room for musicians such as Sanders, Shepp, and Brown, but also letting his own sound be influenced by them. That same sentiment may well be part of what launched Elvin Jones's snare drum against the studio wall that day.

Tommy Lott hears Coltrane's experiments with such an egalitarian and open approach as being rooted in a different place in the African-American music tradition. Lott quotes at length from Zora Neale Hurston's *The Sanctified Church*, and the entire quotation bears repeating here:

> To begin with, Negro spirituals are not solo or quartette material. The jagged harmony is what makes it, and it ceases to be what it was when this is absent. Neither can any group be trained to reproduce it. Its truth dies under training like flowers under hot water. The harmony of the true spiritual is not regular. The dissonances are important and not to be ironed out by the trained musician. The various parts break in at any old time. Falsetto often takes the place of regular voices for short periods. Keys change. Moreover, each singing of the piece is a new creation. The congregation is bound by no rules. No two times singing is alike, so that we must consider the rendition of a song not as a final thing, but as a mood. It won't be the same thing next Sunday.
>
> *Negro songs to be heard truly must be sung by a group, and a group bent on expression of feelings and not on sound effects.*[15]

What Lott is inviting us to pick up on are the references to things like jagged harmony, the importance of dissonance and changing keys, the music's death under training, and the idea that each rendition of a given piece is a new creation. In this sense, on an album such as *Ascension* it is possible to listen as Coltrane gathers his flock

13. Cole, *John Coltrane*, 168.

14. Burns, Interview transcripts for *Ken Burns' Jazz*.

15. Lott, "When Bar Walkers Preach," 107.

into the prayer meeting and invites everyone present to simply go where the Spirit is taking them. He might be the preacher, but this is a church in which the Spirit moves where it will, and that means that anyone and everyone is liable to be caught up and shaken to life. Everyone's voice is needed to keep singing this song.

Here collective group improvisation can be seen as an image of the church at worship, or at least of one manifestation of the church engaged in its particular practice of worship. In this model, what is valued is the way in which the diverse and even disparate voices are drawn together in surprising ways to give voice to what the Spirit is doing—and always threatening to do—in their collective midst. Although Coltrane would have bumped up against this way of being church during his childhood and adolescence in the South, it is not the church in which he was formed. The church of his grandfather would have had an ordered, even practiced, way of being together at worship, with more clearly defined roles of leadership and accountability, and an approach to music more attuned to a well-established set of constraints. Not that the music wouldn't have really swung, or that the preacher wouldn't have cut loose in a dynamic call and response with his congregation. Those would have been very much a part of the experience at St Stephen's African Methodist Episcopal Zion Church. Further, openness to the movement of the Holy Spirit in the singing and preaching would have been assumed, as would the near presence of Jesus as the one to whom faithful discipleship was commanded. And while every member of that church would have been expected to participate in its shared life and ministry, the preachers, elders, prayer leaders, and musicians would have needed to be called or invited to take up those ministries.

This model of the church is much more closely reflected in the work of the classic quartet than it is in a project such as *Ascension*. In that quartet there were four very gifted musicians, all of whom had been called out and recognized by the jazz community as having those gifts. Over the course of several years, the four played together countless times, reaching a collaborative level where they hardly even needed to look at the other to know what each was going to offer into the mix. That level of familiarity and group cohesion is built on—and in turn builds—deep relationship, respect, and trust. Speaking of a not dissimilar experience playing with the Wayne Shorter Quartet, the bassist John Patitucci offered the following reflections:

> With Wayne I'd have to say that in all my life, because of the way that God has blessed that group of people, that's the closest I've ever felt to feeling the divine power of God. In the Wayne Shorter Quartet, you're dealing with people who are all composers and who are also, because of the way Wayne likes to do things, group-oriented as opposed to just individually driven. And we take chances, completely. We start from nothing and improvise music that is tonal, lyrical, and contrapuntal. And then anybody can cue one of Wayne's pieces, and we go in. You'll start from nothing and think "Wow, I don't really have anything tonight," and somebody will do something and you'll think, "wait a minute." And then it's a big journey. I call it the ultimate microcosm of what Christian community would be if people would just be willing to take chances, and get out of the comfort zone and be that other-oriented. I'm speaking of myself too. It is easy for me to do it on the bandstand somehow. Sometimes you're playing and all these things are happening, and you're like "Well, that's God." The "other," meaning the other musicians, but then it spills right into the audience. The spiritual part of it is so thick with that group. That's why I think it has been ten years now. It's been very well received because people are touched by it.[16]

The same day that I interviewed John Patitucci, I had the opportunity to speak with McCoy Tyner about his own experiences as a musician, both in the quartet and during his long tenure as a one of the most influential jazz pianists of the past fifty years. I related to him some of Patitucci's reflections about group improvisation, and specifically how relationships and trust can open the way to experiencing something profound. Without hesitation, Tyner replied, "Tell John that he is right," and then added, "that is a *very* spiritual experience." He then commented that such an experience really is only possible when playing with a regular group, with people you have come to know at a deep level.[17]

In his reflections on his years with Shorter's quartet—"The most trust I've ever experienced. That's a family, a total family"—Patitucci essentially says that intuitively the quartet *knows*

16. Patitucci, personal interview.
17. Tyner, telephone interview.

something that church communities could stand to learn. Such learning would require a willingness to risk moving out of individualistic self-orientation in order to be reoriented toward the other. And as he says, the "other" is not merely the other members of the band—the church community, so to speak—because this other-orientation also "spills right into the audience," or into the neighborhood in which that church community is practicing its risky life. It becomes at this point a picture of an organic engagement with those who, from the edges, have caught a glimpse of something, and can say only, "Look, how those Christians love one another."[18]

Yet Patitucci is also clear that this is not a formulaic approach for either the making of jazz or for the making of a Christian community. There is not a particular set of packaged techniques at work here, but rather a group of people who have been drawn together and who have learned first to *be* together. "The whole idea of the other-orientation and of the compositional component is that you have to compose together, in the moment, and make stuff happen. Or more correctly, *allow* stuff to happen. Share in it, but sometimes you just have to wait."[19] In our conversation, Patitucci also emphasized that part of what makes the Wayne Shorter Quartet able to do what it does is that as a collaborative unit it has deep roots in the history and tradition of jazz. "We're not just playing this very improvised music without any connection to the history. It is deeply rooted; it goes back far."

The elements that John Patitucci identified in our conversation have serious resonance with Samuel Wells' theological reflections on improvisational theater, and how its practices and insights might shape those of the church. Just as through his experiences playing in the context of the Wayne Shorter Quartet, Patitucci has been drawn to look again at how the church is going about its life, so too Wells has been challenged by the practice of improvisation in theater to imagine how the church might be thinking and practicing its faith. Writing of how theatrical improvisation is a practice that both demands and cultivates the courage and trust needed "to embody its tradition in new and often challenging circumstances," Wells makes the point that "this is exactly

18. From Tertullian, *Apologeticum* ch. 39, 7.
19. Patitucci, personal interview.

what the church is called to do."[20] And in writing of what he calls "reincorporation" he offers an insight of particular significance to my reflections in this chapter. Wells writes, "When elements found earlier in the story begin to be reincorporated, then some pattern emerges and a sense of completion is possible." He continues, "The key factor in reincorporation is memory. Memory is much more significant than originality. The improviser does not set out to create the future, but responds to the past, reincorporating it to form a story."[21] And by paying attention to how this works in theater, the church is invited to consider the call to recapitulate its deepest traditions in new and invigorating ways, meaning that, "Free from the paralysis of being original, the pressure to be clever, the fear of the unconscious, and the demand to be solemn, the church can faithfully follow its Lord by improvising . . ."[22]

This is an image of the church as a practiced and disciplined, yet intensely creative and open community, and one no less led by the Holy Spirit than the "sanctified church" of which Hurston wrote. Its life is built for the long haul, and is based on the cultivation of relationships of trust and intimacy, and rooted in *practice* of memory. And memory practiced is a story ever renewing. It is much closer to the classic John Coltrane Quartet finding yet another way to offer "My Favorite Things" than it is to an assembly of eleven musicians launching into the recording that was to become *Ascension*.

That is not to say that *Ascension* is therefore to be dismissed or degraded as a second rate album. It is just that it is doing a different sort of work, speaking something different to the church, maybe even in a different tongue. The wildly free incorporation of players of such differing abilities and sensibilities into a single project in which all are released to participate as equal contributors and creators . . . that too is a potent challenge, and particularly to tightly organized, even buttoned-down churches. Yet that ensemble lasted for just one recording session, while the classic quartet was vitally creative for several years, and the Wayne Shorter Quartet has now moved into its second decade as a unit. While this large format collective certainly made a statement that needed to be heard—and

20. Wells, *Improvisation*, 12.
21. Ibid., 147.
22. Ibid., 68.

one that Coltrane felt he needed to make—the "charismatic" innovation that was the *Ascension* album couldn't last. It is the classic quartet that teaches us something about the shape of the Christian community over the long haul.

I would be remiss to not offer some reflection on the title of this piece, though here I am afraid that I will be working entirely on my own. Not only do the liner notes skip past making any reference to the spiritual and religious significance of the word "ascension," it would appear that Coltrane himself never addressed the meaning of the piece, either in his own writing or with an interviewer. It is almost impossible to think that he selected this title without reference to the story of the ascension of Christ, as told in Acts 1:6–11. I say it is *almost* impossible, and that is partly on account of the other recordings he made shortly before or shortly after the *Ascension* sessions. In the weeks leading up to those June 28, 1965 sessions there was a session on May 26 which included a series of takes of "Dear Lord," one on June 10 which included "Suite" (a twenty-one-minute suite built around the "hours" of prayer that anchor many religious traditions), and finally one on June 16 which included "Vigil," also a word associated with community prayer. After June 28, the next session was on August 26, and it included "Dearly Beloved," "Ascent," and "Amen," while September 2 was the date of the recordings for what would later be released as *First Meditations*. Religious concerns were clearly on Coltrane's mind over these months, and he seemed rather prone to using titles with Christian points of reference. And then there is the piece itself.

More than just a wide-ranging experiment in large ensemble improvisation, something in the raw power of *Ascension* connects it with the story and theological force of the ascension of Christ. Although the Ascension of the Lord is a major feast day in the liturgical calendar, it certainly doesn't have near the profile of Christmas or Easter. At least in North America, the churches that do mark it as a liturgical feast day will likely draw only smallish congregations, and it will be all but invisible in the society outside of those church walls. That is partly because it always falls on a Thursday, which is not typically a day for going to church in our generally pluralistic and secularized society, but I suspect it also has something to do with our modest embarrassment around the story we tell that day. As recorded in the Acts of the Apostles, it is the fortieth day after Easter Day, and having promised his followers that they would soon receive the Holy Spirit, the resurrected Jesus "was lifted up, and a cloud took him out of their sight." (Acts 1:9b). That works very well within a pre-modern cosmology, but now that we know that the earth is a spinning globe and that "up" is really only relative to the vastness of space, what do we do with such an image? This is precisely the objection of the modern liberal, classically voiced by John A. T. Robinson in his popular book from the mid–1960s, *But That I Can't Believe*. While Robinson does get some things very right in his reflections on the deeper meaning of the doctrine of the Ascension, he gets there by way of what seems an attempt to almost embarrass the gathered church out of ever reading the story aloud. "[T]here would be many an intelligent Christian who would be shocked if you said that 'he ascended into heaven' was not a literal statement. This only shows how lazy much of our thinking is. Indeed, I suspect many of us, if we were honest, try to have it both ways, and suppose that Jesus did literally go up in front of his disciples' eyes but that directly he got out of sight it somehow ceased to be a physical event at all and the thing was called off!"[23] I believe, however, that given his roots in the black church and his almost wildly poetic imagination, John Coltrane would not have had any such difficulty reading the story. Not that he would have assumed the worldview of first-century Judea. He was interested in the writings of Albert Einstein, as well as in both astronomy and astrology, and so would have harbored no "flat earth" delusions. But he also would not have shied away from what the narrative from the Acts of the Apostles was attempting to articulate, nor from the lessons he learned in the church of his grandfather. At least at a poetic and intuitive level, he would have known that this belief in Christ's ascension is not about a set of upward directions for getting to heaven, but rather it is about the presence of Christ with the Father in the kingdom of heaven . . . an entirely different matter. And to be fair, it is one more in keeping with what John Robinson suggests the doctrine of the Ascension is all about, when he refers to it as, "the assertion of the absolute sovereignty of Jesus Christ over every part of this universe, the crowning of the cross, the manifest triumph of his way of love over every other force in the world."[24] If in most of the Gospel accounts the risen Christ was readily recognizable as

23. Robinson, *But That I Can't Believe!*, 106–7.
24. Ibid., 109.

the man, Jesus of Nazareth, in his ascension he is proclaimed as Christ the King; the "one seated on the throne" in the Revelation to John, who is worthy "to receive glory and honour and power" (Rev 4:11a). Like the One who speaks to Job from out of the whirlwind (Job 38:1), this ascended Christ is awe-inspiring, and more than just a little overwhelming.

And so we hear from Coltrane and his assembled group something furious, powerful, and at times more than a little over-whelming. In my hearing of it, "Ascension" is an acoustical icon of the ascended and enthroned Christ. Even the section some three quarters of the way through where the intensity of the piece finally lessens—in which the piano of McCoy Tyner is followed by a duet from the two bassists—fits with this iconic reading. In the story from the Acts of the Apostles, following the ascension the disciples return to Jerusalem to keep a kind of vigil, awaiting the gift of the Holy Spirit. It is a breathing space in the narrative, much the same way that this section of "Ascension" is a breathing space in the midst of the intensity of the piece. Or maybe it is the "silence in heaven for about half an hour" that follows the opening of the seventh seal in the Revelation to John, which seems a somehow necessary respite before the whole of creation is carried through crisis toward its fulfillment.

Or maybe John Coltrane had neither of these images in view as he constructed his piece, and aside from wanting to say some-thing about the glory of the ascended Christ, he just let it all unfold as it would. But of this I have little doubt: given all that he said about his own search for God through music, and given what he recorded during the months just before and after these sessions, his choice of the title for the piece was no accident. But we don't stand a chance of hearing what Coltrane manages to say—intentionally or otherwise—unless we are open to a deep engagement with it. As Saliers rightly observes, "The act of listening to music is crucial to the theological significance of music, with or without sacred texts. For 'hearing' music as the bearer of theological import requires not only a 'musical ear,' as we say, but also a sensibility for hearing music *as* revelatory."[25]

---

25. Saliers, *Music and Theology*, 67.

9

"The Father and the Son and the Holy Ghost"

Hearing an Icon of the Trinity

A jazz quartet can utter things in the presence of God that words alone cannot say. A saxophone can lament on behalf of the helpless. A piano may offer intercessions for the needy. A string bass can affirm the firm foundation of faith. Drums and cymbals may call pilgrims to break into joy.

—William Carter, "Singing a New Song"

I refound my faith several years ago. I had already found it and lost it several times. I was brought up in a religious family, I had the seeds of it in me, and, at certain moments, I find my faith again. All of that is connected to the life one leads. . . . It's everything to me; my music is a way of giving thanks to God.

—John Coltrane

I will never forget the first time I sat down to listen to "The Father and the Son and the Holy Ghost," the opening piece in the five-part *Meditations* suite. I can't forget, because that first listening evoked in me the strangest set of reactions. First there was shock—it wasn't *at all* what I had been expecting—and then I fell fast asleep. I still find it hard to make sense of how the one led to the other, but it did. Something about the raw intensity of the piece triggered my whole system to say, "Too much . . . retreat . . ." And I did.

But let me back up a bit and give a bit of context for that experience. "The Father and the Son and the Holy Ghost" is very much a free jazz piece, and at the time I really had no point of access to that genre. I'd been a rock and folk music fan right from early adolescence, and while I'd explored some jazz-fusion during its heyday in the early and mid-1970s, it wasn't until I was in my late thirties that I started to really get into jazz. As is the case for so many people, it was Miles Davis's *Kind of Blue* that first caught my ear, and from there I began to explore other music from around that time. Because Coltrane is on *Kind of Blue,* one of the first albums I picked up was *Giant Steps,* followed by Brubeck's *Take Five,* Davis's *Round About Midnight,* and Charles Mingus's *Mingus Ah Um.* While both *Giant Steps* and *Mingus Ah Um* did push me a little bit—actually, they made me pay attention and really listen—I decided I was indeed a jazz fan. Somewhere around that time, I picked up Ornette Coleman's *The Shape of Jazz to Come,* knowing nothing about it other than its reputation as being yet another one of the really important jazz records released in 1959. I wasn't ready for it; in fact, after trying to listen to it a few times, it basically sat untouched on my CD rack for six or seven years.

Having decided that I liked Coltrane, I borrowed a copy of *A Love Supreme* from the local library, but at that early stage of my explorations I didn't really "get it" either. It opened with that gong, and sometimes the drummer sounded like he was playing tympani, of all things. The closing piece sounded formless to my ears, and as for that chanting of the phrase "a love supreme" in the suite's opening piece; that just sounded cheesy to me. The whole album just didn't feel enough like *jazz* to me.

Well, over the next couple of years I managed to increase my capacity to really listen to this music, which made me far more adventurous than I had been in those very early days. My collection of Coltrane albums began to grow, with *Blue Train* arriving next, and then the album with recorded with Duke Ellington. I decided to give *A Love Supreme* another chance, and lo and behold I loved it.

Still, the snippets of free jazz that I heard from time to time left me cold. I even heard the saxophonist Oliver Lake play in a club sometime around 2007, and his quintet did offer up a couple of free pieces in the course of the evening. It was fascinating and at times even moving to hear and see live, but I remained unconvinced I would ever need to actually own any of it on CD. When would you actually want to listen to it? A year or two after that, I decided that I'd surely developed a capacity to deal with Coltrane's controversial *Ascension* album, and so on the Feast of the Ascension, late at night after attending church, I made an attempt to listen prayerfully through the forty-minute piece. I was committed . . . and I lasted all of ten minutes, before somewhat sheepishly replacing it with my now much-loved and well-played copy of *A Love Supreme*. So much for recordings of free jazz.

Not really knowing the arc of Coltrane's musical career, I'd somehow assumed that *Ascension* was the exception to the rule, and even had it in my mind that maybe it was the last thing he recorded prior to his death. I hadn't really begun to read about jazz yet, and so was just exploring the music by giving albums a listen. Flipping through the jazz section in a local music store, I happened across this Coltrane album from 1966 called *Meditations*. With song titles like "Compassion" and "Love," it seemed reasonable to think it would be a fairly meditative album, so I purchased it and set it aside for a few days. I had a two-day Eastertide retreat scheduled, and imagined that it would be an ideal time to listen meditatively and prayerfully to what I thought must be a recording not unlike *A Love Supreme*.

I was actually making this retreat at home, the rest of my family being away for a few days of the school spring break. I unplugged the phone, unhooked myself from the Internet, kept the woodstove burning, and with my books and music all readily available it was an ideal way to decompress after the intensity of Holy Week and Easter. I spent the first morning out on a long walk with the dog, and then returned to the house to make a bit of lunch before sitting down to listen to *Meditations*. I settled comfortably on the couch, a glass of wine in hand (it was Easter week, after all . . .), and clicked the play button on the stereo remote.

Within seconds I was up on my feet, hurrying over to the stereo to see what had gone wrong. I assumed the disc must have somehow skipped forward to the middle of the track; that is how abruptly "The Father and the Son and the Holy Ghost" begins. Actually, it doesn't so much begin as *explode* into life, with all six musicians in full group improvisational mode. For these recording sessions held in November 1965, the classic quartet of Coltrane,

Tyner, Garrison and Jones has been augmented by Rashied Ali as a second drummer and Pharoah Sanders on tenor saxophone (and tambourine and bells), and from the very opening notes all six musicians are playing hard, with an intensity almost too great to bear. At the forty-eight second mark, Coltrane's tenor is heard picking out what is the closest thing to a melodic line in the piece; an eleven-note run expressing the eleven syllables in the title— "The Father and the Son and the Holy Ghost"—repeated twenty-two times in different keys in just over a minute. The piece then catapults into what seems to be complete chaos. Coltrane solos for four minutes, during which Sanders adds to the barrage of percussion by hammering furiously on a tambourine. Midway through the seventh minute, Sanders puts his horn to his mouth and plays with fury for much of the rest of the piece. Coltrane joins him at the ninth minute, playing hard and free. Coming up to the eleventh minute, Coltrane returns to restate that eleven-note line, again playing it in various keys and this time repeating it twelve times. The two horns return to the percussive style of playing with which the piece opened, which continues to the final twenty seconds of the track, when everything begins to soften and move toward a seamless transition into the album's second track, "Compassion," a far more conventionally structured piece in which Tyner's piano figures prominently. The horns are no longer screaming, the drums and percussion swing, and the exhausted listener is provided with a much-needed bit of breathing space.

Now, when I first heard this piece, what I thought I was hearing was an unstructured barrage of intense sound. I couldn't hear its shape, I couldn't hear any semblance of a melody line, and I certainly couldn't identify the various "voices" that I now hear with such clarity. I just sat back, closed my eyes, and let the intensity roll over me. I think it was because I was in such shock that I fell asleep. As for how long I actually slept, I'm really not sure. The album was still playing when I awoke, but as for which track it was on, I'm afraid that I just don't know. I do remember thinking that I was hearing something that was more conventionally meditative, so I suspect I was probably hearing "Serenity," the piece that closes the album.

There are a number of stories of people hearing Coltrane play live during the final years of his life and having reactions not dissimilar to mine (though I have yet to hear of anyone who fell asleep). Somewhere along the line I read an account of how at the end of a song, a musician who was sitting in the club shot up from his chair and insisted that the person he was with accompany him outside. Afraid that the musician had been offended by Coltrane's music, the friend followed, only to discover that the musician in question simply needed to give himself a break from the intensity before he would dare plunge back in. Of seeing Coltrane at a major event at New York's Lincoln Center, the musician Dave Leibman later wrote, "I was there with a very good friend—we used to go together to see Coltrane a lot. We were just speechless. I couldn't talk for a couple of days."[1] Of course, there are certainly plenty of stories of people leaving these same concerts or clubs in disgust, long before the music ended. Of that same Lincoln Center event, Leibman commented, "I'm not exaggerating—at least half the audience got up and left." Whether or not you appreciate it, there's no denying that this stuff is intense. Intense and controversial.

Now, given that what I first heard as being little more than a sonic explosion actually does have about it a very real structure, there still remains the question of whether or not it actually means anything. Or is it simply an intense experiment in sound, the self-absorbed indulgence of a musician who had begun to believe his own myth? Some reviewers and many Coltrane fans of the day certainly concluded the latter. Of the *Meditations* album as a whole, reviewer Joe Goldberg commented that though he had long been a supporter of Coltrane, "I cannot be scoured or scraped any more," and concluded his review by writing, "I feel only that I am being wildly assaulted, and must defend myself by not listening."[2]

By no means a fan of free jazz, Jeremy Begbie is no doubt correct in his assertion that this genre is "rarely as free from the inheritance of the past as its supporters would like to think."[3] In the case of "The Father and the Son and the Holy Ghost," it is not insignificant to note composer Noel Da Costa's suggestion that the piece picks up its opening theme from the hymn, "Bless this House, O Lord We Pray,"[4] which suggests more structure—more

1. Kahn, *A Love Supreme*, 181.
2. Goldberg, "Meditations," 236.
3. Begbie, *Theology, Music and Time*, 217
4. Porter, *John Coltrane*, 267.

constraint—and more *meaning* than my ears were able to detect on a first listening. Perhaps even more intriguing is the observation shared with me by the biblical scholar Cameron McKenzie, that in this piece he can detect echoes of Charles Wesley's hymn, "O For a Thousand Tongues." The first verse of that hymn—"O for a thousand tongues to sing / my great Redeemer's praise / The glories of my God and King / the triumphs of His grace"—expresses something not unlike Coltrane's ongoing search for a musical language through which he could speak more fully of the divine.

In his review of *Meditations* for *Down Beat*, the jazz critic Don DeMichael writes tellingly of his own reaction to first hearing Coltrane's expanded improvisational group some months before the album was released. "I hated what they were playing," he writes:

> I decided to go home but had a couple beers instead. Intermission. John came over and sat down. What was he trying to do in the music? Just trying to get *it* out, he said, making a scooping motion with his hands away from his chest. But what was all this, I said, pointing at the bandstand? He didn't know for sure; things were not right with the music yet, he said; but he wants to get into rhythm more, and this is what might lead him to it.
>
> The next set I heard it. Experienced it. Not what John talked about so much as what I was grappling with . . . *why* I was repelled, *why* I wanted to run . . .[5]

DeMichael goes on to say that he doubted anyone, including the musicians playing the music, actually *understood* it, but that it somehow opened a part of the self, "that is normally tightly closed, and seldom recognized feelings, emotions, thoughts well up from the opened door and sear my consciousness"[6] Not exactly the stuff one expects to read in a record review.

And again, in spite of my earliest sense that this is a formless piece, it does have about it a very real shape, which I began to hear on probably my third listening. Up front is the first voice, the sometimes honking and squealing horns of the two saxophone players along with Sanders' insistent hammering on a tambourine when he doesn't have the horn in his mouth. Just barely behind this lies the percussive attack of the two drummers, one heard in each of

5. Ratliff, *Coltrane*, 170.
6. Ibid.

the two stereo channels. Yet another step in are the bass and piano, which together provide the ensemble a bare approximation of an anchor. The three voices weave in and through and around each other in a manner entirely in keeping with the trinitarian title of the piece, and I see that as being neither incidental nor accidental.

Given how seldom Coltrane gave interviews during this period, it is impossible to know what was on his mind and in his spirit when he took his expanded group into the recording studio that day. Evidently, the word in the jazz community was that the characters of this trinity were Coltrane, Sanders, and Albert Ayler; Coltrane as "the father" to these two younger sax players generally recognized as being part of the new face of the avant-garde.[7] The playful side of the man might have enjoyed that bit of buzz, but given the character of his spiritual longing, it is difficult to imagine that the piece was created with that in view. If Jeremy Begbie is correct in his assertion about free jazz not being particularly "free from the inheritance of the past," the same might well be said here of Coltrane's theological wisdom and insight. While he might have been pursuing astrology, dropping LSD, learning to chant with the word "Om," and pasting together his own hybrid version of religious truth, I would still want to suggest that deep in his soul there was an "inheritance from the past" upon which he drew to create this piece of music. That he pushed it into territory that would have been unrecognizable to his pastor grandfathers is no surprise. He was, after all, exploring widely and attempting to integrate the ideas and practices of other seekers, regardless of their particular religious locations. But at some deep level, it would appear that his spiritual roots would never quite cut him loose, which, together with the experience of grace he chronicles on *A Love Supreme*, might account for why he can actually say something very important about God's triune character.

As a child growing up in North Carolina, the church pervaded every part of Coltrane's life, and not simply because he was raised in the home of his preacher grandfather. As I've already mentioned, in the view of James Cone, "it would be impossible to grow up black in the south, and not be a product of the church in some way." In a real sense, the church was present in the schools and on

7. Nisenson, *Ascension*, 186. Ayler himself evidently quite liked this take on the title's meaning, and three decades after his death a 2004 multi-disc retrospective of his life's work bears the title, *Albert Ayler: Holy Ghost*.

the front street, as well at home and in the sanctuary. As Herman Gray observes, Coltrane's life was a "ceaseless search for a spiritual life that greatly expanded but was ultimately rooted in the southern black Christian tradition of service, education, and religion within which he was formed."[8] And the specific place within the black church religious tradition in which he was formed—the African Methodist Episcopal Zion Church—was one that sang the spirituals but also drew on a more theologically sophisticated hymnody in which trinitarian doctrine would have been *sung* into his consciousness.

What's more, as Leonard Brown suggests, "One of the principal aesthetics of [black American musical culture] was to play with a sound and energy that deeply touched the people; to play in ways that connected and communicated."[9] This has great resonance with Coltrane's statement in the liner notes for *Meditations* that his goal in making the record was, "to uplift people, as much as I can." "There are always new sounds to imagine, new feelings to get at. And always, there is the need to keep purifying these feelings and sounds so that we can really see what we've discovered in its pure state. So that we can see more and more clearly what we are. In that way, we can give to those who listen the essence, the best of what we are. But to do that at each stage, we have to keep on cleaning the mirror."

So in answer to my question about whether or not this particular piece actually *means* anything, most categorically it does. As I have come to hear it, "The Father and the Son and the Holy Ghost" provides a powerful and important insight into an understanding of the ancient doctrine of the Trinity. Coltrane's insight, which is presumably rooted both in his formation in the black church as well as in his own life-changing spiritual awakening and ceaseless quest, is expressed in the wildness and rawness and intensity of his trinitarian piece. He reminds us that God is like that, too.

Lewis Porter writes of the religious ecstasy conveyed by this piece as being one "taken to exquisitely painful limits."[10] We easily forget just how fraught with risk it is to open ourselves to an encounter with the Divine, thinking instead of comfort and of

8. Gray, "John Coltrane and the Practice of Freedom," 34.

9. Brown, "You Have to Be Invited," 6.

10. Porter, *John Coltrane*, 267.

consolation. Consolation and comfort may well be given, as they clearly were for Coltrane in his experience of being set free from his soul-destroying addictions. Yet his unfolding spiritual search and experience—even as he was met by the sheer grace he celebrates in *A Love Supreme*—was never without risk. "Coltrane's spiritual vision certainly was complex, and his soul's journey not an easy or safe road," writes Nisenson. "The road toward this God . . . is twisting and dangerous, requiring great strength and resilience."[11] And humility, as well, which lies at the heart of both *A Love Supreme* and *Meditations*.

Ever since my years in theological college, I've loved the Christian proclamation of the Trinity. Not as some technical and endlessly elusive doctrinal matter, mind you, but as an extraordinarily poetic and imaginative way of speaking of God's being with and for the world. Like many Christians, I wasn't always particularly clear about what to do—how to think, speak, pray, and believe—with this doctrine of the Trinity. In many respects, I was not unlike the writer and popular biblical commentator William Barclay, who in his *Spiritual Autobiography* confesses that, "to be honest, I find it very difficult to distinguish between the Holy Spirit and the ever present Risen Lord."[12] God as Father—as source and creator—I understood. Jesus Christ the Son, as God Incarnate *and* as the one present when two or three gather in his name; that also worked both theologically and prayerfully. The Holy Spirit? Well, my occasional bumps up against the edges of charismatic Christianity had left me nervous, and while the language of the *paraclete*—of comforter, advocate, guide—on Jesus' lips in the Gospel according to John came much closer to being a part of my faith's mother tongue, practically speaking I was closer to being a functional binitarian than I would have been willing to admit to my professor of systematic theology.

It wasn't until my third year in seminary that my theology came to echo what I had been praying in the liturgy and proclaiming in the creeds. Sitting in Margaret O'Gara's course on "The Triune God," something began to shift. Under Dr. O'Gara's direction, we read widely and deeply in the trinitarian theological tradition, from the early church fathers and the councils through to the likes

11. Nisenson, *Ascension*, 186.
12. Barclay, *Spiritual Autobiography*, 114.

of John Macquarrie, Bernard Longergan, and Karl Rahner. What moved this from being a merely demanding intellectual exercise to being something closer to prayer was O'Gara's passionate engagement with trinitarian theology as poetry and doxology. I will always remember her lecture on Augustine's theology of the Trinity; how she unpacked one after another of his many images of the Three-In-One, and how she conveyed to us the *playfulness* that lay at the heart of Augustine's view. In effect she was saying, "Here's one of Augustine's images, so try it out. If this one doesn't connect, here's another, and another, and still another." One rarely thinks of Augustine as being playful, yet as she lectured O'Gara's face was lit up with delight, crossed by a wide smile, marked by sparkling eyes. Those images danced and sang and swirled about the classroom, hinting at the truth that all of creation dances in a kind of echo of the great *perichoresis*—the mutual indwelling—of Father, Son, and Holy Spirit. No more could the Spirit be left to the wild and woolly charismatic fringes of the church. I had been granted a glimpse of the truth that lies behind those images, and began to have some small sense of the Holy Spirit as "Lord and giver of life;" something I'd been blithely reciting for years every time I said the Nicene Creed. No more could the Three Persons be seen or prayed to in abstraction from the One, and no more could I be a functional binitarian. At the heart of the adventure that is theology now laid the deliciously poetic and playful mystery of the Triune God. Theology had become for me doxology; it had become praise.

And so I came to actually relish preaching on Trinity Sunday, and even more so when I began to discover the connections some theologians had made between the Trinity, creation, and music. For instance, drawing deeply on Gregory of Nyssa, Augustine, and Bach (who he calls "the greatest of Christian theologians"), David Bentley Hart all but sings the connections. "Because God is Trinity, and creation a song shared among the Persons, God is the context in which the polyphony of being is raised up, in which even silenced voices are preserved, and promised a restored share in creation's hymnody. As God is the 'place' of what differs, all distance belongs to God's distance, all true creaturely intervals are 'proportions' and 'analogies' of his infinite interval, *all created music participates in his infinite music.*"[13] What has always held together all of

---

13. Hart, *The Beauty of the Infinite*, 285. Italics added.

these ways of seeing and praying and proclaiming the Trinity is a sense of harmony, of the mutual indwelling as being one of beauty and of a kind of ordered symmetry. From time to time, though, I wondered if I had not at least implicitly superimposed the lines and limits of mathematical coherence over top of the Divine, and maybe come up with the sort of God that Isaac Newton, on a good day at least, could figure on parchment with quill and ink.

In his trinitarian piece, Coltrane pushes hard against any such neatly ordered vision of the Trinity; a push which at least partly accounts for what the jazz critic Nat Hentoff writes in the liner notes for *Meditations*. "The emotions are imperious; they cannot be braked or polished into conventional ways of 'beauty' or 'symmetry.' They must explode as felt—in the rawness of palpable, visceral, painful, challenging, scraping, scouring self-discovery. For there to be unity, there must first be a plunge into and through the agony of separateness." What Hentoff doesn't quite understand is that this piece is not actually about the self or self-discovery, but is rather about God and only secondarily about what one discovers about the self as one searches for God. For all that the mature John Coltrane's religious and spiritual sensibilities placed him at the very edges of a conventional or orthodox Christian theological view—in the interview for those same liner notes in the *Meditations* album, he told Hentoff, "I believe in all religions"—in "The Father and the Son and the Holy Ghost" he manages to express something *true*, something to which orthodox Christianity needs to be recalled. Not to replace images which figure the triune God as *perichoretic*, as "mutual indwelling," but to augment those poetic pictures with another equally poetic one. It would appear that for John Coltrane, the "unity" to which Hentoff refers can only be experienced in and through an honest exposure of the self as one seeks the Divine, and to seek God is an adventure both wondrous and fraught with risk. That is what I hear coming through in the intensity and passion of his sound.

I believe that what John Coltrane managed to achieve with this piece of music is to create something of an acoustical icon of the Trinity. In the Eastern Orthodox tradition, an icon is not simply a painting to be viewed, but is rather a spiritual and religious image that has been "written" to be "read"; a theological visual proclamation meant to be prayerfully engaged. An icon is not thought to be merely or thinly representative of its subject, but instead a window of encounter with that which it represents. "It is important to recognize [that] an icon is not merely the sum total of what it depicts," writes Daniel Siedell. "[I]t is not only an image, it is also an object, a piece of wood panel with paint applied to it. But it is also more than its physical properties. Its making, too, is what gives it power."[14]

In the very making of "The Father and the Son and the Holy Ghost," Coltrane has done something powerfully expressive of a deep theological truth. Not that everyone will necessarily hear it, of course, because to hear it requires deep and prayerful listening. Some people will never get past the sense that the piece is only cacophonous, and some will think its apparent wildness and free-ness is its only point. "Seeing an icon requires also a trained mind and sensibility to 'read' the icon in such a way that the person is gazed upon by the image," writes Don Saliers, and then draw-ing a parallel to "acoustical icons," he continues, "the theological import of music requires a kind of active receptivity that is more akin to prayer, to contemplation, and to attending the world with a sense of awe and wonder."[15]

Now at this point in his musings on the acoustical icon, Sa-liers is writing primarily about music that serves as settings for religious texts. Music without any text can do a different kind of iconographical work, though the risk here is that we become rather overzealous in our presumption to know what the writer intended in creating a particular piece of music. Begbie presses hard on this point, with his reminder that "music does not trans-late into anything like straight-forward statements, theological or otherwise, capable of evaluation and criticism."[16] Yet I would want to cite the observation of the scholar rabbi Abraham Heschel, that "Religious music is an attempt to convey that which is within our reach but beyond our grasp,"[17] and suggest that it is in the ten-sion between "within our reach" and "beyond our grasp" that we should locate the acoustical icon. Begbie might well see this as verging on an unhelpful kind of mysticism—he might even call it

14. Siedell, *God in the Gallery*, 84.

15. Saliers, *Music and Theology*, 69.

16. Begbie, *Theology, Music and Time*, 144–45.

17. Saliers, *Music and Theology*, 31.

romanticism—but I remain undeterred. I think that particularly if one considers both the arc of Coltrane's own spiritual life as well as the way in which his trinitarian piece fits into the *Meditations* suite as a whole, my reading is entirely justified. In other words, I need to now take a look at the *Meditations* suite as a whole.

Clearly conceived as a suite, with no breaks between the five tracks, the more deeply and intentionally I have listened to it, the more convinced I am that it follows an order not unlike that of *A Love Supreme*.

Meditations opens with the power and intensity of "The Father and the Son and the Holy Ghost," which is a statement of what it might mean to dare to draw close to God . . . as well as something about what it might mean to *not* dare to draw near. God is a hurricane and a raging, consuming fire; God is the power and the glory; God will not be domesticated or tamed in any way. That is at least part of the force of the opening piece.

Then comes the track "Compassion." This is a far more conventional jazz piece, with a focus on McCoy Tyner's wonderful work on the piano. It is still not quite meditative or pastoral in tone, in that it clips ahead at a steady pace, with Tyner's solo being highly inventive, and just slightly out of left field. The compassion it seems to express is that of daring to come near to the presence of this untamed God and finding not punishment or condemnation, but rather something closer to a clear and steely-eyed acceptance. As Paul Tillich would have it, this is the knowledge of having been accepted by God, in spite of being, at heart, unacceptable. That's compassion.

"Compassion" folds into the third piece, "Love." Perhaps ironically, "Love" opens with a bass solo of just under two and a half minutes; yet isn't love by its very nature to be shared? There is a sense of loneliness to the solo, which makes it all the more poignant. Then comes Coltrane's saxophone, followed by touches of percussion, and then the piano; each adding but never taking away. Coltrane plays in and around a series of scales throughout the piece, in a way that is both lovely and (finally) meditative. There is no sign of Pharoah Sanders until the closing twenty seconds, and no hint of dissonance. It is a beautiful piece, representing the emotional and spiritual space at which one might arrive, having been accepted and loved in spite of all one's failings. I can't help but think of the recovering heroin addict, sitting in that room in his mother's house in Philadelphia, amazed by grace. He is among the beloved after it all.

Ah, but the appearance of Sanders in those closing seconds marks the movement into "Consequences," the fourth part of the suite. Things begin to get gritty again, with Sanders running up and down his sax, producing squawks and squeals, and Tyner banging hard on his piano. Just after the three-and-a-half-minute mark, Coltrane is back, though now playing with the same squalling sound as Sanders.

When the horns both drop out just after the five-and-a-half-minute mark, Tyner is again the voice the listener really hears. And now he begins to move the piece toward something more lovely . . . though the move is slow and gradual. And the closing forty-five seconds are lovely indeed.

The transition to "Serenity," the fifth and final movement, begins in that closing minute of "Consequences." Coltrane's saxophone is the most prominent voice in this final piece, which actually builds in intensity through the first two minutes and only then resolves into a more serene space in the closing minute. Coltrane's transition to that deeper serenity is wonderful and evocative, but I have to say that I love the fact that he gave Sanders the last word in the whole suite. And for the first time on the whole album, Sanders' playing is subdued and filled with gentleness.

Taken as a whole, I do think this album is tracing something of a second or maybe complementary chapter to *A Love Supreme*. Here we have Coltrane coming in trembling before the fearsome God (part 1), who meets him first with compassionate acceptance (part 2), and then in love (part 3). While love is by definition something mutual and shared, it doesn't come easily at first, and so "Love" begins with that extended bass solo expressing an aching need to learn to respond to love with love. And after that step is taken and love is shared, there can still be a falling away. This is what Coltrane names as his time of "irresolution" in the notes to *A Love Supreme*, and the falling away comes with consequences (part 4). I think it is notable that it is framed in terms of consequences, and not as punishment or judgment; it says to me that at whatever level Coltrane understands grace, he really "gets" it. And as the consequences unfold he will find his feet and make peace in his own self again (God has already made peace with him, so that is not in question), which is represented in the closing minute of this track. "Serenity" (part 5) is finally granted, though because he has learned to face his actions and their consequences, the serenity is not stereotypically serene. There is still work to be done, but always under the assurance of grace and the promise of rest. As a whole, I think this album is extraordinarily wise and insightful.

It is illuminating to compare *Meditations* with an earlier version of the suite; this one recorded by the quartet in September 1965 some two months prior to the *Meditations* session, and eventually released as *First Meditations (for quartet)* in 1977. Aside from the fact that *First Meditations* is a quartet version, the most obvious difference between the two recordings is the absence of "The Father and the Son and the Holy Ghost." Rather than opening with an explosion of trinitarian sound, the earlier version begins with "Love," followed by "Compassion," "Joy" (the one piece not included on the sextet recording), "Consequences," and "Serenity." While the four pieces that appear on both versions are not dissimilar, the spiritual journey traced on *First Meditations* is quite different from that of *Meditations*. On this earlier recording, the path begins with an affirmation of God's love, and then moves into being compassionately stretched toward new growth. The third step is "Joy," and of all of the pieces on *First Meditations*, this one swings the hardest. And then, as with *Meditations*, this earlier version moves toward the culmination that is "Serenity," but only by way of first navigating "Consequences."

If by opening with its powerful acoustical icon of the Trinity *Meditations* begins with Coltrane figuratively on his knees before the Holy, *First Meditations* doesn't find him there until at least "Joy," and probably not until "Consequences." "Joy" is the piece that most seems to explore religious ecstasy—"[It] resembles the shout, the climactic point of a Holiness worship service,"[18] writes Salim Washington—and it does it joyfully. There is nothing here that sounds as if it might overwhelm with awe or with fear, which is so clearly the case in "The Father and the Son and the Holy Ghost." On "Joy" it is a religious ecstasy that dances, and if it lands Coltrane on his knees it is either out of gratitude or from being so swept up in rapturous delight that his legs buckle. He will finally

18. Washington, "'Don't Let the Devil," 124.

go to his knees in penitence before his God on "Consequences," called to account for the ways in which he has strayed.

The spiritual journey traced on this earlier version is actually not unlike those traced by many of the great spiritual writers and mystics of the Christian tradition. The spiritual life begins with that clear sense of being loved; of being compassionately and lovingly prodded into growth, and of knowing the divine presence in ways that are filled with joy and even ecstasy. Then begins the hard and searching work of purgation, often carried out without the consolations of experience and the senses; in the "dark night of the soul" or in the "cloud of unknowing." It is hard, hard work, yet the path does move ever forward toward the promise of the deepest peace, which is the serenity of resting in God. It was quite possibly a familiarity with this way of interpreting the spiritual life that is at work in Coltrane's shaping of the first version of his suite, but ultimately he wasn't happy with it. And while I'm not even going to begin to suggest that John Coltrane is a wiser spiritual and theological guide than someone of the depth and substance of St. John of the Cross, he does make a very sophisticated theological move in his reimagination of the recording. That move has to do with his decision to begin his suite on the spiritual life by writing an acoustical icon of the triune God. He doesn't want the listener to simply hear about the spiritual path; he wants the listener to hear God.

My reading here is very much in keeping with that of Michael Bruce McDonald, who suggests that more than just wanting to create music *about* God, Coltrane's desire was through his music to offer a theophany *of* God; an appearance or manifestation of God, such as what Moses experienced in the burning bush or Elijah in the "still small voice" on the edge of Mount Horeb. Coltrane seems to want to give not just a picture, but rather a window through which to see or hear God. McDonald understands the dissonance of a piece such as "The Father and the Son and the Holy Ghost" as being central to Coltrane's goal, and to his understanding of God and of the nature of the human search for the divine. "The expression of intractable discord *within* an essentially harmonic structure is itself a theophanic proclamation, that is, of the fortunate unattainability of a certain kind of spiritual realization: that which would stake everything on a harmonious state of being while ignoring the dissonances which figure the actual diversity—and thus the varied possibilities—of the human spirit."[19] The dissonance of those jarring horns and crashing percussion is necessary, for it says that life is not always and ever meant to be harmonious, and that spiritual fulfillment often comes with a kind of wounding. To begin *Meditations* with such a statement is to frame the entire search for God as one that will not be completed this side of the grave, and while a place of serenity may be granted, it will take work, humility and the courage to be truthful about our stumblings along the way.

According to most accounts, for Francis of Assisi the high point of his life in God was a wounding, and in different ways it was so for Julian of Norwich, Simone Weil, Dorothy Day, and Dietrich Bonhoeffer, among many, many others. In his Holy Sonnet XIV, John Donne prays, "Batter my heart, three-person'd God," and asks God to, "break, blow, burn, and make me new";

> Take me to you, imprison me, for I,
> Except you enthrall me, never shall [I] be free,
> Nor ever chaste, except you ravish me.

I wonder, do most of us, in our oh-so-safely located churches led by clergy with our oh-so-reasonable theological training have even the faintest idea of what to make of such a prayer, or of that great statement from the Epistle to the Hebrews, that "indeed our God is a consuming fire" (Heb 12:29)? I have had my lovely images for the triune God—images of beauty and of playfulness and of ordered symmetry—virtually all of which are . . . well, without this other image, they're just a bit too safe. For all of his spiritual wanderings, in his aural icon to the triune God, John Coltrane has deepened and enhanced my own theological wrestlings. I will still treasure Augustine's playfulness, and I will always find delight in the *perichoretic* dance of mutual indwelling. And speaking of playfulness, I love to make the claim that a juggler in action, keeping three balls aloft in a steady interweaving motion, offers a most wonderful icon of God. And of course, as I learn to gaze more deeply at an Orthodox icon such as Rublev's famous "Hospitality of Abraham," I am open to seeing more deeply into the mystery. Yet, behind and in and through all of these, I will call to mind the power and the glory and the wildness and the danger of our God, which I first heard with such clarity through the music of John Coltrane.

19. McDonald, "Traning the Nineties," 278.

"Attaining"

Peace/Shalom

By the time of *Sun Ship*, especially on "Dearly Beloved" and
"Attaining," Jones is murderous: it seems impossible that
the saxophone can survive the pounding of the drums.
Coltrane is on the cross, Jones is hammering in the nails.
Prayer turns to scream. If Jones sounds as though he wants
to destroy him, then Coltrane certainly wanted—needed—
him to try.

—Geoff Dyer, *But Beautiful*

And if music is the most fundamentally contemplative of
the arts, it is not because it takes us into the timeless but
because it obliges us to rethink time: it is no longer time for
action, achievement, dominion and power; not even time
for acquiring ideas (you could misinterpret attending to
drama or poetry in these terms). It is simply time for feeding
upon reality; quite precisely like that patient openness to
God that is religious contemplation.

—Rowan Williams, "Keeping Time"

I have to confess that I deliberated for some time before finally
choosing "Attaining" as my final piece in this series of theological explorations. In fact I had pretty much settled on "Suite" from
the *Transitions* album, primarily because it is structured in sections
named for the "hours" or times of daily prayer observed in many
religious traditions. The more I listened to it, though, the more it
seemed that Coltrane was really working out themes similar to

those on *Meditations*, but in a less fully formed way. Though not re-leased until 1970, "Suite" was actually recorded in June 1965, more or less midway between the recording of *A Love Supreme* and *Meditations*. Increasingly I came to hear it as a being a developmental and transitional step between the two, both sonically and spiritually.

I thought it important to work with at least one more piece from the later period, and maybe even one from 1966 or 1967, after the dissolution of the classic quartet. But here I bumped up against another challenge in that almost all of the studio record-ings from this period were released posthumously and without Coltrane's direct input. He certainly did have a hand in the shap-ing of *Expression*, which was released shortly after his death, but in the case of the 1995 release, *Stellar Regions,* the titles for all of the pieces were chosen by Alice Coltrane. Because I believe that particularly in the final four or five years of his life, John Coltrane chose his titles with considerable care, and that they offer a point of entry for theological engagement, I excluded *Stellar Regions* from consideration. I might also note that the piece to which Alice Coltrane attached the title "Stellar Regions" was actually "Venus," from the 1974 release *Interstellar Space.* The "Stellar Regions" ver-sion was recorded with his new quartet on February 15, 1967, and then a week later it was recorded as "Venus" in a session with only Coltrane and his drummer Rashied Ali.

I actually gave some thought to choosing one of the tracks from Coltrane and Ali's *Interstellar Space* project, an album of five quite striking pieces all named for planets. Lewis Porter is quite convinced that given Coltrane's interest in astronomy and astrol-ogy, these titles quite probably were of his own choosing.[1] In terms of my interests here, however, that would mean wandering with Coltrane down one of his more arcane spiritual sidetracks. Short of trying to read that in terms of an appreciation for the wonder of the created universe—"When I look at your heavens, the work of your fingers, the moon and the stars that you have established; what are human beings that you are mindful of them, mortals that you care for them?" (Ps 8:3–4)—this didn't seem to hold much promise. Sometimes it is better to just let Coltrane get sidetracked without trying to haul him back to the road on which I prefer he'd have stayed.

1. Porter, personal interview.

Something of the same must also be said for *Om*, though in this case I wouldn't particularly want Coltrane to bring it back to any road on which I am likely to be walking. Recorded in October 1965 by the classic quartet augmented by three additional musicians, I have to state very clearly that I think *Om* is the single greatest misstep in his entire recording career. The twenty-nine minute piece opens and closes with Coltrane reading from the *Bhagavad-Gita,* but that isn't actually the problem. As I said quite plainly in chapter three, John Coltrane was in many respects the consummate 1960s spiritual seeker, in that he did attempt to incorporate any number of things into his very personal spirituality. I'm not interested in trying to claim him in the name of orthodox Christianity, but instead want to listen for what he might have to say to the Christian theological tradition. However, even if he'd opened and closed this particular recording by reading from the New Testament, I would still find it entirely unhelpful as a theological resource. As has often been suggested, the recording session for *Om* most likely took place under the influence of LSD, which at least partially explains why it is seems so utterly without constraint. There are screaming instruments—and at least one screaming voice—and percussion going in any number of directions, which according to Coltrane was meant to be an expression of the Hindu idea that, "'Om' means the first vibration . . . the first syllable, the primal word, the word of power."[2] Well, whatever its intent, I have to agree with Nisenson's assessment that it is, "undoubtedly the most bizarre album of his career, a genuine artifact of the Sixties."[3] I also suspect that the veteran bass player Bill Crow gives voice to what many others might have thought when they first heard *Om*. While very clear in his respect for what Coltrane could do technically, Crow adds, "I couldn't imagine why he wanted to sometimes." "What's he doing? And then the guys started making less beautiful sounds, like the primal scream thing that was going on there for a while; I really didn't understand that. I mean I understood it psychologically, but the place it had in music? Music is a different game for me than therapy."[4] Thankfully, Coltrane did not remain in that space. Not by any means.

2. Porter, *John Coltrane,* 265.

3. Nisenson, *Ascension,* 183.

4. Crow, personal interview.

In my deliberations as to which piece to choose for this chapter, I found myself drawn to one of two possibilities. I could either work with something from *Expression*, which would be a logical choice given that it was the last album that Coltrane personally shaped, or I could go to one of the later recordings by the classic quartet. It was after a very close listening to the *Sun Ship* album that I finally made the decision to go with the piece, "Attaining." Not that I'm dismissing what Coltrane was attempting with his later group, but in the end I do believe that in his work with the classic quartet he tended to be better positioned to explore and enact theological wisdom and insight. And I will offer some reflections on the *Expression* album in the closing chapter of this book.

Though not released until 1971, *Sun Ship* was recorded in late August 1965, just a week before the sessions that would later be released as *First Meditations,* and three months before the sessions for *Meditations.* Coltrane's explorations on *Sun Ship* sound very much connected to those of the two editions of the "meditations suite," and not at all connected to the *Om* sessions from the middle of that same fall (which is another good reason to judge *Om* as having been a serious miscalculation).

I have been unable to locate any explanation of the meaning of the title of this album, though it is fair to speculate that it has something to do with Coltrane's astrological interests. And while he probably did give the title "Sun Ship" to the song that became the record's opening track, the album name and song order were likely the work of someone at Impulse Records, probably in consultation with Alice Coltrane. The other four pieces on *Sun Ship* bear titles which appear to be drawn from his Christian heritage—"Dearly Beloved" and "Amen"—or at least from conventionally religious language—"Attaining" and "Ascent." In his liner notes to the 1995 CD reissue of the album, David Wild describes *Sun Ship* as, "A meeting of minds, a collaboration of master musicians, expanding, stretching, probing the furthest reaches, the ultimate possibilities of the time-tested 'tenor plus rhythm' format." It is a good description, particularly once you add Wild's observation that while very much a collaborative working group, the quartet had been assembled "to follow one member's restless explorations." At the beginning of "Dearly Beloved" you get a very clear picture of just how collaborative were these recordings. Before the musicians begin to play, Coltrane's voice is quite audible as he gives directions to McCoy Tyner. "Then you go into there. But I think it'd be better to keep it pressing so we, you know, keep a thing happening all through, you know. But you can go through it in the way you feel it; let it happen. Ready?" If the members of the group were in fact following Coltrane's "restless explorations," he in turn demonstrated a great deal of trust in their abilities and instincts to take the explorations in the direction they most needed to go. "But you can go through it in the way you feel it; let it happen," is what he says to his pianist, and here you get a sense as to why McCoy Tyner agreed so readily with what John Patitucci said to me about group improvisation, and how it is so fundamentally dependent on a deep connection amongst the participants: "The most trust I've ever experienced. That's a family, a total family."[5] And of course, this is why it was so difficult when Coltrane began incorporating other musicians, and making forays into music in which the other members didn't necessarily have any idea as to how to begin to "feel it" and "let it happen."

In these sessions, though, there is no question that all four members knew how to let things happen, and "Attaining" is a marvelous example of that. The piece opens with Coltrane's statement of the theme, which Wild characterizes as "dirge-like" and of "pious solemnity," equating it to "a supplicant facing religious immensity." While I don't hear it as being at all dirge-like, I think Wild is otherwise quite accurate in his description, for there is something quite thoroughly solemn being uttered. Porter is certain that this is clear instance of Coltrane offering a recitation of a written text: "It sounds like 'Psalm' [from *A Love Supreme*]; it sounds like a recitation. It doesn't sound like a melody."[6] Unlike the sections in "Alabama" which *may* have been inspired by a text, or even the three pieces from *Crescent*—"Wise One," "Lonnie's Lament" and "The Drum Thing"—which Coltrane actually identified as being based in poems that he had written,[7] the opening theme of "Attaining" sounds virtually spoken on the saxophone. During the course of the very reflective and solemn recitation, underneath and all around it the other members of

5. Patitucci, personal interview.
6. Porter, personal interview.
7. Delorme and Lenissois, "Coltrane, Star of Antibes," 244.

the quartet gradually build an unmetered, percussive tension. At 1:28 Coltrane drops away, followed shortly by Tyner and Garrison, leaving Elvin Jones to hammer his drums with abandon for a quarter of a minute. When at 1:48 Coltrane enters to resume his recitation, he is as steady and contemplative as before, in spite of the fury raging all around him. For the next minute and forty seconds, his voice is an expression of *shalom*; of a steadfast peaceableness granted in the midst of turmoil.

The second time Coltrane drops out it is Tyner's piano that takes the lead, and "Attaining" suddenly finds its blues. For the next four minutes (from 3:10 to 7:15), the piece really swings, and for the most part Jones even keeps time on his drums. Yet, there is a something clearly foreboding in the sound of this section, as again and again it keeps threatening to spring apart. The drumming becomes increasingly intense; Tyner's powerful left hand keeps adding these great accents, and Garrison's bass alternates between holding it all together and being a part of what is going to make it explode. But instead of an explosion, by simply playing a series of increasingly quiet chords, Tyner slowly just pulls it apart, until at 7:15 he drops out entirely. From that point until just shy of the eight-minute mark it is the furiously propulsive percussion that is front and center, and when Coltrane again enters it is almost hard to believe that he could find a way to voice his meditative recitation. Yet, for just over a minute he does, and then for another twenty seconds it is all battering drums, just in case we'd forgotten the intensity of the background against which Coltrane is voicing his prayer.

At 9:27 "Attaining" begins to move toward its climax. The drumming is furious, Tyner is almost equally percussive on the piano, and Garrison has taken out his bow and has begun to draw great lines from his bass. Still, Coltrane is steadfast in his statement, and ever so calm against the storm. There is the one brief window beginning at 10:47, just thirty seconds before the piece ends, when he seems to raise his head and *almost* let go. For just a couple of seconds he begins to move toward the upper register of his sax, and there is just a hint that he is about to really wail on that horn . . . But no, as suddenly as he'd moved toward that upper register, he is not only back down to where he'd been playing all along, but in fact for a moment he plays in the lowest ranges of his instrument. And with one last flurry on the drums and one last crash of the cymbal, "Attaining" fades to silence.

A major part of what gives this piece its coherence and makes it "work" is the way in which it plays with time. There are various sections that are entirely free of meter, as well as the two brief drum solos in which Jones simply refuses to mark time. There is the trio's four-minute blues section that dances just at the edges of dispensing with a steady beat, though never entirely does. Whenever Coltrane's voices his recitative theme the rest of the quartet is playing quite freely, with only occasional hints that there might be a beat tucked away in there somewhere. In his phrasing and pacing, he is clearly following something not unlike a metronome; there is simply a steady pace to what he plays, but no sense that it is characterized by any time signature. And whatever his text, it is clearly more chant-like than it is metrical.

Part of what I find so compelling about this piece is that Coltrane's voice keeps drawing me into the steady, anchoring meditative space that he inhabits. All of this other sound is whirling around, yet his playing embodies and invites a strange stillness in the midst of it all. And the length of the piece is almost impossible to estimate unless you happen to be watching the clock. As Thomas Clifton observes, "There is a distinction between the time which a piece *takes* and the time which a piece presents or *evokes*."[8] What is evoked as Coltrane reads or voices his text on his saxophone is a sense of time as being a sure, steady movement forward through what might otherwise seem like an endless and irresolvable chaos. Certainly the Psalmist's question of "How long, O Lord?" (Ps 13:1a) is present, but so is a sense that the patient singing of an alternate song tells a deeper truth than the clamor against which it is set. As Jeremy Begbie puts it, "Far from abstracting us out of time, the vision opened up by music in this way is one in which to be 'saved' is, among other things, to be given new resources for living 'peaceably' *with* time."[9]

In listening for the theological insights offered in "Attaining," some of Begbie's theological reflections on time are really quite illuminating. I do have to say, though, that given Begbie's critical suspicions regarding free jazz, he might not be entirely in

8. Begbie, *Resounding Truth*, 223.
9. Begbie, *Theology, Music and Time*, 151–52.

agreement with my embrace of this piece of music, nor with how I use some of his material as a source for my own theological explorations. I also need to say that in a few brief paragraphs I will hardly be doing justice to his careful, yet still expansive work.

Among other concerns, Begbie is interested in what he calls "fruitful transience." In hearing music—or at least Western tonal music, which is the primary focus of his work—we hear both movement and direction; and "The motion we hear, is 'pure betweenness, pure passing over.'"[10] "Music is constantly dying, giving way. The next tone in the plainsong melody can only come if the last one is not sung. Musical continuity emerges from transience, from the coming into being and dying of tones, for in this way and only in this way can their dynamic qualities be sensed. The fact that music never solidifies or coagulates to form a thing or substance is critical to its intelligibility."[11] In attending to music's movement, and to its necessary embrace of transience and even death, there are a number of insights to be gleaned. Among these potential gleanings is the knowledge that "change need not imply chaos"; an understanding that patience is required to cope with delayed resolution, and that patience and waiting are also important gifts; and an auditory experience of the "dying" and "giving away" on which music is built, which speaks of a realistic and even hope-filled assessment of transience. St. Benedict's instruction in his Rule that his monks "keep death before you daily" provides something of a parallel. Benedict's words are neither life-denying nor morbid, but instead an invitation to always travel lightly; to live and release each moment in the knowledge that the present is always passing and with a corresponding trust that the future is in God's hands. It is in a similar light that Begbie suggests that "music can serve as a means of discovering afresh and articulating the theological truth that limited duration can be beneficial, and as such, an expression of divine generosity."[12]

In the unmetered and free sections of "Attaining," the trio of drums, piano, and bass offers nothing that could be mistaken as speaking to a movement *through* time. Instead what is offered is a rather different reading *of* time. In these sections, the tones do not

10. Ibid., 49.
11. Ibid., 92.
12. Ibid.

rise and fall in an ordered sequence, and time is not marked by a steady beat. Instead, the sound comes in apparently disordered bursts or even random explosions, which speak to an experience of time as being random, chaotic, and ultimately meaningless. It is against this that Coltrane offers his alternate reading of time and transience. He insistently plays—or reads—his text in *spite* of the chaos, and so weaves into the piece a stubborn statement that there will be resolution. Again, the sense that it is hard to judge how long the piece runs is not insignificant, for this too is an experience voiced in so many of the Psalms. With the presence of Coltrane's voice, the "How long, O Lord?" of Psalm 13 cannot be read in isolation. It is to be heard along with the declaration of patient waiting sung in Psalm 40 (which at times reads like an impatient affirmation of patience), and with the restfulness of Psalm 131. The truth is that over the course of our lives we will need to attend to all three of these voices, and more besides.

One of the quotes at the head of this chapter is taken from Geoff Dyer's *But Beautiful: a Book About Jazz*. At the point in his chapter at which the quote begins, Dyer has turned his attention to the sonic relationship between the playing of Elvin Jones and John Coltrane, suggesting that already in the early 1960s an important creative tension could be heard in their musical interactions. And then Dyer continues, "By the time of *Sun Ship*, especially on 'Dearly Beloved' and 'Attaining,' Jones is murderous: it seems impossible that the saxophone can survive the pounding of the drums." It should be fairly clear by this point that I would agree with this basic reading of Jones' power and fury, though I might not have chosen the word "murderous," in all that it implies. Yet when Dyer goes on to suggest that it is as if, "Coltrane is on the cross, [and] Jones is hammering in the nails," and that "If Jones sounds as though he wants to destroy him, then Coltrane certainly wanted—needed—him to try,"[13] I do think he is really over-reading the tension. At the very least Dyer is giving a highly melodramatic reading of the real drama that the two musicians together could in fact build. And there is little question that the real deal could be marked by what Cornel West calls "antagonistic cooperation," by which he means, "bouncing against one another so that you're giving each other more and more courage to engage in higher

13. Dyer, *But Beautiful*, 203.

levels of collective performance."[14] You can find any number of instances in which Coltrane seems to want or need Jones to take it up yet another notch, as a way of pushing the ferocity of his own playing to a higher level.

You just can't find that on "Attaining." In fact, I'm just not at all clear what Dyer thought he was hearing when he suggests that on this piece, "Prayer turns to scream," because quite frankly it just never does. There's certainly some screaming to be heard on *Sun Ship's* "Dearly Beloved," but part of what really defines Coltrane's work on "Attaining" is that he just won't go there. I hear instead strains similar to those voiced in Psalm 4; not screaming or even loud cries for help, but instead steadfastness in the face of terrible adversity. Psalm 4 begins with an address to God, which is both an affirmation that in the past God has acted—"you gave me room"—and a plea for help—"answer my prayer."

> Answer me what I call, O God of my right!
> You gave me room when I was in distress
> Be gracious to me and hear my prayer. (Ps 4:1)

At verse 4, the Psalmist offers a picture of the sort of peace that will be required to endure the adversity. "When you are disturbed [literally "angry"], do not sin" by lashing back with equal anger. Or maybe even more fatally, do not commit the sin of imagining that you have been defeated. Rather, "ponder it on your beds, and be silent," which is not a defeatist stance, or at least it isn't if the writer trusts that God does indeed "make room." And by the end of the Psalm, the writer is ready to trust.

> You have put gladness in my heart,
> more than when their grain and wine abound.
> I will both lie down and sleep in peace;
> for you alone, O Lord, make me lie down in safety. (Ps 4:7–8)

It is worth noting that the adversaries seem to be reveling in good things like the abundance of grain and wine, yet against this the Psalmist has judged God's gladness to be worth even more. It is precisely this which allows the writer to "lie down and sleep in peace," for God alone can provide true safety and deep peace. Notice that by most measures the tables have not been turned here; the adversary is the one whose storehouse is full, while the

---

14. West, *Hope on a Tightrope*, 118.

Psalmist has only a peaceful sleep. Somehow, though, in the very act of praying for peace, the Psalmist has come to experience an inner peace of infinitely higher value than a storehouse full of mere commodities. Similarly, in looking inward and playing his theme so very evenly through the midst of the clamor that the other members of the quartet are creating, Coltrane conveys to the listener an experience of inner peace. How I would love to know what text he was reading as he played.

Franya Berkman contends that most jazz scholars have tended to set African-American jazz of the 1960s within a narrowly political and civil rights perspective, thus failing to take seriously the spirituality of the musicians. Berkman suggests that this is a deep problem, given that in African-American culture, "the divide between the sacred and secular has been historically nebulous."[15] I take that insight very seriously, and if in this book I have erred it is probably in leaning too heavily in the direction of spirituality and the sacred. So I want to turn to a second text, which like Psalm 4 arises from a place in which the writer is under attack from an adversary. Though I think that in Psalm 4 the writer is anything but oblivious to the social and political context—which actually accounts for why the writer addresses the issue of the obvious abundance that the adversary has in hand—in this second example the connection is even more clearly visible. It is a gospel hymn written in 1958 by Mahalia Jackson and Doris Akers, called "Lord, Don't Move that Mountain." It is significant to note that while two years earlier the Montgomery Bus Boycott had successfully challenged Alabama's laws enforcing racial segregation on public transit, in 1958 the struggle against racial discrimination was really just beginning. In 1958 Martin Luther King, Jr. published his first book, *Stride Toward Freedom: The Montgomery Story*, yet it was at a book signing in Harlem that King was stabbed in the chest and almost killed. 1958 was also the year in which a dynamite bomb was found beside Bethel Baptist Church in Birmingham, Alabama; an apparent attack on the church's pastor, the prominent civil rights leader Fred L. Shuttlesworth. Still on the horizon lay such pivotal events as the 1960 student-led Greensboro, North Carolina, Woolworth's lunch counter sit-in, the 1962 enrollment of James Meredith as the first black student at the University of Mississippi (the

15. Berkman, "Appropriating Universality," 41.

ensuing violent reaction required the intervention of 5,000 federal troops to quell the riots), the 1964 March on Washington, and the bombing of Birmingham's Sixteenth Street Baptist Church. Into a society in which all of this was unfolding, Jackson and Akers sang,

> Now Lord don't move that mountain
> But give me the strength to climb it
> And Lord, don't take away those stumbling blocks
> But lead me all around them

But why not move the mountain, or take away the stumbling blocks? After all, there are spirituals in that tradition that aren't afraid to sing of how "Pharaoh's army got drowned," or of how King Jesus will "ride on" because "No man can hinder him," so why not ask the Lord to knock that mountain down and remove those stumbling blocks? The answer presumably has something to do with some sense that most of the time that isn't the way God works, but I think there are at least two other things that come into play. First of all, in this case I think that it is quite possible that Mahalia Jackson and Doris Akers would have seen the adversary as being not so much the whites who were oppressing them as the very system that made it all possible. If the enemy is Pharaoh and his army, it seems fine to let them sink to the bottom of the Red Sea. But if the enemy is a system and a way of structuring society that prevents people—including church-going people steeped in these very texts—from embracing each other as neighbor, then a different solution is required. Their song was a prayer for strength to climb to the top of the mountain from which (and here I am unashamedly stretching the metaphor) they could stand with Dr. King and share his dream. It is no longer the obstacle, but in fact the way forward.

And secondly, the request that God not take away the stumbling blocks but rather lead the singer around them strikes me as suggesting a victory not unlike that of Psalm 4. Yes, the adversary has the commodities, but we have peace and rest. Yes, we know that there are things that will trip us up, but we have faith that we will be led around them. It is a prayer for deliverance from an arrogant self-assurance that says we can do this all on our own, thank you very much.

I want to suggest that all of this can be heard in John Coltrane's "Attaining." By 1965, the members of the quartet had witnessed the overturning of the segregation laws, but the struggle was hardly resolved. During those days racism was still smoldering everywhere, and not only in the South. In 1968 the slow burn would burst into flames in cities across the North, with riots taking place in any number of urban centers from Detroit to Los Angeles to New York. Further, gangs, drugs, and violence were already crushing the urban neighborhoods that burned in those riots. And all that doesn't even take into account the reality that the United States was involved in an increasingly unpopular war in Vietnam, with a disproportionate number of combat soldiers drawn from the black community. Given all that, it was difficult for many to not get swallowed up in anger, and jazz musicians were no exception. The same year that "Attaining" was recorded, Coltrane's friend and sometime collaborator Archie Shepp announced at a *Down Beat* symposium that he recognized no distinction between playing jazz and political activism, and that jazz was by its very nature both opposed to the war in Vietnam and in full support of Fidel Castro's Cuba.[16]

Coltrane's sound was often misinterpreted as being both angry —and that accusation began to surface in the late 1950s with his intense "sheets of sound"—and as a statement of his imagined political radicalism. It is not that he was disinterested in political issues, or that he didn't have deep affinity for community action and the cultivation of a strong African cultural identity, and in fact he was an active and generous supporter of the Olantunji Center of African Culture in Harlem. It was simply that to be angry, violent, or strident simply was not his way.

What's more, John Coltrane really did believe in the transforming and restorative powers of music. A few years prior to the sessions for *Sun Ship* he actually seemed to hold to rather mystical and even magical ideas about music's potential. In a 1962 interview with the French press he offered the following:

> I want to be able to bring something to people that feels
> like happiness. I would love to discover a process such that
> if I wanted it to rain, it would start raining. If one of my
> friends were sick, I would play a certain tune and he would
> get better; if he were broke, I would play another tune and
> immediately he would receive all the money he needed. But

16. Doggett, *Riot Going On*, 45.

what those pieces are, and what way do you have to go to arrive at knowing them, I don't know. The true powers of music are still unknown. To be able to control them should be, I think, the ambition of every musician. The knowledge of those forces fascinates me.[17]

A statement he made in his 1966 interview with Frank Kofsky gives a good sense of the place to which he had moved: "I think music is an instrument. It can create the initial . . . thought patterns that can create the changes, you see, in the thinking of the people."[18] Even more telling, though, is a story told by the drummer Billy Hart. After being really moved by the music Coltrane had been creating in the final few years of his life, Hart happened to run into him. "And I just told him, 'John, I think you're really beautiful.'" To this Coltrane evidently replied, "Well Billy, you know I'm just trying to clean up . . . can you imagine if you didn't take a bath for thirty or forty years . . . I'm just trying to be clean . . ."[19] Where he had once believed music might have the potential to make it rain or to bring money to friends, John Coltrane came to see it as a path for disciplined and searching self-discovery and purification. And that is the very thing that he came to believe might be shared through his art.

Jost rightly observes that "Coltrane's message of 'peace' and 'love' is not seldom expressed in an apparently chaotic musical context,"[20] though in the case of "Attaining" he has found a way of responding to the chaotic times in which he lived by offering something more deeply rooted. Connecting to the sensibilities of the Psalmist and of the writers of the spirituals, as well as to the vision of Martin Luther King and the Christ from whom King drew his strength, Coltrane spoke through his saxophone a profoundly steadfast peace. Perhaps Dyer was not entirely off the mark in his choice of the language of crucifixion to describe some of the music from Sun Ship. It is just that it wasn't Elvin Jones who was hammering Coltrane to a cross in this music, but instead a whole people who were being crucified in a violent and racist society, and to whom this particular piece of music could speak a word that said,

17. Delorme and Clouzet, "Interview with John Coltrane," 182.
18. Kofsky, "Interview with John Coltrane," 287.
19. Josh Jackson, "On Demand: Interview With Billy Hart."
20. Jost, Free Jazz, 104.

"do not return evil with evil," and "we will lie down and sleep in peace."

Of course that is not necessarily an easy thing to hear, mostly because it doesn't deliver anything that looks like substantial change. This is music written for the long and oftentimes difficult pilgrim journey, and so it is no mistake that it is entitled "Attaining," and not "Attainment." John Coltrane was well aware that he had no more arrived than had anyone else. And you can hear it in his horn.

11

In Memoriam

It was Friday, July 21, and unexpectedly I collided with the sorrow of an age. John Coltrane, the man who gave us *A Love Supreme*, had died. Scores of people were gathering across from St Peter's Church to say goodbye. Hours passed. People were sobbing, as the love cry of Albert Ayler spirited the atmosphere. It was as if a saint had died, one who had offered up healing music yet was not permitted to heal himself. Along with many strangers, I experienced a deep sense of loss for a man I had not known save through his music.

—Patti Smith, *Just Kids*

As long as you care . . . you got to do something, and if you don't the rocks are going to cry out. That's why Coltrane kept blowing his horn, my brother, cause if he didn't blow his horn the rocks were going to cry out. That genius cared.

—Cornel West, "What Kept Coltrane's Horn Blowing"

In using the music of John Coltrane as a starting point for these theological explorations, I have effectively granted to him the status of what Jeremy Begbie calls the "theological musician." In doing this, I don't think I've tried to gloss over the fact that from a Christian point of view his religious views could be rather heterodox, at times a patchwork quilt of the various things that happened to catch his imagination. Given the decade in which most of his deepest spiritual searching took place, he was not entirely atypical. In this final chapter, I need to accomplish three distinct yet overlapping tasks. Firstly, I need to bring the biographical sketch offered in chapter three to a close, and to give some consideration as to how John Coltrane himself has taken on a kind of religious significance. Secondly, I need to give some sense of how his impact on jazz and black culture has been evaluated and interpreted, both positively and negatively. And finally, I need to offer my summary evaluation of Coltrane's overall contribution as a theological musician. At the heart of this summary is my belief that Coltrane's work was not only shaped through his formation in the black church, it is also a significant resource for the church's ongoing theological project.

On July 17, 1967, just two months shy of his forty-first birthday, John William Coltrane died of liver cancer at Huntington Hospital, close to his Long Island home. The cancer had been diagnosed in May of that same year, though there had been at least a few signs that his health might have been failing. Reflecting on the April 23, 1967 concert that was to be his final recorded performance—a benefit concert for the Olatunji Center of African Culture, released in 2001 as *John Coltrane/the Olatunji Concert: The Last Live Recording*—his drummer Rashied Ali notes that though Coltrane's playing was strong, he remained seated on the stage, presumably from pain or exhaustion.[1] With the exception of a May 7 performance in Baltimore, Coltrane was forced to cancel all of his other scheduled concerts.

When he was diagnosed with the cancer, Coltrane declined surgery, quite probably because the prognosis was not good.[2] Instead he returned home to rest and to listen to his recent recordings, and then to attempt to resume work. During this period he continued to make plans for a proposed music center for young people in New Jersey, and stated his intention to pay a visit to Africa to explore traditional music. May 17 found him in Rudy Van Gelder's studio in New Jersey, recording two tracks that remain unreleased, and may in fact have been lost. Even after a second emergency trip to the hospital in early July, Coltrane met with Bob Thiele from Impulse Records to finalize the details for the album that would become his first posthumous release, *Expression*.

1. Porter, *John Coltrane*, 289.
2. Ibid., 290.

Given that this is the last record that Coltrane had a direct hand in shaping, I find it remarkable how little attention it receives in the standard reference works. Porter mentions it only in passing, while the others deal with it only briefly, if at all. The one thing that is often highlighted is Coltrane's statement to Bob Thiele that he really didn't want much by way of liner notes. "By this point I don't know what else can be said in words about what I'm doing. Let the music speak for itself."[3] I suppose it might be said that by giving so little time to this project his biographers have taken him at his word, inadvertently or otherwise, but I suspect the real reason that *Expression* receives so little attention is that it is does not stand as a high point or culminating work in Coltrane's musical journey. Not that it is a bad or even an especially flawed record. It is just that it is not a particularly coherent or integrated whole, of a sort that would have been hoped for as his final recorded statement.

While I am convinced that Eric Nisenson is off-base in placing *Expression* alongside of *Giant Steps* and *Live at the Village Vanguard* in terms of its significance, there is something accurate in his description of *Expression* as "a transitional album, a new turning point rather than an ultimate revelation." "If *Expression* is a genuine clue to the direction Coltrane was heading—which is far from certain, given the fact that he was dying at the time and knew it—it seems clear that his music was on the verge of becoming less abrasively free and more mainstream and accessible."[4] Not dissimilarly, in a 1987 retrospective piece written for *Musician* magazine, the music journalist Peter Watrous describes *Expression* as "yet another new direction." "Spare, mostly calm and rhythmless, it sounds as if Coltrane had reached a level of contentment. The music has neither the exploratory fervor of his earlier 60s works, nor the technique obvious from his music of the late 50s. With *Expression* and *Interstellar Space* (a duet with Ali), Coltrane had reached, through enormous self-discipline and dedication, his last plateau."[5] Although Nisenson hears *Expression* as clearly transitional, and Watrous as a "last plateau," both writers do seem to be suggesting that the album marked a significant departure

3. Cole, *John Coltrane*, 196.
4. Nisenson, *Ascension*, 266–67.
5. Watrous, "John Coltrane: A Life Supreme," 68.

from the sonic explorations that preceded it. With Watrous calling it "mostly calm" and Nisenson suggesting it is an indication that Coltrane's music was becoming "more mainstream," one might expect *Expression* to be a rather accessible and even contemplative record. While it does have moments of being just that, as a whole it is no easier a listen than any of the other records of Coltrane's final years.

It also contains tracks that seem to be as much drawing from the past as looking to the future. On the relatively open and free, sixteen-and-a-half minute piece, "To Be," Coltrane plays the flute in what seems a nod to his friend and former band mate Eric Dolphy, who had died in 1964. Dolphy's mother had entrusted her son's flute and bass clarinet to Coltrane, and it is notable that he used the bass clarinet on another later piece, "Reverend King."[6]

"Offering"—a piece recorded in the sessions for what would be released in 1995 as *Stellar Regions*, and which also appears on that album—incorporates what Ratliff describes as, "huge, repeated, sweeping downward scales [that] can sound like someone frantically, powerfully gathering something, scooping it up, bringing it closer."[7] It might be observed that this is almost a return to, or recapitulation of, what Coltrane was attempting during his "sheets of sound" period, namely using almost impossibly fast runs of notes to fashion a whole. After listening to "Offering" one is left wondering what Watrous meant when he suggested *Expression* "has neither the exploratory fervor of his earlier 60s works, nor the technique obvious from his music of the late 50s." "Offering" has both. And with this choice of this title, Coltrane is continuing his practice of exploring explicitly spiritual themes through his music. Here, his "offering" is his own relentlessly intense and disciplined attempt to speak through his horn.

The track the album opens with is "Ogunde," an apparent reference to a Yoruban deity. "Ogunde" marks something of a reaching back. Ratliff characterizes it as having "the ring of one of his earlier ballads; it was a composition, beyond just a short motif; it had that romantic-contemplative affect, the surface of control, strength, and tenderness."[8] Not that it could ever be confused with his work on

6. Porter, *John Coltrane*, 273.
7. Ratliff, *Coltrane*, 174.
8. Ibid.

the *Ballads* album, or on *John Coltrane and Johnny Hartman*, but it is certainly closer to his work on albums such as *Crescent*, and at a couple of moments even evokes the sound of *A Love Supreme*.

And finally, the title track "Expression," which also contains moments that do seem to hearken back to *A Love Supreme*, particularly in its opening two minutes and closing one. Alice Coltrane's piano solo on this piece, which runs from 2:45 to 5:12, is executed with great confidence and an uncharacteristically strong left hand, making it almost reminiscent of McCoy Tyner's work in the classic quartet. Alongside of "Ogunde," this is the piece that most justifies those descriptions of this album as being calm and even accessible. I don't think it is at all a stretch to describe "Expression" as prayerful and meditative, even during Coltrane's searching and open solo, which runs from 5:12 right into the final minute of the nearly eleven-minute piece. And that final minute brings an extraordinary sense of peacefulness that is built not by the overcoming of Coltrane's tempestuous solo but instead by the blessing of it. Not unlike what I hear in "Attaining," on "Expression," peace/shalom comes in and through the storm, not apart from it.

At the beginning of this brief overview of *Expression*, I suggested that this album is not a particularly coherent or integrated work. This probably has much to do with the fact that Coltrane was drawing it together under the cloud of his own failing health, and did not have the luxury of returning to the studio to continue his work. The album was constructed out of material from four different sessions. With the exception of "To Be," on which Pharoah Sanders plays flute and piccolo, these sessions were all done with the basic "new" quartet of John and Alice Coltrane, Jimmy Garrison, and Rashied Ali. The title track and "To Be" were recorded at two different undated sessions in the spring of 1967, "Offering" at the *Stellar Regions* session on February 15, and "Ogunde" (along with "Number One," a track added to later versions of the album) on March 7. To characterize *Expression* as being in any way simply cobbled together would be unfair, but as is so often true of the final work in any artist's life, be that in music, literature or visual art, it is seldom a life and/or vocation defining work. "Mainly, an artist's final work won't objectively sum up anything," observes Ratliff.

"The idea of a last work acting as a summary or a capstone is a sweet and hopeful construct."[9]

That Coltrane seemed so determined to continue to work—his meeting with Impulse Records to finalize the details for the release of *Expression* took place just three days before his death—can be seen as coming from a basic desire to finish as much as possible while he still had the strength to do so. On the other hand, it might be taken to suggest that he was not particularly willing to admit to himself how little time he had to live. It would be easy to speculate that his aversion to dentists extended to medical care in general, and that he declined treatment for his cancer out of what amounted to fear and denial. As I noted earlier, Lewis Porter suggests that Coltrane's mid-1960s use of LSD might have, for a time, dulled his awareness of his increasing pain, and so compromised his own sense of the seriousness of his condition.[10] On the other hand, some have speculated that Coltrane actually lived for some time with the awareness that his life would not be a long one, which is said to account for why he was so calmly determined to bring his final project to its completion. Taking this even further, the jazz writer Daniel Berger suggests that in the recordings that followed *A Love Supreme*, one can fairly interpret "the madness of his improvisations as panic before death, as a great cry from the precipice, an immense shout before the gods, unknown and mysterious."[11] Similarly, for Wayne Shorter the pace of Coltrane's development over the final decade of his life can be explained as a response to his own sense of the brevity of his life: "He must have known something about his condition . . . Like I gotta do this *fast*."[12]

None of this can be verified, of course. Perhaps like so many of us, John Coltrane simply feared the worst, hoped for the best, and kept looking ahead as best he could. He was certainly very guarded about sharing much information about his condition, which led Miles Davis to comment, "Coltrane's death shocked everyone, took everyone by surprise . . . Trane kept everything close to his vest."[13]

9. Ibid., 174.

10. Porter, *John Coltrane*, 265–66.

11. Ibid., 290.

12. Ratliff, *Coltrane*, 172.

13. Porter, *John Coltrane*, 290.

The funeral was held on July 21, 1967 at St. Peter's Lutheran Church in Manhattan. Under the pastoral leadership of the Reverend John Gensel, St. Peter's had gained a reputation as New York City's jazz church. Over the years, Gensel had come to know Coltrane, and had even secured his promise to play at some point for one of the weekly St. Peter's jazz vespers services. It was fitting, then, that it was Gensel who preached the funeral sermon and led the service, assisted by the Reverend Dale Lind, another member of the St. Peter's staff with a profile in the jazz community. The bulletin for the service bore the title, "A Love Supreme," and the text of that poem was read aloud by the composer and trumpeter Cal Massey, whose association with Coltrane dated back to the late 1940s in Philadelphia. Fittingly, music was offered by the quartets of Ornette Coleman and Albert Ayler; Coleman having been a fellow pioneer with Coltrane in the avant-garde, and Ayler both a disciple of Coltrane and a leader in the movement's continuing explorations. The service opened with Ayler's quartet playing a medley of "Love Cry," "Truth Is Marching In," and "Our Prayer," of which John Gensel said the following:

> She [Alice Coltrane] said she would like to have Ornette Coleman and Albert Ayler play with their quartets in the service. Albert opened the service and, of course, he played very "avant-garde." Twice he removed the saxophone from his lips and literally screamed. The place was completely jammed; people were still trying to get in. It was just as quiet when he did that, and in analyzing or thinking about his particular tribute to John, it brought my attention to two things. His first scream was a cry of despondency or pain and the fact that his mentor was dead. The second was a cry of triumph! He's not dead—he lives![14]

The service closed with "Holiday for a Graveyard" by Ornette Coleman's Quartet, a typically unusual configuration with Coleman's horn backed by the drummer Charles Moffett and both Charlie Haden and David Izenon on bass. Following the funeral, the body was buried at Pinelawn Memorial Park in Farmingdale, Long Island.

It was after Coltrane's death that Alice gave to her deceased husband the Sanskrit spiritual name of *Ohnedaruth*, or "compassionate

---

14. Grey, *Acknowledgment*, 102.

one."[15] By all accounts, her husband's death impacted her very deeply. "Following John's death," notes Tammy Kernodle, "Alice entered a dark period during which she injured herself and was subsequently hospitalized. Meditation and prayer became one of the methods she used to purge herself of her demons . . ."[16] While she had already been interested in Eastern spiritual and religious practices—and along with John had delved into some of the writings of Hinduism and Buddhism—in 1969 her explorations began to move to another level of engagement. Her movement into the Hindu faith evidently provided the spiritual and emotional moorings she most needed at this stage of her life. Influenced by the Swami Satchidananda, she made several trips to India, soon taking on the spiritual name Turiya Aparna. In the early 1970s Alice Coltrane moved her young family to Southern California, where she went on to found first the Vedantic Center (1975) and then the Shanti Anantam Ashram (1983), later renamed the Sai Anantam Ashram (1994).

A piece entitled "Sri Rama Ohnedaruth" appears on Alice Coltrane's 1973 album *Lord of Lords*, the liner notes for which explain that, "The name of Sri Rama has recently been bestowed upon Ohnedaruth John Coltrane, as a result his latest spiritual attainments on his evolutionary Path." Alice Coltrane's notes give some indication of how she came to understand the destiny of her deceased husband's soul, and how she saw his musical genius as having a continuing impact on her own work.

> Many parts of his music were sent direct to my mentality through meditation. Before Ohnedaruth's initiation where he received the name of Sri Rama, his astral globule manifested in my being for my use expressly in music. It is the same container of gross, elementals and cosmic materials he used while living on earth which he no longer has a use for now that he presently moves and works in a finer, lighter ethereal body. Sri means: wealth, prosperity, Rama is one of the highest names of the Lord. It also translates John into English as: Ram. RA also is Universe, MA is world. Ohnedaruth means compassion.

15. Harley, "An Apollonian Scream," 89.
16. Kernodle, "Freedom is a Constant Struggle," 96

Though the name seldom appears in the standard reference books and journal articles, in either its shorter or longer form this "spiritual name" for John Coltrane continues to be used in at least some contexts. In a 2009 interview with Josh Jackson for National Public Radio, the veteran drummer Billy Hart quite casually and comfortably uses the shorter version of the name, simply assuming that the interviewer would make the connection. In its full form, the name is used by the St. John Coltrane African Orthodox Church, a parish in San Francisco that draws on both the Divine Liturgy of the African Orthodox Church and *A Love Supreme* to create what it calls the "Coltrane Liturgy," led by a group named "Ohnedaruth." The website homepage for the church includes the following:

> We thank God for the anointed universal sound that leaped (leapt) down from the throne of heaven out of the very mind of God and incarnated in one Sri Rama Ohnedaruth the mighty mystic known as Saint John Will-I-Am Coltrane. That same healing sound was captured and recorded on the sound disc on the wheel in the middle of the wheel (sound disc recording). Music has the power to make others happy, deliver and set free the mind, hearts and souls of the dear listener. All praise to God. One Mind, A Love Supreme.[17]

The church was founded in 1971 by Franzo Wayne King, himself a saxophonist. Originally called the One Mind Evolutionary Transitional Church of Christ, in its early days the church enjoyed the full approval of Alice Coltrane. However, by 1981 a falling out between King and Alice Coltrane led to her suing the church for what she claimed was the illegal use of the John Coltrane name. The suit failed, and the following year the congregation joined the African Orthodox Church, with King named a bishop in 1984. The church's use of this particular form of their saint's name—St John Will-I-Am Coltrane—is a reference to Exodus 3:14, in which God reveals to Moses the divine name, "I am." The degree to which the church reveres John Coltrane is quite remarkable, as is their willingness to so easily fold together the Hindu spiritual name given him by Alice Coltrane with this stylized "Will-I-Am." And while it is true that the church has not deified Coltrane, they have certainly given him a very robust canonization as a saint. According to an article in the December 2010 edition of the church's newsletter,

17. St. John Coltrane African Orthodox Church, "Welcome," para 3.

Expression, at the service held in honor of the 84th anniversary of the birth of their patron saint—a day they formerly called "Savior's Day"—some members of the congregation experienced "visions of Sri Rama Onedaruth 'The Lord of Compassion, Wealth and Prosperity.'" The same article also notes that his spiritual name "was communicated by way of supreme revelation to the divine mother of the royal family, Turya Coltrane from the Lord of the world."[18]

It is impossible to know what John Coltrane might have thought of all of this. By so many accounts he was a very humble and unassuming man, quite shy and very private. Perhaps too much has been made of an answer he gave to a question during a 1966 interview in Japan. Asked in what kind of a situation he would like to find himself in ten or twenty years, Coltrane responded, "In music, or—as a person . . . I would like to be a saint."[19] This somewhat enigmatic answer provided Rodney Clapp with the title for his essay on Coltrane, "The Saxophonist Who Would be a Saint," in which he wrote, "It is indicative of the seriousness of his searching, ever intense if sometimes scattershot . . ."[20] In his speculations on Coltrane's statement, Nisenson suggests two possible interpretations. He wonders firstly if it "is evidence that Coltrane was perhaps somewhat 'blissed out.'" "Constant studying of mystical texts and intense thought given over to spiritual matters, meditation, special diets and fasting, frequent LSD trips, even his constant practicing, were possibly pushing Coltrane to live an increasingly other-world state. He was not a saint or god after all, although in the late years he seemed to be losing his formerly down-to-earth perspective."[21] Nisenson then adds his second interpretation, namely that, "This statement may have had something to do, however, with his growing awareness that he was seriously ill."[22] In both cases, Nisenson clearly understands Coltrane to have been quite earnest in his statement that he wished to become a saint, whether on account of having lost "his formerly down-to-earth perspective," or due to some inner awareness of his impend-

18. "Church and Community Celebrate 84th Birthday," *Expression Newsletter*, 2.

19. Yui, et al. "Interviews with John Coltrane," 270.

20. Clapp, "The Saxophonist Who Would Be a Saint," 184.

21. Nisenson, *Ascension*, 212.

22. Ibid.

ing death. Not dissimilarly, by simply relating the answer in the context of a consideration of Coltrane's religious beliefs, Ratliff appears to accept the comment as being a straightforward answer to a question. And I have to confess that in my first published explorations[23] of Coltrane's music—with Ratliff and Nisenson as two of my sources—I too took the comment pretty much at face value. This is precisely where things begin to get interesting.

In the published transcript of the Japanese interviews, at least two important things come to light. Firstly, it is not insignificant that on the day in question there was a series of three separate interviews, rather than just a single press conference, as is suggested by Ratliff. While it is true that the comment about wishing to be a saint was given in the context of a press conference, some of the more searching and detailed material on Coltrane's religious beliefs actually surfaced in a private interview with Kazuaki Tsujimoto held later that same day. Unfortunately, this is obscured by the way in which Ratliff presents the material from the interview, which implies that the comment about wishing to be a saint came *after* the more detailed discussion of religious belief. In fact, the two are unrelated.

Secondly, the transcripts are quite clear that as soon as Coltrane makes his sainthood comment, both he and Alice laugh. When the interviewer responds by saying, "You would like to be a saint, huh?" Coltrane again laughs and says, "Definitely." According to the editor and authors of *The John Coltrane Reference*, the meaning of this laughter is quite plain: "This oft-quoted comment has been greatly misunderstood—on the recording he and Alice both laugh, and it is clear that he is joking."[24] Yet Max Hoff, who is both a musician and a deacon at the St. John Coltrane African Orthodox Church, has challenged the conclusion that Coltrane was merely joking. After making it quite evident that he does not believe that Coltrane was predicting his impending death or reaching out for canonization as a saint of the church, Hoff continues, "Clearly John Coltrane understood the concept of 'sainthood' somewhat differently than, say, the Roman Catholic Church. In this concept a 'saint' is a holy person, a devotee, a lover of God—and this is precisely how Coltrane was beginning to view

23. Howison, "God's Mind in the Music," 8–9.
24. DeVito, et al, *The John Coltrane Reference*, 778.

his own life and work."[25] Researcher David Tegnell notes that in an African-American Protestant context, the word "saint" is often applied to all those who are "saved," and so, given Coltrane's own church background his use of the word might not be as exclusive or unusual as it might at first seem. This exchange did spur the authors of *The John Coltrane Reference* to somewhat moderate their earlier conclusion about this comment being nothing more than a joke. Acknowledging that Coltrane's comment probably was connected to his desire "to live a better and more spiritual (or saintly) life," the authors still draw a fairly clear boundary when it comes to taking it all too literally: "That remark has been interpreted by some as though he really wanted to be canonized, an interpretation that goes against all our knowledge of Trane's humility."[26]

This qualified reading of the famous statement is actually quite in line with the things that Coltrane does say in his private interview with Tsujimoto. Referring back to a question about religious faith asked by a student at the second interview session of that day, Coltrane admits that while he tried to answer as best as he could, he hadn't quite managed to say what he most needed to say.

> He felt that I was Christian. And I am by, as far as birth—my mother was, and my father was, and so forth, and my early teachings were of the Christian faith. Now, as I look out upon the world—and it's always been a thing with me—to feel that all men know the truth, see? So therefore I've always felt that even though a man was not a Christian, he could know the truth—or he could *not*. [*laughs*] It's according to whether he knew the truth, and the truth itself doesn't have any name on it, to me, see. Each man has to find this for himself, I think.[27]

A gap in the tape follows, and then Tsujimoto asks him, "In this moment, what do you have in your mind for the future—in a larger sense, what is your theme about your music?"

> Oh, I would—I'll tell you. I believe that men are here to grow themselves into the full—into the *best good* that they can be. At least, this is what *I* want to do. You know? This is

25. *The John Coltrane Reference – updates 1966*. Online: http://www.wildmusic-jazz.com/jcr_1966.htm

26. Ibid.

27. Yui, et al. "Interviews with John Coltrane," 277.

> my belief, that we are supposed to—*I* am supposed to grow
> to the *best good* that I can get to. And as I'm going there,
> becoming this, and what I become, if I *ever* become, this
> will just come out of the horn. So whatever that's gonna be,
> that's what it will be. I'm not so much interested in trying
> to *say* what it's gonna be; I don't know. But I just hope, and
> I realize that good can only bring good.[28]

It is important to note that in his presentation of this material, not
only does Ratliff tie it all in with the sainthood comment; he offers
a significantly edited version of Coltrane's answers. The impact
of Ratliff's presentation is to have Coltrane come across as being
rather more spiritually enigmatic than actually seems to have
been the case. What does come across here is first an acknowledgement of his Christian roots, followed by a statement of his
long-standing sense that truth is not limited to any one tradition.
His is not a generalized universalism, but rather something closer
to a religious relativism, in which truth may be sought and discovered in a variety of ways. As he understands things, the calling to
goodness is a universal one, even if he is rather hesitant to speak
for anyone other than himself: "This is my belief, that we are supposed to—*I* am supposed to grow to the *best good* that I can get
to." Notably, he ties this directly to his music, saying that, "what I
become, if I *ever* become, this will just come out of the horn."

This material really does bear out how Hoff, Tegnell, and ultimately the authors of *The John Coltrane Reference* receive Coltrane's
comment about wanting to become a saint. His goal is to aspire to
truth and goodness—as Hoff has it, to be "a holy person, a devotee, a lover of God"—and to express that in and through his music.
There is no need to read anything particularly mystical into his
remark, other than to say that at least at some level he knew that
he was still very much in process toward becoming what he was
meant to be.

It is fair to say that while his musical voice was one of great
sophistication, John Coltrane found it rather more challenging to
articulate his ideas verbally. One way of reading this is to simply
acknowledge that the language in which he was most comfortable
and articulate was that of music, and to follow the musician and
producer Charlie Peacock in his suggestion that, "Coltrane seemed

28. Ibid.

to do his most significant theological musing with a saxophone in his mouth." "It's not a stretch to say that he was both making music and doing theology, as in reflecting on God, having God-thoughts. Yet, rather than reflecting on the revelation of God to man, Coltrane seemed more intent on having his own personal revelation of God. To say that he approached music and God through the experiential is an understatement. It might be said that his extended solos were so lengthy because he was patiently waiting for God to walk through the room."[29] This is a very positive appreciation of Coltrane's stature as a theological musician, and one that embraces his extended solos and increasingly avant-garde explorations as being not only legitimate, but also spiritually and theologically insightful.

There are other ways of reading his life and work. Aside from Phillip Larkin, it is hard to find anyone quite so dismissive of Coltrane's later work as the essayist and critic Gerald Early. In the transcript of an interview for the Ken Burns documentary *Jazz*,[30] Early speaks of how the jazz avant-garde "got its high priest with John Coltrane." Early is quite intentional in saying that Coltrane "thought of himself as making a religious music," and notes how "people described his saxophone playing with these solos that were going on for forty minutes all in the upper register, speaking in tongues and being possessed by spirits and all this sort of stuff." Yet, from the tone of the interview, it is quite clear that Early doesn't find anything particularly insightful or sophisticated at work in Coltrane's explorations. "I think the avant-garde was really trying to make this kind of meld that was making jazz and spiritual music one," he comments, and based on some of his written essays it is fairly evident that Early is anything but convinced that this is a good thing.

Early gives clear voice to his reservations about Coltrane in his essay "Ode to John Coltrane: A Jazz Musician's Influence on African American Culture," published in 1999, right around the time that the Ken Burns documentary was in production. In this essay Early consistently characterizes Coltrane as being an anti-intellectual, and describes him as "a rather dull man, certainly a

---

29. Peacock, e-mail correspondence.
30. Burns, Interview transcripts for *Ken Burns' Jazz*.

shy, reticent one."[31] While acknowledging that Coltrane was "arguably the best technician of the tenor and soprano saxophone in the history of jazz,"[32] Early also suggests that in terms of his overall creative contribution he simply does not measure up to the likes of Charlie Parker and Duke Ellington. And in terms of Coltrane's impact on the intellectual and religious life of black America, Early is scathing. I have already included part of this quotation in chapter eight, but it bears repeating in full here. "His grasp of religion as either doctrine or emotional experience was not profound, incisive, or especially impressive if the poem/prayer liner notes that he provided for what is arguably his most famous album, *A Love Supreme*, are a fair indication of his thinking. His thinking in this realm seemed positively banal, a kind of pantheistic muddle of God is the universe and truth is the sum total of all religions."[33] Noting the phenomenon of the Coltrane poem, Early wonders why this particular jazz musician gained such an iconographic status for black intellectuals. In answer to his own question, Early notes that "black intellectuals and writers tend to revere all dead black artists," adding that, "Probably only Billie Holiday generates as much sentimentality as Coltrane."[34] Ultimately, it all comes down to the creation of an edifice, and to the way in which the iconic—and therefore artificial—Coltrane could be fitted to the needs of an audience. While this recalls the insights of Herman Gray, who sees a very real and substantial person at work behind the figure of "Trane," Early sees only a flawed artist whose rigorous performing and practice schedule is best characterized as obsessive. In Early's estimation, outside of his technical ability there is nothing to be gained by attending to Coltrane, and much to be lost. "Coltrane represented in remarkably useful ways for his audience and his marketers the ever-growing tendency in jazz to become more nihilistic and more self-consciously technical in its attempt to serve the psychological needs of its marginalized, intellectual audience as well as to become more anti-intellectual as it aspired for transcendence."[35] Early's characterization of Coltrane as anti-

31. Early, "Ode to John Coltrane," 376.
32. Ibid., 372.
33. Ibid., 376.
34. Ibid., 385.
35. Ibid., 379.

intellectual is somewhat odd, given how voraciously he devoured books. It would be more accurate to opt for Clapp's characterization of Coltrane as being "scattershot" in his searching, both intellectually and spiritually. If a concern is to be raised regarding his intellectual life, it is that it was rather undisciplined in terms of any coherence of content or depth of exploration; rather ironic given how disciplined he was in his commitment to musical development and proficiency. There is any number of accounts of friends and fellow musicians sharing books with him, which he seemed to ingest with abandon. Included in this list are A.J. Ayer's *Language, Truth, and Logic*, Inayat Khan's *The Mysticism of Sound*, Cyril Scott's *Music: Its Secret Influence Through the Ages*, Paramhansa Yogananda's *Autobiography of a Yogi*, writings by Albert Einstein and Ghandi, as well as works on both astrology and numerology. Of this approach to spirituality and religion, Franya Berkman writes, "The personalized, eclectic, and global nature of John Coltrane's spirituality was consistent with the new religious culture of the 1960s."[36]

As I trust I have already demonstrated, taken both as a musical prayer and as a statement of theological insight, *A Love Supreme* is hardly banal or muddled. It is true that the written texts of both the liner notes and the prayer/poem are not particularly brilliant when considered apart from the music, but the words were never intended to stand as anything other than a set of very personal written sketches to give context to *A Love Supreme*. As musical theology, the suite does its own work.

In my introductory chapter, I briefly introduced Cornel West's idea of the "organic intellectual" as taken up and qualified by Tommy L. Lott in his essay, "When Bar Walkers Preach." It is now time to briefly revisit Lott's essay, as it provides a powerful counterpoint to Gerald Early's critical view of Coltrane's intellectual standing. As you may recall, Lott takes up West's observation that while the academic world produces a particular kind of intellectual, within the black intellectual tradition there is also the figure of the "organic intellectual," best exemplified by musicians and preachers. In Lott's view, Coltrane is a prime example of this tradition. "His excavation of the system of thought that he inherited from an earlier jazz tradition enabled his further exploration of new ideas that extended that tradition. More important, he began

---

36. Berkman, "Appropriating Universality," 45.

to conceive of music as a sonic language that conveys meanings and allows an exploration of philosophical questions about the nature of reality."[37]

For Lott, John Coltrane "contributed to a history of ideas in music,"[38] and achieved the very thing that the intellectual of the academic tradition generally cannot, namely he advanced African-American music. Add to this Berkman's view that the search for musical, spiritual, and intellectual authenticity carried out by John, and later Alice, Coltrane "had extensive political ramifications during the 1960s as a display of personal liberation and black cultural expression,"[39] and one begins to see something of his significance as an organic intellectual. Quite clearly, Coltrane was not dismissive of other ways of exploring, thinking, and speaking; it is just that his way was one done primary through his music. As he laughingly says in his interview with Frank Kofsky, "the music is enough!" adding, "You know, and that's philosophy."[40]

Unlike Gerald Early, the jazz critic Stanley Crouch does acknowledge the intellectual standing of John Coltrane, and is unflinching in his praise for the work of Coltrane's quartet up through A Love Supreme. In Crouch's estimation, the albums Coltrane, Crescent, and A Love Supreme found the quartet at an all-but-peerless high point, in which together they were able to express a "fusion of passion and intellectual depth," and offer to the listener a "perfect synthesis" of "the inflamed soul and the mind."[41] Yet, when Crouch considers Coltrane's work after A Love Supreme, his appreciation evaporates. Crouch calls the music of this later period an "abyss," and suggests that for reasons unknown, Coltrane "turned his back" against the very things that had made the classic recordings so very strong, namely their "fresh beauty and swinging power."[42] In stark contrast to Early, however, what mystifies Crouch is that Coltrane was "an intellectual giant" who should have known better than to stray so far from his roots.[43]

37. Lott, "Bar Walkers," 104.
38. Ibid., 105.
39. Berkman, "Appropriating Universality," 55.
40. Kofsky, "Interview with John Coltrane," 311.
41. Crouch, "Titan of the Blues," 111.
42. Crouch, "Coltrane Derailed," 215.
43. Ibid., 214.

And in his 2002 article "Coltrane Derailed," Crouch suggests that Coltrane was giving every indication that he was about to return to those roots, and possibly even reunite the classic quartet. Such a move, however, would have been rather unlikely. As Porter observed, not only would this have meant pushing his own wife out of his quartet, there just isn't anything to suggest that Coltrane had any interest in giving up his drummer Rashied Ali in order to go back to the classic quartet.[44]

Part of what is at work for critics such as Crouch—as for the fans and fellow musicians who found the post-*A Love Supreme* work to be so disturbing—is the very fact that Coltrane was making changes at all. Here I find helpful Michael Gilmour's reflections on the way in which fans and critics have reacted to the changes Bob Dylan has made in his own music over the years. Reflecting on Dylan's 1979 movement into his so-called Gospel phase, Gilmour draws from C.S. Lewis's writings on change and relationships to help make sense of the hostile reaction Dylan received. "Change is a threat to Affection," Lewis wrote, suggesting that in a close friendship when one partner becomes deeply engaged in a new interest—"poetry or science or serious music or perhaps undergoes a religious conversion"—the other is often left with a sense of having been deserted or even betrayed.[45] For Gilmour, this dynamic at least partly explains the reaction of many of Dylan's most ardent fans and critical supporters. As was the case with John Coltrane's later music, the reaction to change was often hostile, even mocking. Again, Gilmour's use of Lewis is helpful. "The jealousy will probably be expressed by ridicule. The new interest is all 'silly nonsense,' contemptibly childish (or contemptibly grown-up), or else the deserter is not really interested in it at all—he's just showing off, swanking; it's all affectation."[46] It is not difficult to hear some of this in Crouch's dismissal of Coltrane's late work, as well as in the writings of other similarly mystified critics. I offer only one of the many available examples, the closing sentence from Joe Goldberg's 1967 review of the *Meditations* album in *HiFi/Stereo Review*:

44. Porter, personal interview.
45. Gilmour, *Gospel According to Bob Dylan*, 83.
46. Ibid., 84.

"In this *Meditations* album, I feel only that I am being wildly assaulted, and must defend myself by not listening."[47]

What Gilmour suggests in his use of Lewis's material is that it is quite possible for fans and critics alike to feel connected to a musician in a way that creates a dynamic—albeit a one-way dynamic—not unlike that of a friendship or partnership. In this case, if the partner makes a dramatic change, it can easily upset the "relationship" by changing the terms with which things had formerly worked. Some of this is evident in Dan Morgenstern's *Down Beat* review of Coltrane's appearance at the 1966 Lincoln Center "Titans of the Tenor" concert. "After this display one wonders what had happened to Coltrane," writes Morgenstern. "Has he lost all musical judgment? Or is he putting on his audience? Whatever the answer, it was saddening to contemplate this spectacle, unworthy of a great musician."[48] Others did not share this sense of betrayal, possibly in part due to having at least some sense that Coltrane was moving in precisely the direction they had hoped he would move. This is certainly true of the writer Frank Kofsky who, in his 1966 interview is *so* enthusiastic about the newer material that it seems almost to embarrass Coltrane.

Those of us who came to Coltrane's music only after his death have had the luxury of dealing at our own pace with the changes and developments in his musical work and vision. As Jimmy Greene notes, "In just twelve years the amount that his music changed, and the amount he changed jazz music, is breathtaking."[49] To have been in a place of having to integrate those changes as they were being made left even some of his great supporters feeling breathless, and not in a particularly welcome or positive way. There is no reason to think that the changes and developments would have ceased had he lived. Crouch's hopeful speculations regarding signs that Coltrane was about to return to his roots aside, Coltrane's rather remarkable appetite for music and instruments of wide-ranging provenance—along with his sax, at home he also played guitar, flute, and even bagpipes, and was instrumental in Alice Coltrane taking up the harp—offer no reason to think that he was about to cease his explorations. While he never performed using one, he'd

47. Goldberg, "Meditations," 236.
48. Woideck, "Later Critical Reception," 222.
49. Greene, personal interview.

even accepted an endorsement contract for the electronic Varitone attachment for the saxophone. In the opinion of the noted jazz bassist Christian McBride, we should not be at all hesitant to imagine that Coltrane was still very much in progress in the final years. "To me, listening to Coltrane it was such a natural progression," McBride comments. "It seemed natural to me, like every great innovator in music. It is a natural progression. I firmly believe that had Coltrane lived, he would have wound up doing some musical things that would have been very similar to what Miles Davis did in the late sixties and early seventies. Coltrane was sussing out Ravi Shankar, he was sussing out the Varitone. I can totally see him getting into what is now called 'world music,' with some electronics. Who knows? He could have joined the fusion movement."[50] For many critics and musicians—certainly Stanley Crouch, but also Wynton Marsalis, both of whom have been rather famously dismissive of fusion music—this latter suggestion is all but jazz heresy.

Of course, it isn't just issues of jazz heresy that are at stake in this study. While I would not use the term heretical to describe Coltrane's religious and spiritual views, I do think it is fair to identify him as being theologically heterodox, by which I mean that while he drew deeply from the faith tradition in which he was formed, his theological views were not particularly in keeping with the creedal statements and established theological traditions of historic Christianity. As will be abundantly clear by this point, his views and beliefs often stretched a Christian self-identity to the breaking point, allowing Nat Hentoff to describe him as "a theosophist of jazz." "[H]aving constructed a personal world view (or view of the cosmos) on a residue of Christianity and an infusion of Eastern meditative practices and concerns, Coltrane became a theosophist of jazz. The music was a way of self-purgation so that he could learn more about himself to the end of making himself and his music part of the unity of all being."[51] "Reverend King," Coltrane's tribute to Martin Luther King, Jr., could be offered as a case in point. Recorded in February, 1966 at the same sessions that produced "Peace on Earth," and released in 1968 on *Cosmic Music*—a posthumous album credited to both Alice and John Coltrane—"Reverend King" opens with the band chanting,

50. McBride, personal interview.
51. Hentoff, "John Coltrane," 620.

"A-um-ma-ni-pad-me-hum," a Hindu phrase representing the seven breaths of life. Not that King would have been entirely unsympathetic to the use of a Hindu prayer, given the breadth of his own vision and the degree to which he was influenced by Gandhi. It just seems a somewhat surprising choice, given that Coltrane could easily have hearkened back to the heart of the civil rights movement and drawn a sentence from one of the spirituals, or even from one of King's own addresses. The incorporation of a Hindu chant into "Reverend King" illustrates the hybrid and even syncretistic nature of his belief system; the "all paths lead to God" of A Love Supreme, or the oft-quoted "I believe in all religions," cited in the liner notes to Meditations. Notably, the Cosmic Music album also finds Coltrane and Pharoah Sanders reciting the prayer, "May there be love and peace and perfection throughout all creation, O God."

In an interview for the audio documentary, The Traneumentary, the pianist and composer Gerri Allen offers her own more personal reading of Coltrane's impact on the listener. "[W]hen you hear that music it immediately draws you into a place of very great spiritual depth . . . and you become engulfed by it; you have no other choice but to be involved and I think that that is an amazing gift to humanity, that through the Creator he became a porthole to that . . ."[52] Similarly, the bassist and professed Christian John Patitucci offers his own take on this music. "Coltrane was driven, and part of that was linked to his spiritual thirst. And how could you fully understand when you're given that kind of gift on the horn? To me, when I hear him play, more so than when I hear anybody else play jazz, I hear God's voice. When he plays a ballad, emotionally you hear the cry of the Holy Spirit."[53] "I hear God's voice," Patitucci comments, "you hear the cry of the Holy Spirit," which brings us again to the issue of how the listener is an active part of the construction of the meaning of a piece of music. "Billy Hart said it best," Patitucci continues. "[H]e said 'I don't care what Trane is doing, whether he's playing sheets of sound or one of those killer ballads, he always sounds like he's praying. Even if it is the 'outest' thing—he's screaming, he's doing multi-phonics—it

---

52. "Episode 30," The Traneumentary.
53. Patitucci, personal interview.

just sounds like he's praying."[54] And perhaps it sounds like he's praying because he was. "Undeniably, his spirituality is rooted in his early childhood experience,"[55] claims Lott, and beginning with *A Love Supreme*, Coltrane consistently spoke of his music in terms of its spiritually searching and prayerful purpose. A quick survey of his song and suite titles from the years following *A Love Supreme* bears this out. From 1965 there is "Dear Lord," "Vigil," "Ascension," "Dearly Beloved," "Attaining," "Ascent," "Amen," "Om," as well as the two versions of the *Meditations* suite, and "Suite," with its five-part structure built around the times of daily prayer. The year 1966 added "Reverend King," "Peace on Earth," and "Lead us On," while 1967 brought the song "Offering." Add to this the earlier titles such as "Spiritual" (1961) and "Song of Praise," (1964), and it is hard to argue that prayer and spiritual concerns weren't foremost on Coltrane's mind. Although Porter suggests that of the titles given his later works, "only 'The Father and the Son and the Holy Ghost' is specifically Christian; others such as 'Dear Lord' and *Meditations* are more general,"[56] I believe that it is entirely possible to see the vast majority of these pieces as bearing the imprint of his formation in the black church of his parents and grandparents, "Om" being the most notable and glaring exception. I trust that particularly in my chapter on "The Father and the Son and the Holy Ghost," but also in the other chapters—notably those on *A Love Supreme*, "Attaining" and "Ascension"—I have successfully demonstrated something of the way in which the language and ideas of Coltrane's Christian formation continued to give shape to his thinking, prayer, and music. James C. Hall's observations regarding the liner notes to *A Love Supreme* provide further support for my position. While acknowledging that in both the liner notes and in the accompanying prayer/poem, "Coltrane certainly nods in the direction of his readings in traditional and derivative

54. Ibid.

55. Lott, "Bar Walkers," 110. It is not insignificant to acknowledge that Lott goes on to add the following: "It is important to add, however, that his musical explorations as a means of seeking knowledge of himself and God can also be understood, as in the case of Socrates, in an existential sense that is concerned with self-knowledge and the ultimate meaning of human existence." While in my own writing I have not made this connection to Socrates, I trust that I have addressed the ways in which Coltrane concerns himself with these basic existential issues.

56. Porter, *John Coltrane*, 259.

Eastern religions," Hall sees these texts as having a deep connection to what he calls, "mid-century Protestant angst and American civil religion."[57] "Most commentators have opted for 'mystery' to explain its appeal," Hall suggests, "but the popularity of *A Love Supreme* may have much less to do with its rebelliousness or its opposition than it does with its recognizability."[58] Coltrane was drawing primarily on his religious mother tongue, which was familiar language in the America of the 1960s, particularly so in black America. And at least to some degree that remains the case, even in an increasingly pluralistic and secularized cultural milieu.

In summary, I believe that the imprint of John Coltrane's spiritual formation in the church of his parents and grandparents remained deep on his soul, such that even in the year that found him experimenting with LSD and recording *Om,* he could still articulate something profoundly true about the creedal doctrine of the Trinity. And he did that with music that would have been all but incomprehensible to his preacher grandfathers.

In *But Beautiful: A Book about Jazz*, Geoff Dyer makes an interesting observation regarding the apparent incomprehensibility of the later music. "While Coltrane's concerns were becoming ever more religious, his music for the most part presents a violent landscape filled with chaos and shrieks. It is as if he was attempting to absorb all the violence of his times into his music in order to leave the world more peaceful. Only occasionally, as in the haunting 'Peace on Earth,' does he finally seem able to partake of the repose he hoped to create."[59] While there is a certain amount of melodrama in Dyer's picture of Coltrane "attempting to absorb all the violence of his times into his music in order to leave the world more peaceful," his observation that the music often sounds as if it were in tension with its creator's stated aims is interesting. This is something that Don Saliers flagged for me in a conversation about the *Ascension* project. "Clearly, the kind of religious or theological overlay you get with a title like *Ascension* creates a kind of crick in the brain for the listener, because you're trying to fit it with assumptions about Christ's ascension. And you think, well, everything should go up. It isn't what happens. These are questions

57. Hall, *Mercy, Mercy Me*, 137.
58. Ibid.
59. Dyer, *But Beautiful*, 204.

of realms of acoustical exploration, which carry with them more than the music."[60] Throughout his career, Coltrane was all but captivated by "acoustical exploration," beginning with his "sheets of sound" period in the late 1950s. His modal explorations, his musical recitations of written texts, and certainly his avant-garde and free explorations were as much soundscapes as anything else, and in these he seemed utterly unafraid of exploring territory that was new both to his audience and to himself. To create more than the occasional "crick in the brain" was not something from which he shied away, and particularly not when he believed himself to be articulating something truthful about life, both human and divine. Beauty—at least as it is conventionally defined—was not his goal, though if beauty emerged he would not turn it away.

I will give the final word to John Coltrane himself, taken from a 1962 letter to *Down Beat* editor and writer Don DeMicheal, written before he had fully surfaced from his "period of irresolution."

> Truth is indestructible. It seems history shows (and it's the same way today) that the innovator is more often than not met with some degree of condemnation; usually according to the degree of his departure from the prevailing modes of expression what have you. Change is always so hard to accept. We also see that these innovators always seek to revitalize, extend and reconstruct the status quo in their given fields, whenever it is needed. Quite often they are the rejects, outcasts, sub-citizens, etc. of the very societies to which they bring so much sustenance. Often they are people who endure great personal tragedy in their lives. Whatever the case, whether accepted or rejected, rich or poor, they are forever guided by that great and eternal constant—the creative urge. Let us cherish it and give all praise to God.[61]

60. Saliers, telephone interview.
61. Simpkins, *Coltrane*, 161.

Bibliography

Albert, Richard N. "The Jazz-Blues Motif in Baldwin's 'Sonny's Blues.'" *College Literature* 11:2 (1984) 178–85.

Augustine. *Confessions*. Translated by Henry Chadwick. Oxford University Press, 1991.

Baldwin, James. *The Fire Next Time*. New York: Dell, 1964.

———. *Nobody Knows My Name*. New York: Dial, 1961.

———. "Sonny's Blues." In *The Jazz Fiction Anthology*, edited by Sascha Feinstein and David Rice, 17–48. Bloomington: Indiana University Press, 2009.

Barclay, William. *A Spiritual Autobiography*. Grand Rapids: Eerdmans, 1983.

Beaudoin, Tom. *Virtual Faith*. San Francisco: Jossey-Bass, 1998.

Begbie, Jeremy. *Resounding Truth: Christian Wisdom in the World of Music*. Grand Rapids: Baker Academic, 2007.

———. *Theology, Music and Time*. Cambridge, UK: Cambridge University Press, 2000.

———. "Theology through the Arts," *Faith and Leadership*. No pages. Online: http://faithandleadership.com/multimedia/jeremy-begbie-theology -through-the-arts.

Benson, Bruce Ellis. "Improvising Texts, Improvising Communities: Jazz, Interpretation, Heterophony, and the *Ekklesia*." In *Resonant Witness: Conversations Between Music and Theology*, edited by Jeremy S. Begbie and Steven R. Guthrie, 295–319. Grand Rapids: Eerdmans, 2011.

Berkman, Franya J. "Appropriating Universality: The Coltranes and 1960s Spirituality." *American Studies* 48:1 (2007) 41–62.

Blume, August. "Interview with John Coltrane." In *Coltrane on Coltrane: The John Coltrane Interviews*, edited by Chris DeVito, 9–30. Chicago: A Cappella, 2010.

Bohlman, Philip V. "Is All Music Religious?" *Theomusicology—A Special Issue of Black Sacred Music: A Journal of Theomusicology* 8:1 (1994) 3–12.

Bono, "Introduction." In *The Pocket Canon Psalms*. New York: Grove, 1999.

Branch, Taylor. *Parting the Waters: America in the King Years 1954–63*. New York: Simon and Schuster, 1988.

Brown, Leonard L. "Conversation with Yusef Lateef." In *John Coltrane & Black America's Quest for Freedom,* edited by Leonard L. Brown, 192–204. New York: Oxford University Press, 2010.

———. "In His Own Words." In *John Coltrane & Black America's Quest for Freedom,* edited by Leonard L. Brown, 11–31. New York: Oxford University Press, 2010.

———. "You Have to Be Invited: Reflections on Music Making and Musician Creation in Black American Culture." In *John Coltrane & Black America's Quest for Freedom,* edited by Leonard L. Brown, 3–9. New York: Oxford University Press, 2010.

Brueggemann, Walter. *Spirituality of the Psalms.* Minneapolis: Fortress, 2002.

Burch, Frank. *Good Taste, Bad Taste, & Christian Taste.* New York: Oxford University Press, 2000.

Burns, Ken. "Interview transcripts for *Jazz: A Film by Ken Burns.*" Online: http://www.pbs.org/jazz/about/about_transcripts.htm; http://www.pbs.org/jazz/about/pdfs/Crouch.pdf; http://www.pbs.org/jazz/about/pdfs/Early.pdf.

Carter, William. "Singing a New Song: The Gospel and Jazz." In *Princeton Seminary Bulletin* 19:1 (1998) 40–51.

Clapp, Rodney. "The Saxophonist Who Would Be a Saint." In *Border Crossings,* 177–84. Grand Rapids: Brazos, 2000.

Cobb, Kelton *The Blackwell Guide to Theology and Popular Culture.* Oxford: Blackwell, 2005.

Cole, Bill. *John Coltrane.* Da Capo, 2001.

"Church and Community Celebrate 84th Birthday of Saint John Coltrane," *Expression Newsletter,* (December 2010), 2. Online: http://coltranechurch.org/Expression.pdf

Coltrane, John with Don DeMicheal. "Coltrane on Coltrane." In *Coltrane on Coltrane: The John Coltrane Interviews,* edited by Chris DeVito, 65–71. Chicago: A Cappella, 2010.

Cone, James. "The Cross and the Lynching Tree." No pages. Online: http://www.prattlibrary.org/booksmedia/podcasts/index2.aspx?ID=72459&mark=cross+and+the+lynching+tree

———. *The Spirituals and the Blues: An Interpretation.* 2nd ed. Maryknoll, NY: Orbis, 1991.

Crouch, Stanley. "Coltrane Derailed." In *Considering Genius: Writings on Jazz,* 213–15. New York: Basic Civitas, 2006.

———. "The Negro Aesthetic of Jazz." In *Considering Genius: Writings on Jazz,* 211–12. New York: Basic Civitas, 2006.

———. "Putting the White Man in Charge." In *Considering Genius: Writings on Jazz,* 232–34. New York: Basic Civitas, 2006.

———. "Titan of the Blues," In *Considering Genius: Writings on Jazz,* 111–15. New York: Basic Civitas, 2006.

Crow, Bill. *Jazz Anecdotes.* New York: Oxford University Press, 1990.

Delorme, Michel and Claude Lenissois. "Coltrane, Star of Antibes: 'I Can't Go Farther.'" In *Coltrane on Coltrane: The John Coltrane Interviews,* edited by Chris DeVito, 241–46 Chicago: A Cappella, 2010.

Delorme, Michel and Jean Clouzet, "Interview with John Coltrane." In *Coltrane on Coltrane: The John Coltrane Interviews*, edited by Chris DeVito, 211–16. Chicago: A Cappella, 2010.

Devito, Chris, ed. *Coltrane on Coltrane*. Chicago: Chicago Review, 2010.

DeVito, Chris, et al. *The John Coltrane Reference*. Edited by Lewis Porter. New York: Routledge, 2007.

Doggett, Peter. *There's a Riot Going On*. New York: Canongate, 2007.

Du Bois, W. E. B. *The Souls of Black Folks*. New York: Simon and Schuster Paperbacks, 2009.

Dyer, Geoff. *But Beautiful: A Book About Jazz*. New York: North Point Press, Farrar Straus and Giroux, 1996.

Early, Gerald, "Ode to John Coltrane: A Jazz Musician's Influence on African American Culture." *Antioch Review* 57:3 (1999) 371–85.

Edgar, William "The Deep Joy of Jazz," *byFaith* 11 (2006). No pages. Online: http://byfaithonline.com/page/arts-culture/the-deep-joy-of-jazz.

———. "Heaven in a Nightclub." *Comment* (March 2009) 46–51.

———. "A Love Supreme." *Modern Reformation* 15:1 (2006) 5, 27.

Ellis, Carl F. Jr. *Free At Last? The Gospel in the African American Experience*. Downers Grove, IL: InterVarsity, 2006.

Feinstein, Sascha. "From 'Alabama' to 'A Love Supreme': The Evolution of the John Coltrane Poem." *The Southern Review* 32 (1996) 315–27.

Field, Douglas. "Pentecostalism and All That Jazz: Tracing James Baldwin's Religion." *Literature & Theology* 22:4 (2008) 436–57.

Fraim, John. *Spirit Catcher: The Life and Art of John Coltrane*. West Liberty, OH: Greathouse, 1996.

Fremer, Björn. "The John Coltrane Story." In *Coltrane on Coltrane: The John Coltrane Interviews*, edited by Chris DeVito, 61–64. Chicago: A Cappella, 2010.

Gallegos, Aaron. "Bound for Glory." *Sojourners* 22:9 (1993) 40–41, 43–44.

Gelinas, Robert. *Finding the Groove: Composing a Jazz-Shaped Faith*. Zondervan, 2009.

Gilmour, Michael J. *The Gospel According to Bob Dylan*. Louisville: Westminster John Knox, 2011.

Gitler, Ira. "Trane on Track." In *Coltrane on Coltrane: The John Coltrane Interviews*, edited by Chris DeVito, 41–44. Chicago: A Cappella, 2010.

Goldberg, Joe. "A Love Supreme." In *The John Coltrane Companion: Five Decades of Commentary*, edited by Carl Woideck, 233–34. New York: Schirmer, 1998.

———. "Meditations." In *The John Coltrane Companion: Five Decades of Commentary*, edited by Carl Woideck, 235–36. New York: Schirmer, 1998.

Gracyk, Theodore. "Jazz after 'Jazz': Ken Burns and the Construction of Jazz History." *Philosophy and Literature* 26 (2002) 173–87.

Gray, Herman "John Coltrane and the Practice of Freedom." In *John Coltrane & Black America's Quest for Freedom*, edited by Leonard L. Brown, 33–54. New York: Oxford University Press, 2010.

Grey, De Sayles. *Acknowledgment: A John Coltrane Legacy*. McLean, VA, 2001.

Gussow, Adam. *Seems Like Murder Here: Southern Violence and the Blues Tradition.* Chicago: The University of Chicago Press, 2002.

Hall, James C. *Mercy, Mercy Me: African-American Culture and the American Sixties.* New York: Oxford University Press, 2001.

Harley, Luke. "An Apollonian Scream: Nathaniel Mackey's Rewriting of the Coltrane Poem in *Ohnedaruth's Day Begun.*" *Sydney Studies in English* 36 (2010) 77–107.

Harrison, Carol. "Augustine and the Art of Music." In *Resonant Witness: Conversations Between Music and Theology,* edited by Jeremy S. Begbie and Steven R. Guthrie, 27–45. Grand Rapids: Eerdmans, 2011.

Hart, David Bentley. *The Beauty of the Infinite.* Grand Rapids: Eerdmans, 2003.

Hentoff, Nat. "John Coltrane." In *Reading Jazz: A Gathering of Autobiography, Reportage, and Criticism from 1919 to Now,* edited by Robert Gottlieb, 620–28. New York: Pantheon, 1996.

———. "My Favorite Things." In *The John Coltrane Companion: Five Decades of Commentary,* edited by Carl Woideck, 229–30. New York: Schirmer, 1998.

Howison, Jamie. "God's Mind in the Music: How Coltrane Deepened My Theology of the Triune God." *Didaskalia* (Fall 2009) 1–15.

Jackson, Eric D. "Somebody Please Say, 'Amen!'" In *John Coltrane & Black America's Quest for Freedom,* edited by Leonard L. Brown, 173–81. New York: Oxford University Press, 2010.

Jackson, Josh. "On Demand: Interview With Billy Hart." September 23, 2009. No pages. Online: http://www.npr.org/2011/06/15/113016411/billy-hart-quartet-live-at-the-village-vanguard.

Jones, LeRoi (Amiri Baraka). *Black Music.* New York: Akashi Classics Renegade Reprint Series, 2010.

———. *Blues People.* New York: Quill, 1999.

Jost, Ekkehard. *Free Jazz.* New York: Da Capo, 1994.

Kahn, Ashley. *The House that Trane Built: The Story of Impulse Records.* London: Granta, 2006.

———. *A Love Supreme: The Story of John Coltrane's Signature Album.* Penguin, 2002.

Kernodle, Tammy L. "Freedom is a Constant Struggle: Alice Coltrane and the Redefining of the Jazz Avant-Garde." In *John Coltrane & Black America's Quest for Freedom,* edited by Leonard L. Brown, 73–98. New York: Oxford University Press, 2010.

Koenigswarter, Pannonica de. *Three Wishes: An Intimate Look at Jazz Greats.* New York: Abrams Image, 2008.

Kofsky, Frank. "Interview with John Coltrane." In *Coltrane on Coltrane: The John Coltrane Interviews,* edited by Chris DeVito, 281–318. Chicago: A Cappella, 2010.

Leonard, Neil. *Jazz: Myth and Religion.* New York: Oxford University Press, 1987.

Lind, Dale "John Garcia Gensel: Shepherd to the Night Flock." In *Witness at the Crossroads,* edited by Frederick K. Wentz, 214–26. Gettysburg, PA: The Lutheran Theological Seminary at Gettysburg, 2001.

Lott, Tommy L. "When Bar Walkers Preach." In *John Coltrane & Black America's Quest for Freedom,* edited by Leonard L. Brown, 99–122. New York: Oxford University Press, 2010.

Lynch, Gordon. *Understanding Theology and Popular Culture.* Oxford: Blackwell, 2005.

Mathieu, Bill. "John Coltrane—'Ascension.'" *Down Beat* 33:9 (May 5, 1966) 25.

McDonald, Michael Bruce. "Traning the Nineties, Or the Present Relevance of John Coltrane's Music of Theophany and Negation." *African-American Review* 29:2 (1995) 275–82.

Nisenson, Eric. *Ascension: John Coltrane and His Quest.* New York: Da Capo, 1995.

———. *Blue: The Murder of Jazz.* New York: St. Martin's, 1997.

Odell, Jennifer. "Backstage with Steve Wilson." *Down Beat* 74:11 (November 2007) 15.

Pederson, Ann. *God, Creation, and All that Jazz.* St Louis: Chalice, 2001.

Pickstock, Catherine. "Soul, City, and Cosmos after Augustine." In *Radical Orthodoxy: A New Theology,* edited by John Milbank, et al., 243–77. London: Routledge, 1999.

Porter, Eric. *What is This Thing Called Jazz?* Berkeley: University of California Press, 2002.

Porter, Lewis. *John Coltrane: His Life and Music.* Ann Arbor: University of Michigan Press, 1998.

———. *John Coltrane's Music of 1960 through 1967: Jazz Improvisation as Composition.* PhD diss., Brandeis University, 1983.

Postif, Francois. "John Coltrane: An Interview." In *Coltrane on Coltrane: The John Coltrane Interviews,* edited by Chris DeVito, 129–35. Chicago: A Cappella, 2010.

Price, Emmett G. III. "John Coltrane, 'A Love Supreme' and GOD." *allaboutjazz.com.* No pages. Online: http://www.allaboutjazz.com/coltrane/article_003.htm.

——— "The Spiritual Ethos in Black Music." *John Coltrane & Black America's Quest for Freedom,* edited by Leonard L. Brown, 153–72. New York: Oxford University Press, 2010.

Ratliff, Ben. *Coltrane: The Story of a Sound.* New York: Farrar, Straus and Giroux, 2007.

Robinson, John A. T. *But That I Can't Believe!* New York: The New American Library, 1967.

Rogers, Eugene F. Jr. *Sexuality and the Christian Body.* Oxford: Blackwell, 1999.

Rookmaaker Hans R. *Modern Art and the Death of a Culture.* London: Inter-Varsity, 1973.

———. *New Orleans Jazz, Mahalia Jackson and the Philosophy of Art: Vol. 2 of the Complete Works.* Carlisle, UK: Piquant Editions, 2002.

St. John Coltrane African Orthodox Church. "Welcome." No pages. Online: http://www.coltranechurch.org/

Saliers, Don E. *Music and Theology.* Nashville: Abingdon, 2007.

Sandke, Randall. *Where the Dark and the Light Folks Meet: Race and the Mythology, Politics, and Business of Jazz.* Plymouth, UK: Scarecrow, 2010.

Seerveld, Calvin. *Rainbows for the Fallen World: Aesthetic Life and Artistic Task.* Toronto: Tuppence, 1980.

Shipton, Alyn. *A New History of Jazz.* New York: Continuum, 2007.

Siedell, Daniel A. *God in the Gallery: A Christian Embrace of Modern Art.* Grand Rapids: Baker Academic, 2008.

Simpkins, C. O. *Coltrane: A Biography.* Perth Amboy, NJ: Herndon House, 1975.

Smith, Patti. *Just Kids.* New York: Ecco, 2010.

Snead, Bob. "Jazz Profile: John Coltrane—a Dedicated Musician." In *Coltrane on Coltrane: The John Coltrane Interviews,* edited by Chris DeVito. Chicago: A Cappella, 2010.

Snyder, James. "Coltrane in the Corn Fields." No pages. Online: http://stbene-dictstable.ca/2009/01/coltrane-in-the-cornfields/

Soelle, Dorothee. *Death by Bread Alone: Texts and Reflections on Religious Experience.* Translated by David L. Scheidt. Philadelphia: Fortress, 1978.

———. "The Cross." In *Essential Writings,* selected with an introduction by Dianne L. Oliver, 108–9. Maryknoll, NY: Orbis, 2006.

———. *Memoir of a Radical Christian.* Translated by Barbara and Martin Rumscheidt. Minneapolis: Fortress, 1999.

Spencer, Jon Michael. *Blues and Evil.* Knoxville: The University of Tennessee Press, 1993.

———. "Musicology as a Theologically Informed Discipline." *Theomusicology—A Special Issue of Black Sacred Music: A Journal of Theomusicology* 8:1 (1994) 36–63.

———. "Overview of American Popular Music in a Theological Perspective," *Theomusicology—A Special Issue of Black Sacred Music: A Journal of Theomusicology* 8:1 (1994) 205–17.

———. *Theological Music: Introduction to Theomusicology.* London: Greenwood, 1991.

Steckel, Clyde J. "How Can Music Have Theological Significance?" *Theomusicology—A Special Issue of Black Sacred Music: A Journal of Theomusicology* 8:1 (1994) 13–35.

Stewart, Rex. "The Cutting Sessions." In *Reading Jazz: A Gathering of Autobiography, Reportage, and Criticism From 1919 to Now,* edited by Robert Gottlieb, 387–92. New York: Pantheon, 1996.

Strickland, Edward "What Coltrane Wanted." *The Atlantic Monthly* 260:6 (1987) 100–102.

Tachach, James. "The Biblical Foundation of James Baldwin's 'Sonny's Blues.'" *Renascence* 59:2 (2007) 109–18.

Terpstra, John. *Skin Boat: Acts of Faith and Other Navigations.* Kentville, NS (Canada): Gaspereau, 2009.

Tertullian. *Apologeticum.* Ch. 39, 7. Translated by the Rev. Sydney Thelwell. No pages. Online: http://www.tertullian.org/anf/anf03/anf03-05.htm#39_7.

Tillich, Paul. "Art and Ultimate Reality." In *Theological Aesthetics: A Reader*, edited by Gesa Elsbeth Thiessen, 209–17. Grand Rapids: Eerdmans, 2005.

———. *Theology of Culture*. Oxford: Oxford University Press, 1959.

Thomas, Greg. "Jon Hendricks: Vocal Ease." *allaboutjazz.com*. April 10, 2008. No pages. Online: http://www.allaboutjazz.com/php/article.php?id=28904.

Thomas, J. C. *Chasin' the Trane*. Garden City, NY: Doubleday, 1975.

The Traneumentary: Celebrating the Artistry and Recordings of John Coltrane. No pages. Online: http://traneumentary.blogspot.com/

Viladesau, Richard. *Theological Aesthetics: God in Imagination, Beauty, and Art*. New York: Oxford University Press, 1999.

Washington, Salim. "'Don't Let the Devil (Make You) Lose Your Joy': A Look at Late Coltrane." In *John Coltrane & Black America's Quest for Freedom*, edited by Leonard L. Brown, 123–52. New York: Oxford University Press, 2010.

Watrous, Peter. "John Coltrane: A Life Supreme." In *The John Coltrane Companion: Five Decades of Commentary*, edited by Carl Woideck, 56–71. New York: Schirmer, 1998.

Wells, Samuel. *Improvisation*. Grand Rapids: Brazos, 2004.

West, Cornel. "The Spirituals as Lyrical Poetry." In *The Cornel West Reader*, 463–70. New York: Basic Civitas, 1999.

———. *Hope on a Tightrope*. New York: Smiley Books, 2008.

———. "On Afro-American Popular Music: From Bebop to Rap." In *Prophetic Fragments*, 177–87. Grand Rapids: Eerdmans, 1988.

———. "Subversive Joy and Revolutionary Patience in Black Christianity." In *Prophetic Fragments*, 161–65. Grand Rapids: Eerdmans, 1988.

———. "What Kept Coltrane's Horn Blowing?" *BigThink.com* November 9, 2009. Online: http://bigthink.com/ideas/17242.

Wilder, Amos Niven. *Theopoetic: Theology and the Religious Imagination*. Lima, OH: Academic Renewal Press, 2001 reprint of 1976 ed.

Williams, Terry Tempest. *Finding Beauty in a Broken World*. New York: Pantheon, 2008.

Williams, Rowan. "Keeping Time." In *Open to Judgement: Sermons and Addresses*, 247–50. London: Darton, Longman and Todd, 1994.

Woideck, Carl, ed. *The John Coltrane Companion: Five Decades of Commentary*. New York: Schirmer, 1998.

———. "Later Critical Reception." In *The John Coltrane Companion: Five Decades of Commentary*, edited by Carl Woideck, 221–22. New York: Schirmer, 1998.

Wuthnow, Robert. *All in Sync: How Music and Art Are Revitalizing American Religion*. Berkeley: University of California Press, 2003.

Workman, Reggie. "Harlem Speaks" videotaped interview. National Jazz Museum in Harlem, January 2007.

Yui, Shoichi, et al. "Interviews with John Coltrane." In *Coltrane on Coltrane: The John Coltrane Interviews*, edited by Chris DeVito, 265–80. Chicago: A Cappella, 2010.

Interviews

Bell, Steve. E-mail correspondence. December 15, 2010.

Cone, James. Telephone interview. October 13, 2010.

Crow, Bill. Personal interview. New York City, January 11, 2011.

Edgar, William, Personal interview. New York City, January 3, 2010.

Greene, Jimmy. Personal interview. Winnipeg, February 26, 2010.

Lind, Dale. Personal interview. New York City, January 12, 2011.

McBride, Christian. Personal interview. New York City, January 25, 2011.

McDonald, Earl. Telephone interview. November 8, 2010.

Patitucci, John. Personal interview. Hastings-on-Hudson, New York, January 26, 2011.

Peacock, Charle. E-mail correspondence. October 10, 2010.

Porter, Lewis. E-mail correspondence. August 24, 2010.

Porter, Lewis. Personal interview. Newark, N.J., January 19, 2011.

Saliers, Don. Telephone interview. October 26, 2010.

Schoenberg, Loren. Personal interview. New York City, January 25, 2011.

Seerveld, Calvin. Personal interview. Toronto, January 2010.

Sturm, Ike. Personal interview. New York City, January 6, 2011.

Thomas, Gregory. Personal interview. New York City, January 25, 2011.

Tyner, McCoy. Telephone interview. January 26, 2011.

Wilde, David. E-mail correspondence. October 7, 2010 and February 7, 2011.

Index